SIXTH EDITION

Classrooms That Work
They Can All Read and Write

Patricia M. Cunningham

Wake Forest University

Richard L. Allington

University of Tennessee, Knoxville

Boston • Columbus • Indianapolis • New York • San Francisco • Upper Saddle River
Amsterdam • Cape Town • Dubai • London • Madrid • Milan • Munich • Paris • Montréal • Toronto
Delhi • Mexico City • São Paulo • Sydney • Hong Kong • Seoul • Singapore • Taipei • Tokyo

Editor-in-Chief and Vice President: Jeffery W. Johnston
Executive Editor: Meredith D. Fossel
Program Manager: Maren L. Beckman
Editorial Assistant: Maria Feliberty
Director of Marketing: Margaret Waples
Marketing Manager: Christopher Barry
Project Management Team Lead: JoEllen Gohr
Project Manager: Jessica H. Sykes
Procurement Specialist: Deidra Skahill
Art Director: Diane Lorenzo
Text and Cover Designer: Diane Lorenzo
Full-Service Project Management: Cenveo® Publisher Services
Composition: Cenveo Publisher Services
Printer/Binder: LSC Communications
Cover Printer: LSC Communications
Text Font: Times LT Std

Library of Congress Cataloging-in-Publication Data

Printed in the United States of America

12 2020

www.pearsonhighered.com

ISBN-10: 0-13-408959-6
ISBN-13: 978-0-13-408959-1

Brief Contents

Contents

Preface

IT IS HARD TO BELIEVE we are revising *Classrooms That Work* for the sixth time! Much has changed since we first wrote this book in the early nineties. Systematic phonics programs have replaced whole language as the dominant organizing theme for literacy instruction. Struggling readers are found in the bottom reading group in primary grades and in the low track in intermediate grades. Reading First mandated that all children read at grade level and that their reading progress be regularly monitored. Response to Intervention mandated that schools demonstrate that struggling readers were receiving appropriate classroom instruction and targeted Tier 2 instruction if they were not making adequate progress in their classroom Tier 1 instruction. Common Core State Standards for English/Language Arts, which intend for all students to graduate from high school ready for college or career, were adopted by the majority of states. To date, there is no evidence that these changes have made things better for children who struggle with reading and writing.

In the first edition of *Classrooms That Work*, we applauded the authentic reading and writing experiences provided in whole-language classrooms but expressed our fears that children were not being given enough instruction in decoding and spelling. We made the case for balanced, comprehensive literacy instruction that included authentic reading and writing, along with explicit instruction in the skills that would enable children to successfully engage in reading and writing. Of course, the pendulum has once again swung too far. In many classrooms with a lot of at-risk readers, skills instruction, worksheets, and test prep absorb a huge amount of time and energy, leaving little place for actually engaging in reading and writing.

The most effective classrooms described in Chapter 1 are classrooms that do it all! Authentic reading and writing are combined with explicit skills instruction. Daily instruction includes some whole-class teaching, some one-to-one conferences, and both teacher-led and collaborative groupings. Literacy instruction takes place during the reading/language arts time and throughout the day as the students learn math, science, and social studies. The teachers in these classrooms believe all their students can learn to read and write well and don't believe in an "either–or" approach to their teaching.

The original *Classrooms That Work* argued that all children—particularly children who struggle with reading and writing—need balanced, comprehensive literacy instruction. Our schools today have more children from racial and ethnic minority groups, more children who are learning English, more children from single-parent homes, and more children living in poverty. The need for balanced, comprehensive literacy instruction that pervades the school day and curriculum is greater now than ever. We have revised this book to help you better meet the needs of our increasingly diverse classrooms.

Like many of you, we worry about how Common Core is going to affect the literacy instruction received by struggling readers. Our greatest fear is that because Common Core raises the level of material students are expected to read at each grade level, struggling readers will not be engaging in the on-their-level and easy reading that all readers need to become confident, fluent readers. On the other hand, we are encouraged by the focus of the Common Core on higher-level thinking and comprehension and on including more informational text in our reading instruction at all grade levels. Children who struggle with reading can, and should, be expected to engage in higher-level, and critical, thinking about what they read. Many struggling readers are boys and boys generally prefer informational text over story text. Once they learn how to use the visuals and other special features informational texts provide, they are often more successful at reading informational text.

The other features of the Common Core that we like are its inclusion of the forgotten language arts—listening, speaking, and writing. Children are expected to talk with one another about what they are learning, to write informational and persuasive pieces about what they are learning, and to conduct research and make presentations to extend their learning.

Common Core raises the bar for all children. We have revised *Classrooms That Work* to provide more support for you as you work to help all your children rise to the challenge. Here are the major changes we have made:

New to This Edition

We have added a new chapter on reading informational text. In Chapter 8, you will find many lesson frameworks you can adapt to teach your students how to read informational text. Each lesson framework is illustrated with a sample lesson and each lesson incorporates the Gradual Release of Responsibility Model. At the beginning of the lesson, you model and show your students how they need to think and what they are to do. We call this phase, "I Do and You Watch." "I Do and You Watch" is followed by the "I Do and You Help" phase in which the class helps you to think and do something. Next, students meet in their trios to work together to complete the task. In this "You Do It Together and I Help" phase, students talk to and teach each other how to do the kind of thinking required by the task. As you continue to teach lessons with different text using the same lesson framework, you fade out some of the modeling and help. When your formative assessments indicate that all your students have learned to do the kind of thinking the lesson is focused on, you have them complete the task independently. This is the final phase in the Gradual Release of Responsibility Model, "You Do and I Watch." We believe that using these lesson frameworks specifically designed for informational text and providing lots of scaffolding in the early lessons and gradually fading out that scaffolding will greatly increase the success and confidence of your struggling readers with informational text.

Recognizing the importance of meaning vocabulary to comprehension, the Common Core includes a reading standard and two language standards that pertain specifically to meaning vocabulary. These standards require that students learn how to figure out appropriate meanings for words they encounter. This is particularly important for struggling readers who, when encountering a new word while reading on their own, are very apt to just skip over that word without thinking about what it means. This "Skip it!" habit is probably one of the major reasons most struggling readers have meaning vocabulary deficits, and meaning vocabulary is highly correlated with comprehension. To teach students how to use all the clues in the text—context, pictures, and morphology—to figure out word meanings, we have added a *Word Detectives* lesson framework to Chapter 6. This lesson, like the comprehension lessons, follows the Gradual Release of Responsibility Model. Across the year, you fade the scaffolding provided by you and the small group, and you expect all your students to be able to independently figure out word meanings for new words they encounter in reading.

As in previous editions, the writing chapter, Chapter 9, includes suggestions for making Writer's Workshop the centerpiece of your writing instruction. In addition, this chapter provides lesson frameworks and guidelines for teaching students to write the informational, opinion, and narrative pieces required in the Common Core. Chapter 10 gives you practical suggestions for integrating writing with math, science, and social studies and for teaching lessons that connect reading and writing.

The final big change in this edition can be found in Chapter 12. The first 11 chapters of this book detail for you what we think is the best, most comprehensive Tier 1 classroom instruction. In Chapter 12, you will find diagnostic procedures you can use to truly target your Tier 2 interventions for struggling readers who are not making adequate progress with this "state-of-the-art" classroom instruction. You will learn how to quickly determine whether comprehension, word identification, or fluency is the greatest roadblock for each of your struggling readers and which interventions are apt to be the most effective.

It is hard for us to believe that we are writing the sixth edition of this book and even harder to believe that it was over 20 years ago when we wrote it originally. Back then, we thought we knew all there was to know about teaching all children to read and write. Twenty plus years later, we are smart enough to know we will never know it all!

Thank you to the following reviewers: Christie L. Brown, Clear Spring Elementary School, Hagerstown, MD; Leslie Hopping, Granville Intermediate School, Granville, Ohio; Cerissa Stevenson, Colorado State University; and Victoria A. Tabeek, MacMurray College.

1

Creating Classrooms
That Work

HOW WELL DOES YOUR CLASSROOM WORK? If you are like most teachers, you might respond, "Some days better than others" or "Most days, things work pretty well." Or you might answer the question with a question, "What do you mean by 'work'?"

In 1994, when the first edition of this book was published, it had a bold and optimistic title: *Classrooms That Work: They Can* All *Read and Write.* The claim that *all* children could learn to read and write was, at the time, not widely accepted. In January of 2002, the No Child Left Behind Act (NCLB) was signed into law by President George W. Bush. Reading First specified how NCLB was to be implemented. Reading First required states to assess student progress in reading and schools were penalized if they failed to make AYP—Adequate Yearly Progress. Reading First specified that by 2014, all children were expected to read on grade-level. Unfortunately, this important goal of teaching all children to read well was not achieved by the costly and widely implemented Reading First initiative.

Although Reading First did not require the implementation of specific commercial reading programs, it did require that curricula had to be based on "scientific" research. The effect of this requirement and the way it was implemented was that almost all schools that received federal funds adopted one of a few commercial reading programs. These programs in the early grades focused almost exclusively on phonics instruction and what students read consisted of "highly decodable" texts in which the words were controlled according to which phonics principles had been taught. The programs were also scripted, specifying in the teacher's guide exactly what the teacher should say and how much time should be spent on each part of the lesson. Many school systems, fearful that teachers would deviate from the script, hired monitoring services to ensure fidelity of implementation.

Several large-scale evaluation studies have demonstrated that Reading First was not effective in raising reading achievement scores and that many children were left behind. In the executive summary of the federal government's official final report on the impact of Reading First, the evaluators (Gamse, Jacob, Horst, Boulay, & Unlu, 2008) concluded that there was no consistent pattern of effects over time in the impact estimates for reading instruction in grade one or in reading comprehension in any grade and that there appeared to be a systematic decline in reading instruction impacts in grade two.

In addition to this large evaluation study, results from the National Assessment of Education Progress in Reading (NAEP-Reading) demonstrate the lack of effectiveness of Reading First. In the 2009 NAEP-Reading, seven years into the implementation of Reading First and more than halfway to 2014, 33 percent of America's fourth-graders scored below the Basic level and 67 percent scored below the Proficient level. Only 8 percent performed at the Advanced level (National Center for Educational Statistics, 2010). Moreover, Reading First failed to reduce achievement gaps in reading. The gap between Hispanic and Caucasian fourth- and eighth-graders on the NAEP-Reading Test remained the same size in 2009 as it had been in 1992 (Hemphill & Vanneman, 2010).

The failure of Reading First is a fact. We are left to infer why it failed. The argument that it failed because it wasn't implemented correctly does not hold water because of the scripted reading programs, the extreme pressure on schools to achieve AYP, and the fidelity monitoring many schools put into place. The failure of Reading First can probably be attributed to two factors—the narrow scope of the instruction and the scripted nature of that instruction.

Instruction in the programs adopted by Reading First schools was focused almost exclusively on phonics and fluency. Vocabulary and comprehension instruction were largely left until the later elementary years when students should have mastered phonics skills and be reading fluently. Lesaux and Kieffer (2010) gave a standardized reading comprehension test to 581 urban sixth-graders and found that 45 percent of them scored at or below the 35th percentile. The 262 struggling readers were then given a battery of tests to determine their relative strengths and weaknesses on the major components of reading. Decoding, as measured by nonsense words, was above average for 78.6 percent of the struggling readers and a relative strength for the majority of the rest. Fluency was at least average or a relative strength for the majority of struggling readers. What the struggling readers had most in common was low meaning vocabulary knowledge. This study and others similar to it demonstrate that the near exclusive focus under Reading First on phonics and fluency did not prevent us from having struggling readers or teach them what they would need to know to be able to comprehend satisfactorily when they reach the upper elementary grades and middle school.

One of the most basic principles of effective instruction is that teachers must tailor their instruction to the needs of their students. In a scripted program, you can't do that and if you do deviate from the script and one of the watchers happens to be sitting at the back of your classroom, you will be "called down" for your lack of fidelity.

Teachers we have worked with have cited many instances of this kind of monitoring. The one that is most egregious and hard to believe unless you heard it firsthand was from the African-American first-year teacher who told us he was marked down on the evaluation for not following the script. Following the script from the manual, he introduced the word *Caribbean* before students had read it. A student raised his hand and asked, "Where is that Caribbean?" This fledgling teacher pulled down the map, located the Caribbean, and then continued the lesson as scripted. He received an unsatisfactory evaluation. Locating the Caribbean on the map was not in the script!

In hindsight, we should not be surprised by the failure of Reading First. In fact, if focusing instruction primarily on phonics and fluency and doing that instruction in a scripted way had worked, it would have contradicted much that decades of research, experience, and common sense have taught us.

Observing in the Classrooms of Unusually Effective Teachers

Reading First didn't work but we know what does work. All over the country—in rural, suburban, and urban areas—there are classrooms where, year after year, *all* the children succeed in learning to read and write. We know what happens in these overachieving classrooms. We know what kinds of environment, instruction, and activities the teachers provide that result in all children becoming readers and writers. In this chapter we will invite you into the classrooms of unusually effective teachers by sharing the observations of some very clever researchers. We will then summarize some of the characteristics you would see if you could be a "fly on the wall" in one of these "odds-beating" classrooms.

One of the first research studies that actually observed what was happening in classrooms to try to determine effective classroom practice was conducted by Michael Knapp in 140 classrooms in moderate- to high-poverty areas of California, Ohio, and Maryland (Knapp, 1995). After two years of observations, Knapp concluded that classrooms with the highest achievement gains were classrooms in which teachers:

- Emphasized higher-order meaning construction more than lower-order skills
- Maximized opportunities to read
- Integrated reading and writing with other subject areas
- Provided opportunities to discuss what was read

A team of researchers headed by Ruth Wharton-McDonald (Wharton-McDonald, Pressley, & Hampston, 1998) carried out the first extensive observational study to determine what actually happens in the classrooms of outstanding first-grade teachers. Administrators in school districts in upstate New York nominated "exemplary" first-grade teachers as well as "more-typical—solid but not outstanding"—first-grade teachers. In choosing the exemplary teachers, administrators were asked to consider their own observations of the teacher; teacher, parent, and student enthusiasm; the reading and writing achievement of children in that classroom; and the ability of the teacher to teach children with a wide range of abilities.

Five outstanding teachers and five more-typical teachers were identified, and the researchers made multiple visits to their classrooms across one school year. In addition to being observed, the teachers were interviewed across the year about their teaching and how they made decisions. Throughout the year, the observers also looked for indicators of how well the children in these 10 classrooms were reading and writing.

At the end of the year, the researchers reclassified the teachers according to the achievement of the children. Three classes had unusually high achievement. Most of the students in these three classrooms were reading books at or above first-grade level. They wrote pieces longer than a page in length, and their writing showed reasonably good coherence, punctuation, capitalization, and spelling. These three classes with the highest reading and writing achievement also had the highest levels of engagement. Most of the students were working productively on reading and writing most of the time.

The researchers then looked at the observation and interview data from these three classrooms with the highest levels of reading, writing, and engagement and compared them with the data from other classrooms. Although there were many similarities across all classrooms, the three outstanding first-grade classes differed from the others in significant ways:

- All of the teachers provided both skills instruction and reading and writing, but the teachers in the highest-achieving classrooms integrated skills teaching with reading and writing.
- Every minute of time in the highest-achieving classrooms was used well. Teachers in these classrooms turned even mundane routines into instructional events.
- Teachers in the highest-achieving classrooms used lots of scaffolding and coaching—providing support but always trying to get the most out of every child.
- Teachers in the highest-achieving classrooms constantly emphasized self-regulation and self-monitoring.
- In the high-achieving classrooms, reading and writing instruction was often integrated. Reading and writing were also integrated with content areas, and teachers made many cross-curricular connections.
- Teachers in the high-achieving classes had high expectations for their children—both for their learning to read and write and for their behavior. Students knew how they were expected to act and behaved accordingly most of the time.
- Teachers in the high-achieving classrooms were excellent classroom managers.

Encouraged by the results of the Wharton-McDonald study and supported by a large grant, faculty at the University of Albany and other researchers planned and carried out an observational study of first-grade classrooms in five states (Pressley, Allington,

Wharton-McDonald, Block, & Morrow, 2001). Thirty exemplary or typical teachers were identified in New York, New Jersey, Texas, Wisconsin, and California, and year-long observations and interviews were conducted in their classrooms. At the end of the year, each teacher identified six students—two low achieving, two middle achieving, and two high achieving—and these children were administered a standardized reading test. Based on the results of this test, a most effective and a least effective teacher were identified for each of the five locations. Comparing observations in the classrooms of the most and least effective teachers revealed the following characteristics of the most effective classrooms:

- Skills were explicitly taught and related to reading and writing.
- Books were everywhere and used in a variety of ways—read aloud by the teacher and read and listened to on tape by the children.
- Children did a lot of reading and writing throughout the day and for homework.
- Teachers had high but realistic expectations of children and monitored progress regularly.
- Self-regulation was modeled and expected. Children were taught to check and reflect on their work and to make wise choices.
- Cross-curricular connections were made as children read and wrote while studying science and social studies themes.
- Classrooms were caring, positive, cooperative environments, in which discipline issues were handled quickly and quietly.
- Classroom management was excellent and teachers used a variety of grouping structures, including whole class, one-to-one teaching, and a variety of small groups.
- Classrooms showed high student engagement. Ninety percent of the students were engaged in their reading and writing work 90 percent of the time.

The researchers followed up their first-grade observational study by looking at exemplary teachers in fourth grade (Allington & Johnson, 2002). Thirty fourth-grade teachers from five states were identified. Classroom observations took place for 10 days in each classroom. Teachers and children were interviewed. Samples of student writing, reading logs, and end-of-year achievement tests provided information about the reading and writing abilities of the children. From their observations, interviews, and data, the researchers concluded that the following variables distinguished the most effective fourth-grade classrooms from the less effective fourth-grade classrooms:

- All kinds of real conversations took place regularly in the most effective classrooms. Children had conversations with each other and teachers had conversations with children.
- Through their conversations and in their instruction, teachers constantly modeled thinking strategies. More emphasis was put on How could we find out? than on right and wrong answers.
- All kinds of materials were used for reading and writing. Teachers "dipped" into reading, science, and social studies textbooks but rarely followed the lesson plans for these materials. Students read historical novels, biographies, and informational books. Magazines and the Internet were used to gather information.

- Word study focused on building interest in words and on looking for patterns in words.
- Learner interest and engagement were important variables in the teachers' planning. Teachers taught the standard curriculum but tailored it to their students' interests, needs, strengths, and weaknesses.
- *Managed choice* was a common feature in these classrooms. Students were often presented with a topic or problem and allowed to choose which part of it they would pursue and what resources they would use.
- Instruction took place in a variety of formats. Whole-class, various types of small groups, and side-by-side teaching were seen throughout the day.
- Students were expected to work collaboratively and take responsibility for their learning. Working together was valued. When problems occurred, teachers helped students figure out how to solve these problems so the group could successfully complete its task.
- Reading and writing were integrated with science and social studies. Many of the books chosen for the class to read tied into science and social studies topics.
- Teachers evaluated student work with consideration for improvement, progress, and effort. Self-evaluation was also encouraged and modeled.

In the late 1990s, Barbara Taylor, David Pearson, and other researchers at the Center for the Improvement of Early Reading Achievement (CIERA) began investigating school and classroom practices in schools with unexpectedly high achievement and compared them to what was happening in similar schools in which the children were not "beating the odds" (Taylor, Pearson, Clark, & Walpole, 2000). They identified 70 first-, second-, and third-grade teachers from 14 schools in Virginia, Minnesota, Colorado, and California. Teachers were observed monthly and kept weekly logs of instructional activities. They also completed a questionnaire on their reading/language arts instructional practices. Some of the teachers and principals also participated in interviews. In each classroom, data were gathered for two low and two average readers in the fall and in the spring. When comparing the classroom practices of the most effective teachers with those of the less effective teachers, researchers concluded that the most effective teachers shared these qualities:

- Had higher pupil engagement
- Provided more small-group instruction
- Provided more coaching to help children improve in word recognition
- Asked more higher-level comprehension questions
- Communicated more with parents
- Had children engage in more independent reading

For a peek into preschool and kindergarten classrooms that work, we invite you into classrooms observed by Connie Juel and associates (Juel, Biancarosa, Coker, & Deffes, 2003), who followed 200 low-income urban children from preschool to first grade. Juel and her associates tracked the development of these young children in two important areas—decoding and oral vocabulary. While it is generally accepted that young children need to develop phonemic awareness and phonics skills to become successful readers, meaning vocabulary—that is, the number of words students have meanings for in their speaking and listening vocabularies—is often ignored. Meaning vocabulary, however, is essential to comprehension, and deficits in the oral vocabularies of young children are apt to show up as comprehension deficits in future years.

When the 200 children were evaluated on their decoding and meaning vocabulary skills as they entered preschool, most showed deficits in both areas. The children improved in their decoding skills each year. By the middle of first grade, their average decoding scores were slightly above national norms. Although the children did make gains in oral vocabulary between preschool and first grade, they never caught up to national norms. In their vocabulary development, these low-income children were as far behind (nearly one standard deviation) in first grade as they had been in preschool.

Juel and her associates then looked at their classroom observations and coded all the instruction observed into five categories: letter-sound, oral language, anchored word, reading, and writing. The only category of activities that had a positive effect on oral vocabulary was anchored word instruction. Anchored word instruction was defined using an example from Pat Hutchins's *Rosie's Walk*:

> The teacher had printed the words *pond, mill* and *haystack* on large cards which she places on the floor in front of her students. As she rereads the story, she points to the word cards and asks the students to walk around them the way Rosie walks around each of the locations in the book. The class discusses the meaning of the words *pond, mill* and *haystack.* (p. 13)

The article goes on to explain that the teacher then helps children with the sounds in the words *pond, mill,* and *haystack* but only after having the children actively involved in adding these words to their oral vocabularies. Choosing important words from reading, printing them on cards, and focusing specifically on their meanings is what Juel defines as *anchored word instruction.*

First-graders who had experienced more anchored word instruction had higher oral vocabulary scores. This increase occurred for children who entered preschool with low, average, and high levels of oral vocabulary. Conversely, the oral vocabulary scores of children in classrooms that spent the largest amount of time in letter-sound instruction decreased. This decrease in scores occurred for children who entered preschool with low, average, and high levels of oral vocabulary. Juel concluded her research with one of the best arguments for the need for balanced instruction at all grade levels:

> Ultimately, effective early reading instruction must help students learn to identify words and know their meanings. With so much research emphasizing the importance of early development in both word reading and language skills, we must consider how to provide instruction that fosters students' vocabulary development without losing the promising results of effective instruction in decoding. It does little good, after all, to be able to sound out the words *pond, mill* and *haystack* if you have no idea what they mean. (p. 18)

Observing in the Most Successful Schools

In 2005, Pat Cunningham conducted a study of effective schools (Cunningham, 2006; 2007). She identified six schools with high levels of poverty and large numbers of children who passed their states' literacy tests. The six schools were located in five different states. All but one school were located in medium-sized cities in the midwest, northeast, and southeast. The non-urban school was on an army base. The percentage of children in these schools who qualified for free/reduced-price lunch ranged from 68 to 98 percent. Students in two of the schools were predominately Hispanic and most of these students were English language learners. One school was almost exclusively African American. Two of the schools had mixed populations of children, with approximately half Caucasian and half African-American students. In the army base school, 70 percent of the students were Caucasian. The tests taken by the students varied according to the states in which they were located. Scores on the 2005 state literacy tests indicated that between 68 and 87 percent of students met or exceeded the state's standards for proficiency. All six schools scored better on their literacy tests than other schools in their districts that had lower levels of poverty.

The third factor all six schools shared was that they used the Four Blocks framework to organize their literacy instruction. Four Blocks, a framework for balanced literacy in the primary grades, began in the 1989 school year in one first-grade classroom (Cunningham, Hall, & Defee, 1991). Since then, it has expanded to include a Building Blocks framework in kindergarten and a Big Blocks framework in upper grades. At all grade levels, instructional time and emphasis is divided between a Words Block, which includes sight words, fluency, phonics, and spelling; a Guided Reading Block, which focuses on comprehension strategies for story and informational text and building prior knowledge and meaning vocabulary; a Writing Block, which includes both process writing and focused writing; and a Self-Selected Reading Block, which includes teacher read-alouds and independent reading.

The six schools had three things in common: They had large numbers of poor children, they had done better than expected on their states' literacy tests, and they all used the Four Blocks framework. What did they do that allowed them to achieve their success? To attempt to answer this question, 12 factors were identified that research suggests are important to high literacy achievement: assessment, community involvement, comprehensive curriculum, engagement, instruction, leadership, materials, parent participation, perseverance, professional development, specialist support, and time spent reading and writing. Through interviews and school visits, it was determined that all 12 factors were valued by all six schools and played important roles in school decision making. To determine which of the 12 factors was most important to the schools' success, teachers and administrators completed a survey in which they ranked these 12 factors according to their perceived importance.

None of these factors is unimportant, but when the teachers and administrators in these schools were forced to decide what contributed most to their success, *time spent reading and writing*, the *engagement* of their students in the literacy activities, and their *perseverance* in sticking with the Four Blocks framework were ranked as the most important factors.

The final evidence of what works in raising reading achievement comes from Chula Vista, California (Fisher, Frey, & Nelson, 2012). Chula Vista is a large school district with more than 27,000 K–6 students. The high level of poverty in Chula Vista is evidenced by the fact that 45 percent of their students qualify for free/reduced-price lunch and only 13 percent of the students are Caucasian. In 2002, only two of Chula Vista's 44 elementary schools performed satisfactorily according to the California Academic Performance Index (API). Chula Vista implemented Reading First by purchasing a commercial reading program, providing teachers with 120 hours of professional development on how to use the reading program, and observing teachers daily to ensure the fidelity of implementation. By 2004, after two years of using the scripted reading program, nine of 44 schools performed satisfactorily on the API.

In 2005, Chula Vista abandoned the idea that scripted instruction could achieve their goals of teaching all children to read and adapted a model based on developing teacher expertise in reading instruction and supporting teachers in teaching reading lessons based on the needs and interests of students. They adopted the Gradual Release of Responsibility Model of instruction (Pearson & Gallagher, 1983) in which teachers first modeled and scaffolded the comprehension strategies they were teaching, then had the students practice the strategies in small groups, and, finally, asked students to perform the strategies independently. Across the next several years, leadership teams conducted regular classroom walk-throughs and provided professional development to teachers based on the instruction they observed. Scores on the 2011 tests indicated that 41 of Chula Vista's 44 schools now performed satisfactory on the California API.

What We Know About Effective Classrooms

Based on the research studies of effective classrooms and schools, we can draw some firm conclusions about what it takes to create classrooms in which all the children learn to read and write.

The Most Effective Classrooms Provide Huge Amounts of Balanced, Comprehensive Instruction

Balance is an overused word these days, but it is still an important concept in classroom instruction. Balance can be thought of as a multiple vitamin. We know that many vitamins are required for good health, and we try to eat a balanced diet. Many of us take a multiple vitamin each day as extra insurance that we are getting all the most important nutrients. The most effective teachers provide all the important ingredients that go into creating thoughtful, avid readers and writers. Exceptional teachers teach skills and strategies and also provide lots of time each day for children to read and write. The Juel study, in particular, points out the importance of balance (Juel et al., 2003). When teachers spend too much time on one component—teaching decoding—the development of another important component—meaning vocabulary—suffers.

Children in the Most Effective Classrooms Do a Lot of Reading and Writing

We have long known that the amount of reading and writing children do is directly related to how well they read and write. Classrooms in which all the students learned to read and write are classrooms in which the teachers gave more than "lip service" to the importance of actually engaging in reading and writing. They planned their time so that children did a lot of reading and writing throughout the day—not just in the 100 minutes set aside for reading and language arts.

Science and Social Studies Are Taught and Integrated with Reading and Writing

In a misguided effort to raise test scores, some schools have eliminated science and social studies in the primary grades and asked teachers just to focus on "the basics." Unfortunately, children who have not had regular science and social studies instruction usually enter the intermediate grades with huge vocabulary deficits. Science and social studies are the "knowledge" part of the curriculum. Young children need to be increasing the size and depth of their meaning vocabularies so that they can comprehend the more sophisticated and less familiar text they will be reading as they get older. Exemplary teachers don't choose reading and writing over science and social studies. Rather, they integrate reading and writing with the content areas. As children engage in science and social studies units, they have daily opportunities to increase the size of their meaning and knowledge stores and real reasons for reading and writing.

Meaning Is Central and Teachers Emphasize Higher-Level Thinking Skills

In today's society, where almost every job requires a high level of literacy, employers demand that the people they hire be able to communicate well and thoughtfully as they read and write. Low levels of literal comprehension and basic writing are no longer acceptable in the workplace. The most effective teachers emphasize higher-level thinking skills from the beginning. They ask questions that do not have just one answer. They engage students in conversations and encourage them to have conversations with one another. They teach students to problem solve, self-regulate, and monitor their own comprehension. Classrooms in which all the children learn to read and write are classrooms in which meaning is central to all instruction and activities.

Skills and Strategies Are Explicitly Taught, and Children Are Coached to Use Them While Reading and Writing

Excellent teachers know what strategies children need to be taught, and they teach these explicitly—often through modeling and demonstration. More importantly, these excellent teachers never lose sight of the goals of their instruction. When working with children in a small group or in a one-on-one reading or writing setting, these teachers remind children to use what they have been taught. Because the children are doing a lot of reading and writing, they have numerous opportunities to apply what they are learning and to do so independently.

Teachers Use a Variety of Formats to Provide Instruction

The argument about whether instruction is best presented in a whole-class, a small-group, or an individual setting is settled when you observe excellent teachers. Teachers who get the best results from their children use a variety of formats, depending on what they want to accomplish. In addition to providing whole-class, small-group, and individual instruction themselves, excellent teachers use a variety of collaborative grouping arrangements to allow children to learn from one another. Excellent teachers group children in a variety of ways and change these groupings from day to day, depending on what format they determine will best achieve their goals.

A Wide Variety of Materials Are Used

In some schools today, there is a constant search for the "magic bullet" to increase reading achievement. "What program should we buy?" is the question these schools ask. Not a single one of the exemplary teachers found in the various observational studies was using only one program or set of materials. All the teachers gathered and used the widest range of materials available to them. Administrators who restrict teachers to any one set of materials will find no support for this decision in the research on outstanding teachers.

Classrooms Are Well Managed and Have High Levels of Engagement

In order to learn, children must be in a safe and orderly environment. If there are many disruptions and behavior management issues in a classroom, they will take the teacher's time away from teaching and the children's focus away from learning. All the teachers in the most effective classrooms had excellent classroom management. They expected children to behave in a kind and courteous manner and made these expectations known. These classrooms all had high levels of engagement. Almost all the children were doing what they were supposed to be doing almost all the time. If this seems a bit unreal to you, think about all the factors underlying these well-managed, highly engaging classrooms. Instead of doing a lot of worksheets and repetitive drills, the children were engaged in a lot of reading and writing. Because the teachers took into account the interests and needs of the children, the students were interested in what they were reading and writing. The fourth-grade classrooms, in particular, featured a great amount of managed choice and collaborative learning. Children spent time investigating topics they cared about with friends with whom they were encouraged to have conversations. Teachers focused their evaluations on improvement and progress, and they guided the children in becoming self-reliant and responsible for their own learning. Classrooms in which the activities seem real and important to the children are classrooms in which children are more engaged with learning and less apt to find reasons to be disruptive.

Common Core Raises the Bar

While schools across the nation were working to implement Reading First and becoming increasingly frustrated with the results they were getting, the National Governors Association and the Council of Chief State School Officers were working to develop high-quality education standards. These Common Core State Standards for English Language Arts (CCSS-ELA) specify what K–12 students should be able to do at each grade level in the areas of reading, writing, language, speaking, and listening (National Governors Association Center for Best Practices [NGA] & Council of Chief State School Officers [CCSSO], 2010). In developing these standards, the governors and chief state school officers worked backward from their previously developed College and Career Readiness (CCR) standards. The standards are very rigorous and require elementary students to engage in higher-level thinking, synthesis, and analysis, as they read or listen, to write well-formulated, mechanically correct opinion, informational and narrative pieces, and to conduct and summarize research. By the end of fifth grade, students are expected to be able to integrate information from several texts on the same topic in order to write or speak about the topic knowledgeably—a task that would be challenging for many college graduates!

The majority of states have adopted the CCSS-ELA standards and teachers are working to provide instruction that will help students meet the very high standards and pass the tests that will evaluate how well the students—and teachers—are doing in the quest to be college and career ready!

Creating Your Classroom That Works

From the first edition to the current edition, we have been writing this book for you—the classroom teacher. It has been clear to everyone for decades that the teacher is the most important variable in how well children learn to read and write. In 1967, the results of the first-grade studies were reported. Teams of investigators examined the effectiveness of programs and approaches for teaching beginning reading. The principal finding of this seminal and national study was summarized by Bond and Dykstra (1967):

> "to improve reading instruction, it is necessary to train better teachers of reading rather than to expect a panacea in the form of methods and materials" (p. 416).

The critical role of the teacher in determining reading achievement was confirmed by Nye, Konstantopoulos, and Hedges (2004) in a large study that showed that teacher effects were more powerful than any other variable, including class size and socioeconomic status. Although there are many restrictions on what elementary classroom teachers can do, most teachers are still given a great deal of freedom in deciding exactly how their classrooms will be run, how the various materials will be used, what the daily schedule will be like, what kinds of instructional formats they will use, how they will monitor and assess the progress of their students, and how they will create a well-managed, engaging environment. By learning from the most exemplary teachers—teachers who "beat the odds" in helping all their children achieve thoughtful literacy—you can create classrooms that work *even better* than they have in the past. You can teach all your students to read and write at the high levels required for them to be college and career ready.

2

Creating
Independent Readers

IN CHAPTER 1, we described the characteristics of classrooms that work—classrooms in which all the children become the very best readers and writers they can be. These classrooms share many important features. Teachers in these classrooms provide a comprehensive curriculum and devote time and energy to all the important components of literacy. They model, demonstrate, and encourage. They emphasize meaning and integrate reading and writing with each other and with the content areas. They use a variety of groupings and side-by-side teaching. They use a wide assortment of materials and are not tied to any one published program. They have excellent classroom management, based primarily on engaging their students in meaningful and worthwhile endeavors. Children spend a lot of their time actually engaged in reading and writing.

In this chapter, we will focus on the essential component that must be in place in any classroom where all the children learn to read and write. In order to become literate, children must become readers. Readers are not just children who *can* read—they are children who *do* read. The amount of reading children do is highly correlated with how well they read. The number of words in your meaning vocabulary store is directly related to how much you read, and your reading comprehension is heavily dependent on having meanings for the words you read. *Fluency*—the ability to read quickly and with expression—is also related to how much you read.

Reading is complex, and teaching children to read is equally complex. The fact that children must do a lot of reading to become good readers, however, is simple and straightforward. Because creating enthusiastic and independent readers is the essential foundation on which all good instruction can be built, we begin this book by describing how to create classrooms in which all children become readers. We hope that as you think about how to make your classroom one in which all children become readers, you will begin by considering how much and how willingly they read and what steps you can take to increase both those levels.

Assess and Document Your Students' Independent Reading

One of the characteristics of the most effective teachers is that they regularly assess how children are progressing toward meeting important goals and then adjust their instruction based on these assessments. Suppose that having all your children read more enthusiastically is one of your most important goals. You will be more apt to achieve this goal if you have some way of knowing where your children are early in the year and how they are progressing toward that goal.

Many teachers do a status assessment early in the year to determine how the children feel about themselves as readers. They file these assessments away and then have the children respond to the same questions halfway through the year and at the end of the year. After the children assess themselves halfway through the year, the teachers give them the reports they completed early in the year and have them compare how they are "growing up" as readers. Both the early-in-the-year reports and the midyear reports are then filed away. At the end of the year, the teachers have children self-report their reading habits one last time. After the students complete the final report, the teachers give them the first and second reports and have them write paragraphs summarizing their change and growth as readers. Many children are amazed (and proud!) to see how much more they like to read. The "Reading and Me" form is one example of the type of report you might use to help you and your students assess their growth as readers.

Make a Teacher Read-Aloud an Everyday Event

Do you read aloud to your students at least once every day? Teacher read-alouds have been shown to be one of the major motivators for children's desire to read. In 1975, Sterl Artley asked successful college students what they remembered their teachers doing that motivated them to read. The majority of students responded that teachers reading aloud

● Reading and Me ●

My name is _____.

Here is how I feel about reading as of _____ (today's date).

The best book I ever read was _____.

I like it because _____.

The best book I read in the last 4 months was _____.

I like it because _____.

My favorite author is _____.

My favorite kind of book is _____.

When I am home, I read: (Circle one)

    Almost Never   Sometimes   Almost Every Day   Every Day

This is how I feel about reading right now: (Circle one)

    I love reading.   I like reading.   I don't like reading.   I hate reading.

to the class was what got them interested in reading. More recently, elementary students were asked what motivated them to read particular books. The most frequent response was "My teacher read it to the class" (Palmer, Codling, & Gambrell, 1994). Ivey and Broaddus (2001) surveyed 1,765 sixth-graders to determine what motivates them to read. The responses of this large group of diverse preteens indicated that their major motivation for reading came from having time for independent reading of books of their own choosing and teachers reading aloud to them.

Reading aloud to children is a simple and research-proven way to motivate children of all ages to become readers. When thinking about your struggling readers, however,

Common Core Connections: Teacher Read-Aloud and Independent Reading

Speaking and Listening is one of the four major strands of the CCSS-ELA and Standard 2 relates directly to text read-aloud. Children in kindergarten and first and second grade are expected to describe and answer questions about key details in a text read aloud. Third-, fourth-, and fifth-graders are expected to determine main ideas and details and summarize text read aloud to them. Including daily read-alouds of a variety of texts through the elementary grades will help your students meet Listening and Speaking Standard 2.

Reading Standard 10 requires children to read grade-level stories, plays, poems, and informational and technical texts independently and proficiently. Your instruction, as described in the next chapters, will teach students how to read and comprehend a variety of texts. Independent reading time is their opportunity to independently apply what you are teaching them to materials of their own choosing.

I (Pat) first heard this report on female/male preferences for fiction versus informational texts on *All Things Considered* while driving home from a workshop I had just done on motivation to read. I was instantly transported back to a fourth-grade class I taught many years ago. I had five "resistant" readers—all boys—who I tried all kinds of things with to motivate them to read. I can clearly hear their voices telling me that they didn't want to read because "Reading is dumb and silly." At the time, I thought this was just their way of rationalizing the fact that they weren't good readers.

I read to my fourth-graders every day, but I am embarrassed to admit I can't think of a single nonfiction title I read aloud. I read *Charlotte's Web* but never a book about real spiders. What if their "reading is dumb and silly" attitude was engendered by the fanciful text I so enjoyed reading to them?

Reading to children motivates many of them to want to read—and particularly to want to read the book the teacher reads aloud. I wonder if my struggling boys' attitude toward reading was an unintended consequence of years of being read to by female teachers who were reading their favorite books—which just happened to be mostly fiction! If I could go back in time, I would resolve to read equal amounts of fiction and informational text. Yes, I would still read *Charlotte's Web,* but I would also read Gail Gibbon's wonderful book *Spiders.*

you also need to consider *what* you are reading aloud. Did you know that most of the fiction sold in bookstores is sold to women and most of the informational texts are sold to men? Now, this doesn't mean that women never read informational texts or that men never read fiction; it just means that males seem to have a preference for information and females for fiction.

Include Both Fact and Fiction

Reading aloud matters to motivation, and what you read aloud may really matter to your struggling readers. In *True Stories from Four Blocks Classrooms* (Cunningham & Hall, 2001), Deb Smith describes her daily teacher read-aloud session. Each day, Deb reads one chapter from a fiction book, a part of an information book, and an "everyone" book. She chooses the "everyone" book by looking for a short, simple book that "everyone in her class will enjoy and can read." (She *never* calls these books "easy" books!) By reading from these three types of books daily, Deb demonstrates to her students that all kinds of books are cherished and acceptable in her classroom. Deb follows her teacher read-aloud with independent reading time. The informational books and "everyone" books are popular choices, especially with her boys who struggle with reading.

Reading aloud to students is more common in primary grades than in upper grades, even though it might be even more important for teachers of older children to read aloud. Most children develop the reading habit between the ages of 8 and 11. Reading aloud to older children provides the motivation for them to read at the critical point when they have the literacy skills to take advantage of that motivation. Intermediate teachers need to make a special effort to read books from all the different sections of the bookstore. Most of us who are readers established our reading preferences in these preteen years. If you read *Cam Jansen* mysteries then, you probably still enjoy reading mysteries today. If you read *Star Wars* and *Star Trek* books then, you probably still enjoy science fiction today. If you packed biographies of famous people and informational books about sports to take to camp, the books you pack in your vacation travel bags today are probably still more information than fiction.

One way you can motivate more of your students to become readers is to read some books in a series and some books by authors who have written many other books. Remember that your students often want to read the book you read aloud. Read aloud one of David Adler's *Cam Jansen* mysteries, and then show students several more of these mysteries that you wish you had time to read aloud to them. Read aloud one of Gail Gibbon's informational books on animals—perhaps *Sharks* or *Whales* or *Dogs*—and then show students the other 40 Gibbon animal books you wish you had time to read to them. Your students who like mysteries may have "choice anxiety" trying to decide which *Cam Jansen* mystery they want to read first, and your animal lover informational readers will not know where to begin with all of Gail Gibbon's wonderful animal books. Unlike most anxiety, this kind of choice anxiety is a good thing!

Male Reading Models

Most elementary teachers are women, and most struggling readers are boys. A lot of boys believe that "Real men don't read books!" Many schools have reported an increase in students' motivation to read after some "real men" came in to read books to their classes.

Finding these real men and getting them to come to school regularly is not easy, but if you are on the lookout for them, they can often be found. Service organizations such as the Jaycees and the Big Brothers are a place to begin your search. City workers, including policemen and firemen, may also be willing to help. Would the person who delivers something to your school each week be flattered to be asked to come and read to your class? If some construction is being done in your neighborhood, the construction company may feel that it is good public relations to allow its workers to volunteer to come into your classroom for a half hour each week and read to your class.

Cindy Visser (1991), a reading specialist in Washington, reported how her school formed a partnership with the local high school football team. Football players came once a month and read to elementary classes. Appropriate read-aloud books were chosen by the elementary teachers and sent to the high school ahead of time. Interested athletes chose books and took them home to "polish their delivery." On the last Friday of the month, the athletes donned their football jerseys and rode the team bus to the elementary school. The arrival of the bus was greeted by cheering elementary students, who escorted the players to their classes. There, they read to the children and answered questions about reading, life, and, of course, football. This partnership, which was initiated by an elementary school in search of male reading models, turned out to be as profitable for the athletes as it was for the elementary students. The coach reported a waiting list of athletes who wanted to participate and a boost in the self-esteem of the ones who did.

You may want to make a list of different genres, titles, and authors, on which you can record the books you have read aloud. By keeping a Teacher Record Sheet, you can be sure you are opening the doors to all the different kinds of wonderful books there are.

If you teach older children, you can show your students the whole range of items that adults read by bringing real-world reading materials, such as newspapers and magazines, into the classroom and reading tidbits from these with an "I was reading this last night and

It's Never Too Late! Become a Book Whisperer!

If you need inspiration and lots of practical tips for turning older children on to books, read Donalyn Miller's *The Book Whisperer*. Donalyn is a teacher who requires her sixth-graders to read 40 books during the year they spend in her classroom! Most of her students, including her English learners, reach or exceed this goal. She begins the books by describing the dilemma many teachers of teens and tweens face:

> So many children don't read. They don't read well enough; they don't read often enough; and if you talk to children, they will tell you that they don't see reading as meaningful to their life. (p. 2)

If you can hear yourself saying these very words, read Donalyn's book and you will be empowered to change this in your classroom and change the future for many of your struggling readers.

• Teacher Record Sheet: •
Books and Magazines Read Aloud This Year

Type	Title	Author
Mystery	_____	_____
Science Fiction	_____	_____
Fantasy	_____	_____
Contemporary Fiction	_____	_____
Historical Fiction	_____	_____
Multicultural Fiction	_____	_____
Sports Fiction	_____	_____
Other Fiction	_____	_____
Sports Informational	_____	_____
Animal Informational	_____	_____
Multicultural Informational	_____	_____
Science Informational	_____	_____
Other Informational	_____	_____
Biography	_____	_____
Easy Chapter-Series	_____	_____
Authors with Other Books	_____	_____
Magazines	_____	_____

just couldn't wait to get here and share it with you" attitude. You may also want to keep a book of poetry handy and read one or two poems whenever appropriate. No intermediate-aged student can resist the appeal of Jack Prelutsky's or Judith Viorst's poems. In addition to poetry, your students will look forward to your reading to them if you often read snippets from *The Guinness Book of World Records* and from your favorite joke and riddle books. Be sure to include some of the wonderful new multicultural books in your read-aloud, so that all your students will feel affirmed by what you read aloud to them.

Talking Partners

Many teachers use a "Turn and Talk" routine to increase student talk and engagement. Before introducing Turn and Talk to your students, think carefully about who you will pair with whom. If you have children learning English, do you have other children who speak their language and whose English is more advanced so they could do some translating? Do you have a "budding teacher" who, although not able to speak the language of the child learning English, would enjoy teaching that child? If you have a child with attention or behavior problems, could you pair that child with someone he or she is friends with and thus more likely to want to talk with and listen to? Thinking about what kind of support you want the partners to provide for the various activities and assigning partners purposefully are the secrets to the success of this collaborative grouping.

After you have decided on the talking partners, think about when you want to have the partners turn and talk, and seat your talking partners together for this activity. Many teachers use Turn and Talk regularly during their teacher read-aloud so they assign places on the carpet to the talking partners. Periodically, they stop during their reading and pose a question and give students 30 seconds to turn and talk.

> "Turn and talk to your partner about what you see in the pictures. How many things can you name?"
> "Turn and tell your partner what you think is going to happen next."
> "Turn and tell your partner if you think the boy has a plan that will work."
> "Would you like to take a trip to the moon? Tell your partner why or why not."
> "Do you think the things in this story could really happen? Explain to your partner what you think and why."

The possibilities for Turn and Talk during teacher read-aloud are endless. When you incorporate Turn and Talk into your read-aloud, you can raise both the level of thinking your students do and their active engagement with the text. After students talk with one another, resist the temptation to let everyone share with the whole group. This will slow your read-aloud down considerably and you have accomplished what you wanted to accomplish by letting them share their thinking with each other. After the 30 seconds, return to your read-aloud and acknowledge their thinking with a general response.

> "You named a lot of the things in the picture. Listen and see if you called them what the author called them."
> "I heard lots of good predictions. Let's see what did happen."
> "Some of you think yes and some of you think no. Let's read on and see."
> "Thumbs up if you told your partner you would like to go to the moon."
> "Most of you thought the story was imaginary. Here are some of the good reasons I heard you use to explain your thinking."

English Language Learners

Approximately 25 percent of the children in U.S. elementary schools speak a language other than English as their home language. That means that one out of every four children in our classrooms must learn to *speak* English as they learn how to read and write English. Use your teacher read-aloud time as one vehicle for developing English vocabulary. Be sensitive to vocabulary that might not be understood and ask your students to explain what unfamiliar words mean. Be sure to include "everyone" books and informational books with lots of pictures as part of your teacher read-aloud. When reading an easy book, record that reading and let your English language learners listen to that book several times. If possible, include some books that reflect the culture of your English language learners.

Schedule Time Every Day for Independent Reading

The goal of every elementary teacher should be to have all children read for at least 20 minutes each day from materials they have chosen to read. Use an analogy to help your students understand that becoming good at reading is just like becoming good at anything else. Compare learning to read with learning to play the piano or tennis or baseball. Explain that in order to become good at anything, you need three things: (1) instruction, (2) practice on the skills, and (3) practice on the whole thing. To become a good tennis player, you need to (1) take tennis lessons, (2) practice the skills (backhand, serve, etc.), and (3) play tennis. To become a good reader, you also need instruction, practice on the important skills, and practice reading! Point out that sometimes we get so busy that we forget to take the important time each day to read. Therefore, we must schedule it, just like anything else we do.

At least 20 minutes daily for independent reading is the goal, but you may want to start with a shorter period of time and increase it gradually as your children establish the reading habit and learn to look forward to this daily "read what you want to" time. Consider using a timer to signal the beginning and end of the independent reading time. When engaging in activities regularly, some natural time rhythms are established. Using a timer to monitor independent reading will help children establish these rhythms. When the timer sounds at the end of the session, say something like "Take another minute if you need to get to a stopping point."

When the time for independent reading has begun, do not allow your students to move around the room, looking for books. You may want to suggest to the children that they choose several pieces of reading material before the time begins. Alternately, place a crate of books on each table, and let children choose from that crate. Every few days rotate the crates from table to table so that all the children have access to many different books "within arm's reach." Depending on the arrangement of your classroom, you might want some of your students to read in various spots around the room. Make sure that they all get to their spots before the reading time begins and they stay in that spot until the time is up. Help your students understand that reading requires quiet and concentration and that people wandering around are distracting to everyone.

Establishing and enforcing the "No wandering" rule is particularly important for struggling readers. If your students have not been successful with reading in the past and they are allowed to move around the room to look for books during the independent reading time, then they will be apt to spend more time wandering than reading. Remember

English Language Learners

Support your English language learners in choosing books they can read during independent reading time. Provide them with alphabet and simple picture dictionaries. If they can read in their home language, help them find books in that language. When they demonstrate that they can read some materials, encourage them to take those items home and share them with their families, who will be delighted with the progress their children are making in learning English.

that one of your major reasons for committing yourself to this daily independent reading time is that you know how much children read plays a critical role in how well they read. If your good readers read for almost all the allotted time and your struggling readers read for only half the time, the gap between your good and poor readers will further widen as the year goes on. Having a large variety of materials within arm's reach is crucial if your struggling readers are going to profit from this precious time you are setting aside each day for independent reading.

If you begin with just five or six minutes, kindergarteners and early first-graders can engage in independent reading even before they can read. Think about your own children or other young children you have known. Those who have been read to regularly often look at their books and pretend they are reading. Encourage your kindergarteners and early first-graders to get in the habit of reading even before they can do it. Many teachers of young children encourage them to "Pretend that you are the teacher and you are reading the book." Kindergarten children are also very motivated to read when they are allowed to pick a stuffed animal or a doll to read to!

Big Buddy Readers

Having easy-to-read books available for older struggling readers will not get you anywhere if those readers refuse to be seen reading "baby books"! One way to get older children to read easy books is to give them a real-life reason to do so. In some schools, older children (big buddies) go to the kindergarten and read aloud to their little buddies books that they have practiced ahead of time. Arranging such partnerships allows older poor readers to become reading models. The buddy system also serves another critical function in that it legitimizes the reading and rereading of very easy books.

Once you have a buddy system set up, you can have the kindergarten teacher send up a basket of books from which each of your big buddies can choose. Tell them that professional readers always practice reading a book aloud several times before reading it to an audience. Then, let them practice reading the book—first to themselves, then to a partner in the classroom, and finally to a tape recorder.

Accumulate the Widest Possible Variety of Reading Materials

To have successful independent reading, it is crucial that students choose their own reading materials and have plenty of materials to choose from. Collecting a lot of appealing books requires determination, cleverness, and an eye for bargains. In addition to obvious sources—such as getting free books from book clubs when your students order books, asking parents to donate, begging for books from your friends and relatives whose children have outgrown them, and haunting yard sales and thrift shops—there are some less obvious sources. Libraries often sell or donate used books and magazines on a regular basis. Some bookstores will give you a good deal on closeouts and may even set up a "donation basket," where they will collect used books for you. (Take some pictures of your eager readers and have them write letters that tell what kind of books they like to read for the store to display above the donation basket.)

Many classrooms subscribe to some of the popular children's magazines. You will have far fewer resistant readers if the latest issue and back copies of *Your Big Backyard, Children's Digest, Cricket, Soccer Junior, Ranger Rick, 3-2-1 Contact, Sports Illustrated for Kids, National Geographic for Kids,* and *Zoobooks* are available for your students to read during independent reading.

Another inexpensive source of motivating reading materials is the variety of news magazines for children, including *Scholastic News, Weekly Reader,* and *Time for Kids.* They generally cost about $4.00 per year, and you get a "desk copy" with an order of 10 to 12. Teachers across a grade level often share the magazines, with each classroom receiving two or three copies. These news magazines deal with topics of real interest to kids, and reading interest is always heightened on the day that a new issue arrives.

The Rotating Book Crates Solution

The goal of every teacher of struggling readers should be to have a variety of appealing reading materials constantly and readily available to the children. In one school, four intermediate teachers became convinced of the futility of trying to teach resistant children to read with almost no appealing materials in the classroom. The teachers appealed to the administration and the parent group for money and were told that it would be put in the budget "for next year." Not willing to "write off" the children they were teaching this year, each teacher cleaned out her or his closets (school and home), rummaged through the bookroom, and used other means to round up all the easy and appealing books they could find. Then they put these materials into four big crates, making sure that each crate had as much variety as possible. Mysteries, sports, biographies, science fiction, informational books, cartoon books, and the like were divided up equally.

Since the teachers did this over the Christmas holiday, they decided that each classroom would keep a crate for five weeks. At the end of each five-week period, a couple of students carried the crate of books that had been in their room to another room. In this way, the four teachers provided many more appealing books than they could have if each had kept the books in his or her own classroom.

The four-crate solution was one of those "necessity is the mother of invention" solutions that the teachers came up with to get through the year without many books; fortunately, it had serendipitous results. When the first crate left each classroom at the end of the initial five-week period, several children complained that they had not been able to read certain books or that they wanted to read some again. The teacher sympathized but explained that there were not enough great books to go around and that their crate had to go to the next room. The teacher then made a "countdown" calendar and attached it to the second crate. Each day, someone tore off a number so the children would realize that they had only 10, 9, 8, 7, and so on days to read or reread anything they wanted to from this second crate. Reading enthusiasm picked up when the students knew that they had limited time with these books.

When the third crate arrived, students dug in immediately. A race-like atmosphere developed as children tried to read as many books as possible before the crate moved on. When the fourth (and final) crate arrived, children already knew about some of the books that were in it. Comments such as "My friend read a great mystery in that crate, and I am going to read it, too" let the teachers know that the children were talking to their friends in other classes about the books in the crates!

While the enthusiasm generated by the moving crates of books had not been anticipated by the teachers, they realized in retrospect that it could have been. We all like something new and different, and "limited time only" offers are a common selling device. The following year, even with many more books available, the teachers divided their books up into seven crates and moved them every five weeks so that the children would always have new, fresh material.

Schedule Conferences So You Can Talk with Your Students About Their Reading

Early in the year, when you are getting your students in the habit of reading every day and gradually increasing the time for independent reading, circulate around and have whispered conversations with individual children about their books. Once the self-selected reading time has been well established, set up a schedule so that you can conference with one-fifth of your students each day. Use this time to monitor your children's reading, to encourage them in their individual reading interests, and to help them with book selection if they need that help.

If your reading conferences are going to be something your students look forward to (instead of dreading!), you need to think of them as conversations rather than interrogations. Here are some "conference starters" you can use to set a positive and encouraging tone for your conferences:

> "Let's see. What have you got for me today?"
>
> "Oh good, another book about ocean animals. I had no idea there were so many books about ocean animals!"

"I see you have bookmarked two pages to share with me. Read these pages to me, and tell me why you chose them."

"I never knew there was so much to learn about animals in the ocean. I am so glad you bring such interesting books to share with me each week. You are turning me into an ocean animal expert!"

"I can't wait to see what you bring to share with me next week!"

One way to make sure your conferences are kid-centered conversations, rather than interrogations, is to put the job of preparing for the conference on your students. Before you begin conferences, use modeling and role-playing to help children learn what their job is in the conference. Your children are to choose the book (or magazine) they want to share and bookmark the part they want to discuss with you. Make sure your students know they must prepare and be ready for the conference, since you will only have three or four minutes with each student. After role-playing and modeling, many teachers post a chart to remind children what they are to do on the day of their conference.

Rather than arbitrarily assigning one fifth of the class to the different conference days, consider dividing your struggling and avid readers across the days. Spend an extra minute or two with the struggling reader scheduled for the day. Many of these readers need help selecting books they can read. After your struggling reader shares the book chosen for that day, take a minute to help that student select some books or magazines to read across the next week. Advanced readers also often need an extra minute for help with book selection. These excellent readers are sometimes reading books that are very easy for them. Although reading easy books is good for all of us, it is nice to take a minute to nudge them forward in their book selection. Clever teachers do this in a "seductive" rather than a heavy-handed way.

"Carla, I know you love mysteries. The other day when I was in the library, I found two mysteries that made me think of you. Listen to this." (Teacher reads "blurb" on the back of each mystery to Carla.) "Now, I have to warn you: These mysteries are a little longer and harder than the ones you usually read. But you are such a good reader. I know you could handle them if you wanted to read them."

• Getting Ready for Your Reading Conference •

1. Choose the book or magazine you want to share.

2. Pick a part to read to me and practice this part.

3. Write the title and page number on a bookmark and put the bookmark in the right place.

4. Think about what you want to talk to me about. Some possibilities are:
   - What you like about this book
   - Why you chose this part to read to me
   - Other good parts of the book
   - What you think will happen (if you haven't finished the book)
   - What you are thinking about sharing with me next week
   - Who you think would also like this book

Carla will probably be delighted that you thought of her and believed she could read harder mysteries. She will very likely "take the bait" and go off with some mysteries closer to her advanced reading level.

Reading books you want to read motivates you to read more. Sharing those books once a week with someone who "oohs and aahs" about your reading choices is also a sure-fire motivator.

Make Time for Sharing and Responding

Children who read also enjoy talking to their classmates about what they have read. In fact, Manning and Manning (1984) found that providing time for children to interact with one another about reading material enhanced the effects of sustained silent reading on both reading achievement and attitudes.

One device sure to spark conversation about books is to create a classroom bookboard. Cover a bulletin board with white paper, and use yarn to divide it into 40 or 50 spaces. Select 40 to 50 titles from the classroom library, and write each title in one of the spaces. Next, make some small construction paper rectangles in three colors or use three colors of small sticky notes. Designate a color to stand for various reactions to the books.

- Red stands for "Super—one of the all-time best books I've ever read."
- Blue indicates that a book was "OK—not the best I've ever read but still enjoyable."
- Yellow stands for "Yucky, boring—a waste of time!"

Encourage your students to read as many of the bookboard books as possible and to put their "autographs" on red, blue, and yellow rectangles and attach them to the appropriate titles. Every week or two, lead your class in a lively discussion of the reasons for their book evaluations. If some books are universally declared "reds," "blues," or "yellows," ask your students to explain why the books were so wonderful or so lame. The most interesting discussions, however, can be centered on those books that are evaluated differently by your students. When most of your students have read some of the books on your bookboard, begin a new bookboard. This time, you may want to let each student select a book and label/decorate the spot for that book.

Another way to have your students share books with each other is to end the independent reading time with a *Reader's Chair,* in which one or two children do a book talk each day. Each child shows a favorite book and reads or tells a little about it and then tries to "sell" this book to the rest of the class. The students' selling techniques are quite effective, since these books are usually quickly seen in the hands of many of their classmates.

Another popular sharing option is to hold "reading parties" one afternoon every two or three weeks. Your students' names are pulled from a jar and they form groups of three or four, in which everyone gets to share his or her favorite book. Reading parties, like other parties, often include refreshments such as popcorn or cookies. Your students will develop all kinds of tasty associations with books and sharing books!

Finding time for children to talk about books is not easy in today's crowded curriculum. There is, however, a part of each day that is not well used in most elementary classrooms—the last 15 minutes of the day. Many teachers have found that they can successfully schedule weekly reading sharing time if they utilize those last 15 minutes one day each week. Here is how this sharing time works in one classroom.

Every Thursday afternoon, the teacher gets the children completely ready to be dismissed 15 minutes before the final bell rings. Notes to go home are distributed. Book bags are packed. Chairs are placed on top of the desks. The teacher has previously written down each child's name on an index card. The index cards are now shuffled and the first five names—which will form the first group—are called. These children go to a corner of the room that will always be the meeting place for the first group. The next five names that are called will form the second group and will go to whichever place has been designated for the second group. The process continues until all five or six groups have been formed and all the children are in their places. Now, each child has two minutes to read, tell, show, act out, or otherwise share something from what he or she has been reading this week. The children share in the order that their names were called. The first person called for each group is the leader. Each person has exactly two minutes and is timed by a timer. When the timer sounds, the next person gets two minutes. If a few minutes remain after all the children have had their allotted two minutes, the leader of each group selects something to share with the whole class. If you establish a regular sharing time, you will find that your students are more enthusiastic about reading. Comments such as "I'm going to stump them with these riddles when I get my two minutes" and "Wait 'til I read the scary part to everyone" are proof that your students are looking forward to sharing and that this anticipation is increasing their motivation to read. The popularity next week of books shared this week is further proof of the motivation power of book sharing.

Do Incentive Programs and Book Reports Demotivate Reading?

Many schools set up reading incentive programs in an attempt to get children to read real books. These programs can take many different forms. In some, children are given T-shirts that proclaim "I have read 100 books!" and in others, whole classes are rewarded with pizza parties if they have read "the most" books.

These reward systems are set up with the best intentions and may even motivate some children to begin reading. Unfortunately, another message can get communicated to children who are exposed to such incentive programs. The message goes something like "Reading is one of those things I must do in order to get something that I want." Reading thus becomes a means to an end, rather than an end in itself. Many teachers (and parents) report that children only read "short, dumb books" so that they can achieve the "longest list."

Doing book reports is another device used to motivate reading that can often have the opposite effect to what was intended. When adults are asked what they remember about elementary school that made them like reading, they mention having their teachers read books aloud to the class, being allowed to select their own books, and having time to read them. When asked what things teachers did that made them dislike reading, doing book reports is most commonly mentioned. Likewise today, few children enjoy doing book reports, and their dislike is often transferred to the act of reading. Some children report on the same books year after year, and others even admit lying about reading books and copying their book report from the summary on the Internet!

Children who are going to become readers must begin to view reading as its own reward. This intrinsic motivation can only be nurtured as children find books that they "just can't put down" and subsequently seek out other books. Incentive programs and book reports must be evaluated on the basis of how well they develop this intrinsic motivation.

Summary

The more you read, the better you read! Nagy and Anderson (1984) showed that good readers often read 10 times as many words as poor readers during the school day. Guthrie and Humenick (2004) analyzed 22 studies of reading achievement and found that access to interesting books and choice about what to read were strongly correlated with reading achievement scores. Stanovich (1986) labeled the tendency of poor readers to remain poor readers as "the Matthew effect" and attributed the increasing gap between good readers and poor readers in part to the difference in time spent reading.

Summer reading loss by low-income children is a well-documented fact. Cooper, Nye, Charlton, Lindsay, and Greathouse (1996) reviewed 13 studies representing approximately 40,000 students and found that, on average, the reading proficiency levels of students from lower income families declined over the summer months, while the reading proficiency levels of students from middle-income families increased. In one year, this decline resulted in an estimated three-month achievement gap between more advantaged and less advantaged students. Allington (2013) summarizes the results of an attempt to stem this summer reading loss by providing low-income children with 12 free self-selected books to read in the summer. The poor children who were provided with these books actually showed gains in reading achievement over the summer months while the control children who were not provided books lost ground.

Wide reading is highly correlated with meaning vocabulary, which, in turn, is highly correlated with reading comprehension. Students who read more encounter the same words more frequently, and repeated exposure to the same words has been shown to lead to improvements in fluency (Topping & Paul, 1999). A. E. Cunningham and Stanovich (1998) found that struggling readers with limited reading and comprehension skills increased vocabulary and comprehension skills when time spent reading was increased.

Wide reading is also associated with the development of automatic word recognition (Stanovich & West, 1989). Share (1999) reviewed the research and concluded that self-teaching of word recognition occurs while readers are decoding words during independent reading. Good decoders teach themselves to recognize many words as they read for enjoyment.

This chapter has described classroom-tested ways to create a classroom in which your students read enthusiastically and independently. Reading aloud to your students from all the different types of books and magazines is your best tool for motivating independent reading. Scheduling time every day for independent reading demonstrates to your students the importance of reading and ensures that all your students spend some time every day developing the reading habit. Having a wide variety of books and magazines available is critical to the success of independent reading—particularly with your struggling readers, who may not yet have discovered the perfect books for them. Sharing what they are reading in a weekly conference with you and periodically with their peers further motivates students to read and is consistent with a sociocultural view of literacy.

How Well Does Your Classroom Support the Creation of Independent Readers?

1. Do I set aside time to read aloud to my students?
2. Do I read aloud from a wide variety of fiction and informational books and magazines?
3. Do I seize opportunities to build meaning vocabulary when I read aloud to my students?
4. Do I set aside time for my students to engage in independent reading?
5. Do I let my students choose what they want to read from a wide variety of materials?
6. Do I conference with my students about their independent reading?
7. Do I set aside time for students to share what they are reading?
8. Have I considered how I might provide self-selected books to my needy children to read over the summer?

3

Building the Literacy Foundation

ASK MOST ADULTS when they learned to read, and most will tell you about their experiences in kindergarten or first grade. In reality, learning to read begins much earlier for many children. Think back to your own preschool years. You probably couldn't read in the way we usually think of it. You probably couldn't pick up a brand-new book and read it by yourself. But you probably did have some literacy skills in place before you were ever given any reading instruction in school.

Did you have a favorite book that someone read to you over and over? Did you ever sit down with a younger child or a stuffed animal and pretend you could read that book? Perhaps it was a predictable book, such as *Are You My Mother?* or *Pat the Bunny* or *Brown Bear, Brown Bear, What Do You See?* You probably didn't know all the individual words in the book, but you could sound like you were reading by telling in book language what was happening on the different pages.

Pretend reading is a stage that many 3- and 4-year-olds go through and is probably crucial to the ease with which they learn to read once they start school. Children who pretend to read a book know what reading is—that it has to "sound right" and "make sense." They also know that reading is enjoyable and something all the "big people" can do and thus something they are very eager to be able to do, too. Pretend reading is a way of experiencing what reading feels like even before you can do it and is an indicator of future success in reading.

Did you write before you came to school? Could you write your name and the names of your siblings, cousins, pets, or favorite restaurants?

Did you ever write a note like this?

Did you ever make a sign for your room that looked like this?

Many 4-year-olds love to write. Sometimes they write in scribbles.

Young children want to do everything that grown-ups can do. For the things they can't do yet, they just pretend they can! They pretend to drive, to take care of babies, to cook—and if they grow up in homes where the grown-ups read and write, they pretend they can read and write. As they engage in these early literacy behaviors, they learn important concepts.

Concepts That Form the Foundation for Literacy

Why We Read and Write

Ask 5-year-olds from strong literacy backgrounds why people read and write, and they reel off a string of answers:

> "Well, you have to able to read. You read books and signs and cereal boxes and birthday cards that come in the mail and recipes and ... You write notes and stories and signs and lists and you write on the computer and you send postcards when you are on a trip and you write to your aunt and ..."

You can tell from these answers that children who come to school with clear ideas about the functions of reading and writing have had many real-world experiences with reading and writing. Reading and writing are things all the bigger people they know do, and they intend to do them, too!

Background Knowledge and Vocabulary

A lot of what we know about the world, we have learned from reading. This is also true of young children. When parents or other people read to young children, they don't just read; they also talk with the children about what they are reading:

> "Do you know what that animal is called?"
>
> "Yes, it's a bear. The bears in this story are not real bears. We can tell because we know that real bears don't wear clothes or live in houses. Where could we go to see a real bear?"
>
> "Maybe we can find a book about real bears the next time we go to the library."

Comprehension is very highly correlated with prior knowledge and vocabulary. The more you know about any topic, the greater will be your understanding of what you read related to that topic. Your store of background knowledge and vocabulary directly affects how well you read. Young children who have had many books read to them simply know more than children who haven't.

Print Concepts

Print is what you read and write. Print includes all the funny little marks—letters, punctuation, spaces between words and paragraphs—that translate into familiar spoken language. In English, we read across the page in a left-to-right fashion. Because our eyes can see only a few words during each stop (called a *fixation*), we must actually move our eyes several times to read one line of print. When we finish that line, we make a return sweep and start all over again, left to right. If there are sentences at the top of a page, a picture in the middle, and more sentences at the bottom, we read the top first and then the bottom. We start at the front of a book and go toward the back. These arbitrary rules about how we proceed through print are called *conventions*.

Jargon refers to all the words we use to talk about reading and writing. Jargon includes such terms as *word, letter, sentence,* and *sound.* We use this jargon constantly as we try to teach children how to read:

> "Look at the **first word** in the **second sentence**."
> "How does that **word begin**?"
> "What **letter** has that **sound**?"

Children who have been read to and whose early attempts at writing have been encouraged often walk in the door of kindergarten knowing these critical print conventions and jargon. From being read to in the "lap position," they have noticed how the eyes "jump" across the lines of print as someone is reading. They have watched people write grocery lists and thank-you letters to Grandma, and they have observed the top-to-bottom, left-to-right movement. Often, they have typed on the computer and observed these print conventions. Because they have had people to talk with them about reading and writing, they have learned much of the jargon. While writing down a dictated thank-you note to Grandma, Dad may say,

> "Say your **sentence** one **word** at a time if you want me to write it. I can't write as fast as you can talk."

When the child asks how to spell *birthday,* he may be told,

> "It **starts with** the **letter *b***, just like your dog, Buddy's, name. *Birthday* and *Buddy* **start with the same sound and the same letter**."

Knowing these print concepts is an essential part of the foundation for becoming literate. Young children who have had lots of informal early experiences with reading and writing have already begun to develop understandings about print conventions and jargon.

Phonemic Awareness

The ability to recognize that words are made up of a discrete set of sounds and to manipulate those sounds is called *phonemic awareness,* and children's level of phonemic awareness is very highly correlated with their success in beginning reading. Phonemic awareness develops through a series of stages, during which children first become aware that language is made up of individual words, that words are made up of syllables, and that syllables are made up of phonemes. It is important to note here that it is not the jargon children learn. Five-year-olds cannot tell you there are three syllables in *dinosaur* and one syllable in *Rex.* What they can do is clap out the three beats in *dinosaur* and the one beat in *Rex.* Likewise, they cannot tell you that the first phoneme in *mice* is *m,* but they can tell you what you would have if you took the "mmm" off *mice—ice.* Children develop this phonemic awareness as a result of the oral and written language they are exposed to. Nursery rhymes, chants, and Dr. Seuss books usually play a large role in this development.

Phonemic awareness is an oral ability. You hear the words that rhyme. You hear that *baby* and *book* begin the same. You hear the three sounds in *bat* and can say these sounds separately. Only when children realize that words can be changed and how changing a sound changes the word are they able to profit from instruction in phonics.

Children also develop a sense of sounds and words as they try to write. In the beginning, many children let a single letter stand for an entire word. Later, they put in more letters and often say the word they want to write, dragging out its sounds to hear what letters they might use. Children who are allowed and encouraged to "invent-spell" develop an early and strong sense of phonemic awareness.

Some Concrete Words

In addition to print concepts and phonemic awareness, children who have been exposed to lots of reading and writing activities know some words. If you were to sit down with children in their first week of school and try to determine if they can read by giving them a simple book to read or testing them on some common words, such as *the, and, of,* and *with,* you would probably conclude that most of them can't read yet. But many young children do know some words. The words they know are usually "important-to-them" concrete words—*David, tiger, Pizza Hut, Cheerios.* Knowing a few words is important, not because you can read much with a few words but because in learning these first words, you have accomplished a critical task. You have learned how to learn words, and the few words you can read give you confidence that you can learn lots of words.

Some Letter Names and Sounds

Many children know some letter names and sounds when they come to school. They can't always recognize all 26 letters in both upper- and lowercase, and they often don't know the sound of *w* or *c,* but they have learned the names and sounds for the most common letters. Usually, the letter names and sounds children know have come from those concrete words they can read and write. Many children have also learned some letter names and sounds through repeated readings of alphabet books and through making words with magnetic letters on the refrigerator. In addition, children have learned some letter names and sounds as adults have spelled out words they were trying to write. This immersion in print has allowed children to make connections between the most common letters and sounds.

Desire to Learn to Read and Write

Children who have had lots of early literacy encounters can't wait to learn to read! All the big people can do it, and they want to, too! We all know of children who have come home disappointed after the first day of school because "We were there all day and didn't learn to read!" This "can't wait" attitude motivates and sustains them through the work and effort required to learn to read.

The Foundation

From early reading and writing experiences, children develop these critical concepts:

- Why we read and write
- Background knowledge and vocabulary
- Print concepts
- Phonemic awareness
- Some concrete words
- Some letter names and sounds
- Desire to learn to read

These concepts are not, however, all or nothing. Some children come to school with all the concepts quite well developed. Some children come with some developed but not all. Some children come with few of these concepts. Successful classrooms for young children are filled with lots of activities to help all children move along in their development of these crucial concepts.

Activities for Building the Foundation

Reading to Children and Independent Reading Time

The previous chapter outlined the importance of doing activities to promote enthusiastic and independent readers. If you have committed yourself to reading aloud to children and including a time for independent reading each day, you are well on your way to helping children build a firm foundation for learning to read. Many children are read to at home and are encouraged as they "pretend read" favorite books and attempt to read signs, labels, and other environmental print. For these children, your teacher read-alouds and independent reading encouragement will just move them further along in their literacy development. For children who have not had these experiences before coming to school, daily teacher read-alouds and independent reading time will give them a successful start in building the foundation for literacy.

Reading to children and providing time for them to read independently will also help children build their oral vocabularies. You may want to capitalize on an anchored vocabulary activity found to be effective in helping low-income young children build their oral vocabularies by picking important words from the books you read aloud to them and focusing their attention on those words. Find or copy a picture to go with each word. Put these words together in a book, with each page having one picture and the word that goes with it. Label the book according to the category the word belongs in. Make these books available for self-selected reading, and you will have lots of simple books that even your most struggling readers can find success with and enjoy.

Supporting and Encouraging Writing

Some people believe that if children are allowed to write before they can spell and form the letters correctly, they will get into bad habits that will be hard to break later. There is a certain logic in this argument, but the logic does not hold up to scrutiny when you actually look at what children do before they come to school. Just as many children "read" before they can read by pretend reading a memorized book, they "write" before they can write. Their writing is not initially decipherable by anyone besides themselves, and sometimes they read the same scribbling different ways! They write with pens, markers, crayons, paint, chalk, and normal-sized pencils with erasers on the ends. They write on chalkboards, magic slates, paper, and, alas, walls! You can encourage and support fledgling attempts at writing in numerous ways.

Model Writing for the Children　As children watch you write, they observe that you always start in a certain place, go in certain directions, and leave spaces between words. In addition to these print conventions, they observe that writing is "talk written down." There are numerous opportunities in every classroom for the teacher to write as the children watch—and sometimes help with what to write.

In many classrooms, the teacher begins the day by writing a morning message on the board. The teacher writes this short message as the children watch. The teacher then reads the message, pointing to each word and inviting the children to join in on any words they know.

Dear Class,

　　Today is Thursday, October 24. It is a very windy day! We will need our jackets when we go outside. Did you wear your jacket to school today?

　　Love,

　　Miss Williams

Sometimes, the teacher takes a few minutes to point out some things students might notice from the morning message:

　　"How many sentences did I write today?"
　　"How can we tell how many there are?"
　　"What do we call this mark I put at the end of this sentence?"
　　"Who can come and circle some words that begin with the same letters?"
　　"Who can come and underline some words you can read?"

These and similar questions help children learn the conventions and jargon of print and focus their attention on words and letters.

Provide a Variety of Things to Write With and On　Young children view writing as a creation and are often motivated to write by various media. Many teachers grab free postcards, scratch pads, counter checks, pens, and pencils and haunt yard sales—always on the lookout for an extra chalkboard or an old but still working typewriter. A letter home to parents at the beginning of the year, asking them to clean out desks and drawers and donate writing utensils and various kinds of paper, often brings unexpected treasures. In addition to the usual writing media, young children like to write with sticks in sand, with paintbrushes or sponges on chalkboards, and with chocolate pudding and shaving cream on tables.

Help Children Find Writing Purposes through Center Activities   Children need to develop the basic understanding that writing is a message across time and space. Once they have that understanding, they are able to identify a purpose for a piece of writing. For most young children, the purpose of writing is to get something told or done. Children will find some real purposes for writing if you incorporate writing in all your classroom centers. Encourage children to make grocery lists while they are playing in the housekeeping center. Menus, ordering pads, and receipts are a natural part of a restaurant center. An office center would include various writing implements, a typewriter or computer, along with index cards, phone books, and appointment books.

Children can make birthday cards for friends or relatives or write notes to you or their classmates and then mail them in the post office center. They can make signs (Keep Out! Girls Only!) and post them as part of their dramatic play. When children put a lot of time into building a particularly wonderful creation from the blocks, they often do not want to have it taken apart so that something else can be built. Many teachers keep a large pad of tablet paper in the construction center. Children can draw and label records of their constructions before disassembling them.

Once you start looking for them, there are numerous opportunities for children to write for real purposes as they carry out their creative and dramatic play in various centers.

Provide a Print-Rich Classroom   Classrooms in which children are encouraged to write have lots of print in them. In addition to books, there are magazines and newspapers. There are also charts of recipes made and directions for building things. Children's names are on their desks and on many different objects. There are class books, bulletin boards with labeled pictures of animals under study, and labels on almost everything. Children's drawings and all kinds of writing are displayed. In these classrooms, children see that all kinds of writing are valued. Equally important, children who want to write "the grown-up way" can find lots of words to make their own.

Accept the Writing They Do   Accepting a variety of writing—from scribbling to one-letter representations to invented spellings to copied words—is the key to having young children "write" before they can write. Talk to your students on the very first day of school about the forms they can use for writing. Show them examples of other children's scribbles, pictures, single letters, vowel-less words, and other kinds of writing. Tell them they all started out at the scribble stage, and they will all get to conventional writing. For now, they should write in the way that is most comfortable to share the message they have.

Teach Concrete Words

All children need to be successful in their first attempts at word learning. If the words you focus on with your beginners are the most common words—*the, have, with, to*—then those children who have not had many literacy experiences are going to have a hard time learning and remembering these words. The problem with the most common words is that they do not mean anything. *The, have, with,* and *to* are abstract connecting words. Children do need to learn these words (lots more about that in Chapter 4), but doing so will be much easier if they have already learned some concrete important-to-them words. Most kindergarten and first-grade teachers begin their year with some get-acquainted activities. As part of these activities, they often have a "special child" each day. In addition to learning about each child, you can focus attention on the special child's name and use that name to develop some important understandings about words and letters.

To prepare for this activity, write all the children's first names (with initials for last names, if two first names are the same) in permanent marker on sentence strips. Cut the strips so that long names have long strips and short names have short strips. Each day, reach into the box and draw out a name. This child becomes the "King or Queen for a Day," and his or her name becomes the focus of many activities. Reserve a bulletin board and add each child's name to the board. (Some teachers like to have children bring in snapshots of themselves or take pictures of the children to add to the board as the names are added.) The following sections describe some day-by-day examples of what you might do with the names.

Day 1　　Close your eyes. Reach into the box, shuffle the names around, and draw one out. Crown that child "King (or Queen) for a Day!" Lead the other children in interviewing this child to find out what he or she likes to eat, play, or do after school. Does she or he have brothers? Sisters? Cats? Dogs? Mice? Many teachers record this information on a chart or compile a class book, with one page of information about each child.

David Cunningham

> David likes to play basketball. Carolina is his favorite team. His dad teaches at Carolina and they go to the games. David's favorite food is spaghetti. His favorite color is blue. David does not have any brothers or sisters. He doesn't have any pets because his mom is allergic! David's birthday is September 20.

Now focus the children's attention on the child's name—*David.* Point to the word *David* on the sentence strip and develop children's understanding of jargon by pointing out that this *word* is David's name. Tell them that it takes many *letters* to write the word *David,* and let them help you count the letters. Say the letters in *David*—D-a-v-i-d—and have the children chant them with you. Point out that the word *David* begins and ends with the same letter. Explain that the first and the last *d* look different because one is a capital *D* and the other is a small *d* (or uppercase/lowercase—whatever jargon you use).

Take another sentence strip and have the children watch as you write *David.* Have them chant the spelling of the letters with you. Cut the letters apart and mix them up. Let several children come up and arrange the letters in just the right order so that they spell *David,* using the original sentence strip on which *David* is written as a model. Have the other children chant to check that the order is correct.

Give each child a large sheet of drawing paper, and have all of them write *David* in large letters on one side of their papers using crayons. Model at the board how to write each letter as the children write it. Do not worry if what they write is not perfect (or even if it does not bear much resemblance to the letter you wrote). Also resist the temptation to correct what they write. Remember that children who write at home before coming to school often reverse letters or write them in funny ways. The important understanding is that names are words, that words can be written, and that it takes lots of letters to write them. Finally, have everyone draw a picture of David on the other side of the drawing paper. Let David take all the pictures home!

Day 2 Draw another name—*Caroline*. Crown "Queen Caroline" and do the same interviewing and chart making that you did for David. (Decide carefully what you will do for the first child because every child will expect equal treatment!) Focus the children's attention on Caroline's name. Say the letters in *Caroline,* and have the children chant them with you. Help the children count the letters and decide which letter is first and last. Write *Caroline* on another sentence strip and cut it into letters. Have children arrange the letters to spell *Caroline,* using the first sentence strip name as their model. Put *Caroline* on the bulletin board under *David,* and compare the two. Which has the most letters? How many more letters are in the word *Caroline* than in the word *David?* Does *Caroline* have any of the same letters as *David?* Finish the lesson by having everyone write *Caroline* as you model the writing and draw a picture of *Caroline* on the back of their paper. Let Caroline take all the pictures home.

Day 3 Draw the third name—*Dorinda*. Do the crowning, interviewing, and chart making. Chant the letters in Dorinda's name. Write it, cut it up, and do the letter arranging. Be sure to note the two *d*'s and to talk about first and last letters. As you put *Dorinda* on the bulletin board, compare it to both *David* and *Caroline*. This is a perfect time to notice that both *David* and *Dorinda* begin with the same letter and the same sound. Finish the lesson by having the children write *Dorinda* and draw pictures for Dorinda to take home.

Day 4 *Mike* is the next name. Do all the usual activities. When you put *Mike* on the bulletin board, help the children realize that *David* has lost the dubious distinction of having the shortest name. (Bo may now look down at the name card on his desk and call out that his name is even shorter. You will point out that he is right but that Mike's name is the shortest one on the bulletin board right now. What is really fascinating about this activity is how the children compare their own names to the ones on the board, even before their names get there. That is exactly the kind of word/letter awareness you are trying to develop!)

When you have a one-syllable name with which there are many rhymes (*Pat, Jack, Bo, Sue,* etc.), seize the opportunity to develop phonemic awareness by having children listen for words that rhyme with that name. Say pairs of words, some of which rhyme with Mike—*Mike/ball, Mike/bike, Mike/hike, Mike/cook, Mike/like*. If the pairs rhyme, everyone should point at Mike and shout "Mike." If not, they should shake their heads and frown.

Day 5 Next, the name *Cynthia* is drawn from the box. Do the various activities, and then take advantage of the fact that the names *Caroline* and *Cynthia* both begin with the letter *c* but with different sounds. Have Caroline and Cynthia stand on opposite sides of you. Write their names above them on the chalkboard. Have the children say *Caroline* and *Cynthia* several times, drawing out the first sound. Help them understand that some letters can have more than one sound and that the names *Caroline* and *Cynthia* demonstrate this fact. Tell the class that you are going to say some words, all of which begin with the letter *c*. Some of these words will sound like *Caroline* at the beginning, and some of them will sound like *Cynthia*. Say some words and have the children say them with you—*cat, celery, candy, cookies, city, cereal, cut.* For each word, have the children point to Caroline or Cynthia to show which sound they hear. Once they have decided, write each word under *Caroline* or *Cynthia.*

Day 6/Last Day Continue to have a special child each day. For each child, do the standard interviewing, charting, chanting, letter arranging, writing, and drawing activities. Then take advantage of the names you have to help children develop an understanding about how letters and sounds work. Here are some extra activities many teachers do with the names:

● Write the letters of the alphabet across the board. Count to see how many names contain each letter. Make tally marks or a bar graph, and then decide which letters are included in the most names and which letters are included in the fewest names. Are there any letters that no one in the whole class has in his or her name?

● Pass out laminated letter cards—one letter to a card, lowercase on one side, uppercase on the other. Call out a name from the bulletin board, and lead the children to chant the letters in the name. Then let the children who have those letters come up and display the letters and lead the class in a chant, cheerleader style: "David—D-a-v-i-d—David—Yay, David!"

Learning Other Concrete Words The activities just described for names can be used to teach many concrete words. Many teachers bring in cereal boxes as part of a nutrition unit. In addition to talking about the cereals, children learn the names of the cereals by chanting, writing, and comparing. Places to shop is another engaging topic. Ads for local stores—Walmart, Kmart, Sears—are brought in. Children talk about the stores and, of course, learn the names by chanting, writing, and comparing. Food is a topic of universal interest. Menus from popular restaurants—Burger King, McDonald's, Pizza Hut—spark lots of lively discussion from children, and, of course, children love learning to read and spell these very important words. You can teach the color words through chanting, writing, and drawing. When studying animals, add an animal name to an animal board each day. Children love chanting, writing, and drawing the animals.

These activities with the children's names and other concrete words can be done even when many children in the class do not know their letter names yet. Young children enjoy chanting, writing, and comparing words. They learn letter names by associating them with the important-to-them words they are learning.

Develop Phonemic Awareness

Phonemic awareness is the ability to take words apart, put them back together again, and change them. Phonemic awareness activities are done orally, calling attention to the sounds—not the letters or which letters make which sounds. Here are some activities to include in your classroom to ensure that all your children continue to develop in their ability to hear and manipulate sounds in words.

Use Names to Build Phonemic Awareness Capitalize on your children's interest in names by using their names to develop a variety of phonemic awareness skills. The first way that children learn to pull apart words is into syllables. Say each child's name, and have all the children clap the beats in that name as they say it with you. Help children to discover that *Dick* and *Pat* are one-beat names, that *Manuel* and *Patrick* are two beats, and so on. Once children begin to understand, clap the beats and have all the children whose names have that number of beats stand up and say their names as they clap the beats with you.

Another phonemic awareness skill is the ability to hear when sounds are the same or different. Say a sound, not a letter name, and have all the children whose names begin with that sound come forward. Stretch out the sound as you make it: "s-s-s." For the "s-s-s" sound, Samantha, Susie, Steve, and Cynthia should all come forward. Have everyone stretch out the "s-s-s" as they say each name. If anyone points out that *Cynthia* starts with a *c* or that *Sharon* starts with an *s,* explain that they are correct about the letters but that now you are listening for sounds.

You can use the names of some of your children to help them understand the concept of *rhyme.* Choose the children whose names have lots of rhyming words to come forward— *Bill, Jack, Brent, Kate, Clark.* Say a word that rhymes with one of the names (*hill, pack, spent, late, park*), and have the children say the word along with the name of the rhyming child. Not all your children's names will have rhymes, but the children who do will feel special and appreciated because they are helping everyone learn about rhyming words.

All your children will feel special if you call them to line up by stretching out their names, emphasizing each letter of each name. As each child lines up, have the class stretch out his or her name with you. The ability to segment words into sounds and blend them back together is an important phonemic awareness ability.

Encourage Phonics Spelling   Think about what you have to do to "put down the letters you hear" while writing. You have to stretch out the sounds in the word. Children who stretch out words develop the phonemic awareness skill of *segmenting.* When children are just beginning, it doesn't really matter if they represent all the sounds with the right letters. What matters is the stretching out they are doing to try to hear the sounds. As phonics instruction continues, their phonics spelling will more closely match the actual spelling of the word.

Count Words   This activity lets you build math skills as you develop the basic phonological awareness concept of separating words. For this activity, each child should have 10 counters in a paper cup. (Anything that is manipulative is fine. Some teachers use edibles, such as raisins, grapes, or small crackers, and let the children eat their counters at the end of the lesson. This makes clean-up quick and easy!) Begin by counting some familiar objects in the room, such as windows, doors, trash cans, and the like, having each child place one of the counters on the desk for each object.

Tell the children that you can also count words by putting down a counter for each word you say. Explain that you will say a sentence in the normal way and then repeat the sentence, pausing after each word. The children should put down counters as you say the words in the sentence slowly and then count the counters and decide how many words you said. As usual, children's attention is better if you make sentences about them:

> "Carol has a big smile."
> "Paul is back at school today."
> "Last night I saw Jawan at the grocery store."

Once the children catch on to the activity, let them make up the sentences. Have them say the sentence—first in the normal way, then one word at a time. Listen carefully as they say their sentences, because they usually need help saying them one word at a time. Not only do children enjoy this activity and learn to separate words in speech but they are also practicing basic counting skills!

Clap Syllables   In addition to using your students' names to develop syllable awareness, you can use any of the environmental print words that you are helping children learn. *Cheerios* is a three-beat word. *Kix* takes only one clap and has one beat. When children can clap syllables and decide how many beats a given word has, help them see that one-beat words are usually shorter than three-beat words—that is, they take fewer letters to write. To do this, use your sentence strips and write some words that children cannot read. Cut the strips into words so that short words have short strips and long words have long strips. Have some of the words begin with the same letters but be of different lengths. This will require the children to think about word length in order to decide which word is which.

For the category of animals, choose animal names that begin the same but are quite different in length. Create picture cards with the name on one side and a picture of the animal on the other side. This lesson uses the words *horse* and *hippopotamus, dog* and *donkey, ant* and *alligator,* and *rat, rabbit,* and *rhinoceros.* Show the children the pictures of the animals whose names begin with the same letter and have the children pronounce the names. Have children say the names of animals and clap to show how many beats each word has. (Do not show them the words yet!) Help children to decide that *horse* is a one-beat word and that *hippopotamus* takes a lot more claps and is a five-beat word. Now, show children the two words and say, "One of these words is *horse,* and the other is *hippopotamus.* Who thinks they can figure out which one is which?" The children will probably quickly guess that *horse* in the short word and *hippopotamus* is the really long word. Turn the card to the picture side to show them that they correctly figured out which word was which. Continue with the other sets of words that begin alike and help children notice that short words have just a few letters but long words have many letters!

Play Blending and Segmenting Games   In addition to using the names of your children to help them learn to blend and segment, you can use a variety of other words that help build their meaning vocabularies while simultaneously practicing blending and segmenting. Use pictures related to your unit or from simple concept and alphabet books. Let each child take a turn saying the name of the picture (one sound at a time), and call on another child to identify the picture. In the beginning, limit the pictures to five or six items whose names are very different and short—*truck, frog, cat, pony, tiger,* for example. After children understand what they are trying to do, they love playing a variation of "I Spy," in which they see something in the room, stretch out its name, and then call on someone to figure out what was seen and to give the next clue.

Read Rhyming Books and Chant Rhymes   One of the best indicators of how well children will learn to read is their ability to recite rhymes when they walk into kindergarten. Since this is such a reliable indicator and since rhymes are so naturally appealing to children at this age, kindergarten and first-grade classrooms should be filled with rhymes. Children should learn to recite these rhymes, sing the rhymes, clap to the rhymes, act out the rhymes, and pantomime the rhymes. In some primary classrooms, they develop "raps" for the rhymes.

As part of your read-aloud, include lots of rhyming books, including such old favorites as *Hop on Pop; One Fish, Two Fish, Red Fish, Blue Fish;* and *There's a Wocket in My Pocket.* As you read the book for the second time—once is never near enough for a favorite book of young children—pause just before you get to the rhyme and let the children chime in with the rhyming word.

Read and Invent Tongue Twisters Children love tongue twisters, which are wonderful reminders of the sounds of beginning letters. Use children's names and let them help you create the tongue twisters. Have students say them as fast as they can and as slowly as they can. When students have said them enough times to have them memorized, write them on posters or in a class book.

Teach Letter Names and Sounds

Through all the activities just described, children will begin to learn some letter names and sounds. You can accelerate this learning with some of the following activities.

Use Children's Names to Teach Letter Names and Sounds When you focus on a special child each day, chanting and writing that child's name and then comparing the names of all the children, many children will begin to learn some letter names and sounds. Once all the names are displayed, however, and most of the children can read most of the names, you can use these names to solidify knowledge of letter names and sounds.

Imagine that these children's names are displayed on the word wall or name board:

David	Rasheed	Robert	Catherine	Cindy
Mike	Sheila	Larry	Joseph	Julio
Amber T.	Matt	Erin	Shawonda	Bianca
Erica	Kevin	Adam	Delano	Brittany
Bill	Tara	Amber M.	Octavius	Kelsie

Begin with a letter that many children have in their names and that usually has its expected sound. With this class, you might begin with the letter *r.* Have all children whose names have an *r* in them come to the front of the class, holding cards with their names on them. First count all the *r*'s. There are 12 *r*'s in all. Next, have the children whose names contain an *r* divide themselves into those whose names begin with an *r*—*Robert* and *Rasheed;* those whose names end with an *r*—*Amber T.* and *Amber M.*; and those with an *r* that is not the first or the last letter—*Brittany, Erica, Tara, Erin, Catherine,* and *Larry.* Finally, say each name slowly, stretching out the letters, and decide if you can hear the usual sound of that letter. For *r,* you can hear them all.

Now choose another letter, and let all those children come down and display their name cards. Count the number of times that letter occurs, and then have the children divide themselves into groups according to whether the letter is first, last, or in between. Finally, say the names, stretching them out, and decide if you can hear the usual sound that letter makes. The letter *D* would be a good second choice. You would have *David* and *Delano* beginning with *d; David* and *Rasheed* ending with *d; Cindy, Shawonda,* and *Adam* having a *d* that is not first or last. Again, you can hear the usual sound of *d* in all these names.

Continue picking letters and having children come up with their name cards until you have sorted for some of the letters represented by your names. When doing the letters *s, c, t,* and *j,* be sure to point out that they can have two sounds and that the *th* in *Catherine* and the *sh* in *Sheila, Shawonda,* and *Rasheed* have their own special sounds. You probably should not sort out the names with an *h* because although *Shawonda, Sheila, Rasheed, Catherine,* and *Joseph* all have *h*'s, the *h* sound is not represented by any of these. The same would go for *p*, which only occurs in *Joseph*. When you have the children come down for the vowels—*a, e, i, o,* and *u*—count and then sort the children according to first, last, and in between but do not try to listen for the sounds. Explain that vowels have many different sounds and that the children will learn more about the vowels and their sounds all year.

Use Favorite Words with Pure Initial Sounds as Key Words   Capitalize on the concrete words you have been teaching your children by choosing one or two of these words to represent each of the important sounds. Use your children's names when they have the appropriate sounds and then use other concrete words you have been learning.

When teaching the first letter–sound relationships, begin with two letters that are very different in look and sound and that are made in different places of the mouth—*b* and *l,* for example. Also choose two letters for which your children's names can be the examples. Show the children the two words, *Bill* and *Larry,* which will serve as key words for these letters. Have the children pronounce the two key words and notice the positions of their tongues and teeth as they do. Have Bill stand in the front of the room and hold the word *Bill.* Also have Larry hold a card with his name on it. Say several concrete words that begin like *Bill* or *Larry*—*bike, lemon, box, book, ladder, lady, boy*—and have the children say them after you. Have them notice where their tongues and teeth are as they say the words. Let the children point to the child holding the sign *Bill* or *Larry* to indicate how each word begins.

The Alphabet Song and Alphabet Books   "The Alphabet Song" has been sung by generations of children. Not only do children enjoy it, but it seems to give them a sense of all the letters and a framework in which to put new letters as they learn them. Many children come to school already able to sing "The Alphabet Song." Let them sing it and teach it to everyone else. Once the children can sing the song, you may want to point to alphabet cards (usually found above the chalkboard) as they sing. Children also enjoy "being the alphabet" as they line up to go somewhere. Simply pass out your laminated alphabet cards—one to each child, leftovers to the teacher—and let the children sing the song slowly as they line up. Be sure to hand out the cards randomly, so that no one always gets to be the *A* and lead the line or has to be the *Z* and bring up the rear every day!

Wonderful alphabet books are also available. You can read these books aloud over and over. Your children can select these books to "read" during their independent reading. Teacher aides, as well as parent and grandparent volunteers, can "lap read" these in

the reading corner and so on. Your class can create its own alphabet book modeled after the children's favorite alphabet books. Be sure to focus on the meanings of the words in all alphabet books you use, so that children will add words to their oral vocabularies.

Letter Actions   Young children love movement! Teach children actions for the letters, and they will remember those letters. Write a letter on one side of a large index card and an action on the other. The first time you teach each letter, make a big

Source: Patricia Cunningham

deal of it. Get out the rhythm sticks and the marching music when you *march* for *M*. Go out on the playground and do *jumping jacks* for *J*. Play *hopscotch* and *hop* like bunnies for *H*.

When the children have learned actions for several letters, you can do many activities in the classroom without any props. Have all the children stand by their desks and wait until you show them a letter. Then, they should do that action until you hide the letter behind your back. When they have all stopped and you have their attention again, show them another letter and have them do that action. Continue this with as many letters as you have time to fill. Be sure to make comments such as "Yes, I see everyone marching because *M* is our marching letter."

In another activity, pass out the letters for which children have learned the actions to individual children. Each child then gets up and does the action required and calls on someone to guess which letter he or she was given. In "Follow the Letter Leader," the leader picks a letter card and does that action. Everyone else follows the leader, doing the same action. The leader then chooses another card and the game continues.

Teachers have different favorites for letter actions, and you will have your own favorites. Try to select actions with which everyone is familiar and that are only called by single names. Following is a list of actions we like:

bounce	hop	nod	vacuum
catch	jump	paint	walk
dance	kick	run	yawn
fall	laugh	sit	zip
gallop	march	talk	

The action for *s* is our particular favorite. You can use it to end the game. Children say, "It is not an action at all," but remember that "*s* is the sitting letter." You may want to take pictures of various members of your class doing the different actions and make a book of actions they can all read and enjoy.

English Language Learners

Using concrete words, alphabet picture books, and actions will help all your students learn letter names and sounds. Your English language learners will reap the extra benefit of adding these words to their oral vocabularies.

Summary

Emergent literacy research began with the work of Charles Read (1975) and his mentor, Carol Chomsky (1971). Read's work described for many of us at the time what we were seeing in the writing of young children. Read taught us that young children's spellings are developmental and could be predicted by analyzing the consonant and vowel substitutions students consistently made. Chomsky's article, "Write First, Read Later," was seminal in helping to shift instruction toward the field that came to be known as *emergent literacy*.

Much of the emergent literacy research has been done in the homes of young children, tracing their literacy development from birth until the time they read and write in conventional ways (Sulzby & Teale, 1991). From this observational research, it became apparent that children in literate home environments engage in reading and writing long before they begin formal reading instruction. These children use reading and writing in a variety of ways and pass through a series of predictable stages on their voyage from pretending and scribbling to conventional reading and writing. When parents read to children, interact with them about the print they see in the world (signs, cereal boxes, advertisements), and encourage and support their early writing efforts, children establish a firm foundation for learning to read.

This chapter has summarized the crucial understandings essential to building the foundation for success. Through early reading and writing experiences, children learn why we read and write. They develop background knowledge and vocabulary, print concepts, and phonemic awareness. They learn some concrete important-to-them words and some letter names and sounds. Most important, they develop the desire to learn to read and gain self-confidence in their own ability to become literate. Classrooms in which all children develop a firm foundation of emergent literacy provide a variety of reading, writing, and word activities to help all children get off to a successful start in literacy.

How Well Does Your Classroom Help Children Build the Literacy Foundation?

1. Do I read aloud to children and provide a print-rich classroom so that my children will all know why we read and write?

2. Do I build meaning vocabulary when I read aloud to my students and during other activities throughout the day?

3. Do I model writing and do other activities from which all children can learn the conventions and jargon of print?

4. Do I use a variety of activities to teach all the phonemic awareness skills?

5. Do I include activities from which all children can learn to read and write some concrete words?

6. Do I use concrete words and other activities to teach letter names and sounds?

7. Do I establish a climate in my classroom so that all children develop the desire to learn to read and write and the confidence that they can?

4

Fluency

SOMETIMES TO UNDERSTAND what something is, you have to understand what it is not. To experience what it feels like to read without fluency, read this paragraph **aloud** WITHOUT first reading it to yourself. When you have finished reading it, cover it and summarize what you read.

FLUENCYISTHEABILITYTOREADMOSTWORDSINCONTEXTQUICKLYAND
ACCURATELYANDWITHAPPROPRIATEEXPRESSIONFLUENCYISCRITICAL
TOREADINGCOMPREHENSIONBECAUSEOFTHEATTENTIONFACTOR
OURBRAINSCANATTENDTOALIMITEDNUMBEROFTHINGSATATIMEIF
MOSTOFOURATTENTIONISFOCUSEDONDECODINGTHEWORDSTHERE
ISLITTLEATTENTIONLEFTFORTHECOMPREHENSIONPARTOFREADING
PUTTINGTHEWORDSTOGETHERANDTHINKINGABOUTWHATTHEYMEAN

If you paused to figure out some of the words and if your phrasing and expression was not very smooth, you have experienced what it feels like when you cannot read something fluently. If your summary lacked some important information, you have experienced the detrimental effects of the lack of comprehension. If you are developing a headache, you have experienced what a painful task reading can be to readers who lack fluency.

Fluency is the ability to read most words in context quickly and accurately and with appropriate expression. It is critical to reading comprehension because of the attention factor. Our brains can attend to a limited number of things at a time. If most of our attention is focused on decoding the words, there is little attention left for the comprehension part of reading—putting the words together and thinking about what they mean.

The paragraph you just read is exactly the same as the one written in caps with no punctuation and no spaces between words. If, this time, you read it quickly and effortlessly and with good comprehension, you read it the way you normally read everything—fluently.

In order to become avid and enthusiastic readers who get pleasure and information from reading, children must develop fluency. Children who have to labor over everything they read, as you did with the paragraph with no spacing or punctuation opening paragraph, will only read when forced to read and will never understand how anyone can actually enjoy reading!

Fluency is not something you have or don't have. In fact, how fluent a reader you are is directly related to the complexity of the text you are reading. If you are reading a text on a familiar topic with lots of words you have read accurately many times before, you probably recognize those familiar words immediately and automatically. All your attention is then available to think about the meaning of what you are reading. If you are reading a text on an unfamiliar topic with lots of new words, you will have to stop and decode these words in some way—using the letter–sound and morphemic patterns you know to turn the printed letters into sounds and words. In order to comprehend what you have read, you may have to reread the text once or even twice so that your attention is freed from decoding and available for comprehending.

The National Reading Panel (2000) explains this relationship between reading comprehension and fluency:

> If text is read in a laborious and inefficient manner, it will be difficult for the child to remember what has been read and to relate the ideas expressed in the text to his or her background knowledge. (p. 11)

Fluency is fast, expressive reading. Close your eyes and try to imagine the voices of your good and struggling readers as they read aloud. The good readers probably sound "normal." They identify almost all the words quickly and accurately and their voices rise and fall and pause at appropriate points.

Some of your struggling readers, however, read one word at a time hes—si—ta—ting and and and re—peat—ing words. Every teacher has had the experience of working with students who can read many words but for whom reading is a tortured, labored, word-by-word, sometimes syllable-by-syllable, process. Dysfluent reading is slow, labored, and lacking in expression and phrasing. Fluency is the ability to quickly and automatically

Common Core Connections: Fluency

Reading: Foundational Standard 4 recognizes the importance of fluency to young readers. First- and second-graders are expected to read grade-level text orally with accuracy, appropriate rate, and expression on successive readings and to use context to confirm or self-correct word recognition and understanding. Foundational Standard 3 recognizes that, in English, many of the most common words (*they, want, of*) cannot be decoded and requires that first-, second-, and third-graders read grade-appropriate irregularly spelled words.

identify the words. Fluent reading is not saying one word at a time. Fluent reading puts words together in phrases and has the expression you would use if you were speaking the words. All your students can become fluent readers. This chapter will describe activities you can use to make it happen.

Mandate Easy Reading for Everyone

Most of the reading you do is not at your reading level. In fact, most of what you read is much too easy for you! If your reading in the past month has included the latest best-selling novel, a travel guide in preparation for your summer break, a journal article on effective teaching strategies, and your favorite section of your local newspaper, all this reading was most likely at your independent level. Because these are all things you chose to read and were interested in, you had huge amounts of background knowledge for these topics and you instantly recognized 98 to 99 percent of the words.

The best readers in your classroom—the ones whose instructional reading levels are above the grade level they are placed in—also spend most of their time reading text that is very easy for them. The science and social studies textbooks in their desks are written at the average reading level for the grade but they are easy for your best readers who read above grade level—so are the books you assign them for guided reading and take-home readers. The books and magazine articles they choose to read for independent reading time at home and school are also probably very easy for them. Your best readers became fluent readers by reading and rereading lots of easy books. Many of these children have favorite books at home in their own personal libraries and have read these books over and over. Many good readers get "hooked" on a series of books—the Arthur books or the Babysitter Club books, for example—and they devour these books.

Now think about the materials your struggling readers are reading. They probably have the same grade-level science and social studies books in their desks and these books are much too hard for them to read. Hopefully, the books you assign them for guided reading and as take-home readers are at their level—but that doesn't mean they are easy. The reading level of most children is determined to be the level at which they can read 90 to 95 percent of the words and can comprehend 75 percent of the ideas. Even in material that is determined to be at their instructional reading level, they will encounter a word they don't recognize every two or three sentences. When they encounter these unfamiliar words, they have to stop and use whatever decoding strategies they have to figure out these words, and this stopping to decode interrupts their fluency and interferes with comprehension.

Our best readers are fluent readers who spend a huge proportion of their reading time reading things that are easy for them. Our struggling readers spend a huge proportion of their reading time struggling through text that is much too hard and only spend a little bit of time working to read material that is at their level. When reading both the too-hard text and the on-their-level text, they have to work hard to read and their reading is not fluent. The first commitment you have to make to help all your students become fluent readers is to make sure all your students are spending some of their time reading easy text—text in which they are interested, and thus have background knowledge, and text in which they can recognize 98 to 99 percent of the words.

Donors Choose

Are you excited about providing all your students with easy reading materials but short on funds? Go to www.donorschoose.org and enter your request there. Donors Choose is a clever but simple idea. Many people are concerned about schools that lack the resources to provide their students with the extras often provided by PTOs in wealthier communities. Teachers can write short grants that explain what they need and why and how much the items will cost. Donors can log on and use their credit cards to fund worthy projects. Donors Choose is available in all 50 states and the District of Columbia.

At this point, you may be thinking, "Easier said than done! I struggle to find appropriate materials at the instructional levels of my struggling readers. Where will I find easy books? And if I find easy books, won't my students be insulted if I offer them these 'baby' books?"

Finding easy materials for your struggling readers and getting them to read them is actually easier than you think, and we have already shared some ideas clever teachers use to accomplish this. Look at Chapter 2 and think about Deb Smith including an "everyone book" as part of her teacher read-aloud. An "everyone book" is a book that everyone can read and that would be easy for even your struggling readers. Fortunately, many publishers have recently published sets of small informational books. These books have very little text on the page and the text is accompanied by engaging pictures—often photos. Because these books are informational and on high-interest topics—trucks, turtles, magnets, football, and much more—your students won't perceive them as "baby" books. Because you include them in your read-aloud (they only take two minutes to read!), and you marvel at all the interesting facts in the book, your students won't be embarrassed to be seen reading and enjoying the books you obviously enjoy.

Chapter 2 contains another clever way you can lure your struggling readers into reading easy books. Set up a buddy reading program with a kindergarten class. Gather some classic kindergarten favorites—such as *Hop on Pop, Go Dog Go,* and *Mr. Brown Can Moo*—and have your struggling readers choose one and practice reading it in preparation for reading to their little buddy. (If you don't have these books, consider asking your students' parents if they have any books their kids have outgrown and would like to donate, borrow some from a kindergarten or first-grade teacher, or check the local thrift shops.) Many of your struggling readers are familiar with these books but were not able to read them when they were younger. They will be delighted to be able to read them now, and the repetition of sight words and rhyming words in these books will go a long way toward increasing the fluency of your struggling readers.

Depending on the age of your children, a magazine subscription to *Zoobooks, Your Big Backyard,* or another magazine easy enough for your struggling readers to read may provide the needed easy reading resources. With magazines, it is not essential that the children be able to read every word or every article. Just as adults do, children tend to pick and choose from magazine articles and read the ones they are most interested in. Those high-interest articles will be easier to read because they are usually on a topic on which your struggling reader has a lot of background knowledge and vocabulary.

Independent reading is a critical daily component of a balanced reading program in any classroom. Some significant amount of time every day in every classroom should be devoted to children choosing something to read for themselves and then settling down to read it. Independent reading is often promoted in terms of the motivation and interest children develop as they have time to pursue their own personal interests through books. In addition, reading easy materials during independent reading promotes fluency. In Chapter2, it was suggested that you conference with one-fifth of your students each day during their independent reading time and that you spread your struggling readers out across the days. Use the opportunity of this weekly conference to monitor what your struggling readers are reading and entice them into reading some easier books if they are consistently choosing books that are too hard for them to read fluently.

For your struggling readers who don't yet read fluently, you need to think about increasing the amount of easy reading they do beyond the independent reading time. Consider getting some volunteers to come to your classroom and "drop in when they drop off." Parents who drive or walk their children to school are often willing to come to a classroom for 20 minutes when they know a child is counting on them to read a book to them and then listen to them read from a book they have been reading during independent reading time. Consider letting your students choose books they want to take home to read to a younger brother, sister, or cousin. Make sure they have practiced the book they are taking home and that they can read the book fluently.

If you have lots of struggling readers, consider forming an "After Lunch Bunch" reading club in your classroom. Each day, invite five or six of your children to read with you some "just plain fun" books. Include all your students at least once each week but include the struggling readers on several days. Choose "old favorites" and read the books chorally with your students. Remember that all good readers spend a significant amount of time reading easy materials. Provide your struggling readers with a lot of easy reading opportunities and watch them become fluent readers.

Model Fluent, Expressive Reading

In addition to making sure everyone in your classroom has some easy reading in their reading diets, you can promote fluency by modeling fluent reading. Be sure that you are reading as expressively as possible whenever you read aloud to students. Give your students the opportunity to practice expressive reading by doing echo reading and choral reading with plays and poems.

Echo Reading

One teacher had been doing echo reading for months when a child suddenly asked, "What's an echo?" The teacher invited class members to explain what an echo is and discovered that many children hadn't heard an echo. After some "field research," the teacher located a spot in the auditorium where sound would echo and the class all got to hear their voices echoing back to them. Echo reading made a lot more sense to them after that and they tried to "be the echo." It is easy to forget that our students don't know everything we know. If your children haven't heard an echo, you might try to find a place to take them where they can have firsthand experience with echoes.

Echo reading is the perfect venue for modeling expressive oral reading because in echo reading, your voice is the first voice and your students are trying to make their voice sound just like your voice. Echo reading is usually done one sentence at a time and is fun to do when the text has different voices. If you teach young children, consider using some of their favorite big books for echo reading. Children enjoy doing the different voices in *Brown Bear, Brown Bear; I Went Walking;* and *Hattie and the Fox.* Echo reading also works well for stories such as *There's an Alligator Under My Bed* in which one boy is telling the story. Stories told in the first person format are called *"I" stories.* When you echo read "I" stories, try to sound the way the different voices would sound. Some favorite "I" stories include *One of Three* by Angela Johnson, *Enzo the Wonderfish* by Cathy Wilcox, and *My Friend* by Taro Gomi.

Elementary children of all ages enjoy plays, and echo reading is the perfect format for reading plays. There are many books of reproducible plays available and several sets of leveled readers include plays.

In addition to plays you find, you can easily turn some of your children's favorite stories into plays using a Readers' Theatre format. The trick to turning a story into a play is to choose a story with a lot of dialogue and to include a narrator who describes what you can't describe with dialogue. Imagine that your students have read *The Little Red Hen*—or you have read it aloud to them. Here is the beginning of the Readers' Theatre you could easily create:

Narrator: The Little Red Hen was walking in the barnyard. Her friends—the cat, the pig, and the duck—were playing. The Little Red Hen found a grain of wheat.

Hen: "Who will help me plant this wheat?"

Cat: "Not I!"

Dog: "Not I!"

Pig: "Not I!"

Narrator: So, the Little Red Hen planted the wheat herself. The wheat grew and grew.

Hen: "Who will help me cut this wheat?"

Cat: "Not I!"

Dog: "Not I!"

Pig: "Not I!"

As you can see, you don't need any particular talents to turn a favorite story with a lot of dialogue into a Readers' Theatre play. If you teach older students, you can have them take a story and turn it into a play. Let different groups create different plays. Make copies for everyone and use the echo reading format to model fluent, expressive reading of all the plays. Have students take the plays home and corral their family members into reading the plays at home. This is one take-home reading assignment the whole family will willingly participate in.

Choral Reading

Another format you can use to model expressive oral reading is choral reading. When you do choral reading of plays, assign groups of students to the different roles. If you are doing a choral reading of *The Little Red Hen*, for example, divide your students into five groups and let different groups chorally read the parts of the narrator, hen, cat, dog, and pig. Reassign the parts and read it several times so that all your students get to read all the parts. Make sure that you assign your struggling readers to the easier parts first. For much of *The Little Red Hen*, the cat, dog, and pig roles only require the students to read, "Not I!" After a couple of readings, your struggling readers may be able to fluently read the hen's part. If your struggling readers are very dysfluent readers, you should probably not assign them the narrator's part, which always requires the most sophisticated reading skills.

In addition to choral reading of plays and Readers' Theatres, consider leading your students in reading some poetry you have arranged in a choral reading format. Nursery rhymes and other rhymes and finger-plays are naturals for choral reading. Begin by reading the rhyme to your children using the echo reading format. After the echo reading, assign different groups of voices to read different parts. Keep the choreography simple by having the children count off to read different parts or assigning girls and boys to read different parts. Here is an example for the beginning of *Five Little Monkeys:*

All: Five little monkeys jumping on the bed.

Voice 1: One fell off and bumped his head.

All: Momma called the doctor and the doctor said,

Voice 2: "No more monkeys jumping on the bed!"

After reading it the first time, reassign the students so that those who were voice 1 now read the part of voice 2.

Many of these poems lend themselves to pantomiming. Divide your class into actors and readers. For actors, you will need five monkeys, the doctor, and the momma. Have all the readers read the first line chorally—*Five little monkeys jumping on the bed.* Then stop the readers so the five monkeys can pantomime jumping on the bed. Continue leading your readers to read and stopping them so the actors can act. Read the poem several times so that all your students get to be actors as well as readers.

Sometimes, fluency is talked about as if it is only rate of reading. Some tests (the Diebels, for example) claim to measure fluency but really only measure how quickly and accurately students read. Reading with expression (called *prosody*) is a critical part of fluency. When we read fluently, our voices go up and down in pitch at the right times, we pause, and we group words together in phrases. If you want your students to read with expression, you have to model how expressive reading sounds. When you regularly engage your students in echo and choral reading of plays and poetry, you are modeling for them and giving them opportunities to practice fluent, expressive reading.

Provide Engaging Rereading Opportunities

One of the major ways that we become fluent readers is to read something over several times. The first time, a lot of our attention is on identifying the words. The second time, we are able to read in phrases as our brain puts the phrases together into meaningful units. The third time, we read more rapidly, with good expression and in a seemingly "effortless" way. Good readers often reread favorite books. Do you remember the stage in your life when you were hooked on a favorite series of books such as Nancy Drew, American Girl, Junie B. Jones, or Harry Potter? Did you ever go back and reread some of the first ones you read? If you were lucky enough to have a magazine subscription when you were a child, did you save these magazines and return to *American Girl, Zoobooks, Highlights,* or *Ranger Rick* and reread some of your favorite articles?

Rereading is important for fluency and if you reread the previous sections of this chapter, you will find that getting your students to reread text plays a role in many of the activities. In the section on easy reading, we suggested that you pair your struggling readers with a "drop-off, drop-in" volunteer and that after the volunteer had read to the student, that student read something he had already read to the volunteer. That section also suggests that students will do more easy reading if you let your struggling readers choose something they enjoyed to take home and read to family members, especially younger siblings and cousins. When you model expressive reading through echo and choral reading, you lead the students through several readings of the plays and poems. Having your students take copies of the plays and poems home and engage their families in echo and choral reading provides more opportunities for rereading.

Easy reading, echo reading, and choral reading all provide opportunities for rereading. You can provide more opportunities for rereading if you include some recorded reading and fluency development lessons in the fluency instruction portion of the balanced reading diet you are providing your students.

Recorded Reading

Children—and many adults—enjoy listening to recorded books. Many of these books are recorded by authors or professional readers and they are marvelous models of fluent expressive reading. For your readers who need to work on fluency, have them select a book on their reading level and then let them listen to that book as many times as they need to until they can read the book fluently. When your students are able to read the selection fluently without the aid of the recording, let them show off their fluency skills by reading the book to whomever you can commandeer to listen. Send them to a class of younger-aged students and let them read the book to a small group in that class. Let them take the book home and challenge them to see how many signatures they can collect on an "I can read this book" card. Young children like to read to their pets and stuffed animals. Grandparents would love to hear their precious grandchild reading the book over the phone.

Consider recording some of the books and magazine articles as you are reading them aloud to your students. Have your students participate by clapping as a turn-page signal. Likewise, you may want to record some of the echo and choral reading you do with your students. If you record just a few pieces you are reading to your students, you will soon have a large recorded library customized to the interests of your students. Children often want to read the book the teacher has read to them. Recording some of what you read to your students makes this possible for more of your students.

Fluency Development Lessons

In 1998, Tim Rasinski and Nancy Padak published a study that drew everyone's attention to how widespread fluency problems are for readers who are in remedial or special education classes. They had looked at a large number of remedial readers and evaluated their abilities in comprehension, decoding, and fluency. Almost all the children were well below grade level in all three areas, but fluency was by far the biggest area of concern. The children read the test passages in such a slow and laborious manner that the investigators were surprised that they had any comprehension at all. In response to their findings, Rasinski and Padak developed a lesson for teaching fluency they call a Fluency Development

Lesson, or FDL (Rasinski & Padak, 2013). Here is how the Fluency Development Lesson strategy works. This is adapted from a more detailed and rich explanation in Tim Rasinski's (2003) wonderfully practical book, *The Fluent Reader*.

The teacher chooses a short passage—often a poem—that is apt to be appealing to the students and reads the passage aloud several times, modeling fluent reading. Meaning for the poem or passage and for any difficult vocabulary words is built through discussion.

Using individual copies of the poem or the poem written on a chart, the teacher and the class do a choral reading of the poem. The poem is read chorally several times, often with different children reading different parts or verses.

The children are paired and take turns reading the passage to each other. Each person reads the passage three times. The children help each other and respond to each other's reading with praise, support, and encouragement.

When the class gathers together again, children can volunteer to read the passage aloud for everyone. If possible, children read the passage to other classes or to other school personnel.

The children choose two or three words from the passage to add to their personal word banks. They study these words and often use them in a variety of word sorts and games.

Children put one copy of the text in their poetry folder and are given a second copy to take home. They are encouraged to read the passage to whoever will listen. Children and parents alike report that this is one "homework" assignment they all look forward to.

The following day, the previous day's passage is read again and then the whole cycle begins with a new passage. Rasinski recommends a fast pace for this activity and suggests that once the class learns the routines, the whole FDL can be completed in 15 to 20 minutes.

Fluency Development Lessons are easy to do and enjoyed by both teachers and students. Rasinski reports that children engaged in these lessons made greater gains in reading than a similar group of children who read the same passages but did not use the FDL procedure. Fluency Development Lessons would be a welcome addition to any classroom routine but would be especially helpful in remedial and special education classes.

Use a Word Wall to Teach High-Frequency Words

Did you know that approximately 100 words make up half of all the words we read and write our whole lives? To read and write fluently, your students must quickly and automatically recognize and spell these most common words. Unfortunately, the most common words are often the hardest words for beginning readers to learn. Most of these words— *of, and, the, is*—are meaningless, abstract, connecting words. Young children use these words in their speech, but they are not aware of them as separate entities. Read these sentences in a natural speech pattern, and notice how you pronounce the italicized words:

> *What do* you see?
> I want that piece *of* cake.
> What are *they?*

In natural speech, the *what* and the *do* are slurred together and sound like "wadoo." The *of* is pronounced like "uh." The *they* is tacked on to the end of *are* and sounds like "ah-thay."

All children use high-frequency words such as *what, of,* and *they* in their speech, but they are not as aware of these words as they are of the more concrete, tangible words, such as *birthday* and *pizza.* To make learning to read and write even more difficult, many of these high-frequency words are not spelled in regular, predictable ways. *What* should rhyme with *at, bat,* and *cat. Of* should be spelled *u-v. They,* which clearly rhymes with *day, may,* and *way,* should be spelled the way many children do spell it—*t-h-a-y.*

When you consider that most high-frequency words are meaningless, abstract words that children use but do not realize are separate words and that many of these words are irregular in spelling/pronunciation, it is a wonder that any children learn to recognize and spell them! In order to read and write fluently, however, children must learn to instantly recognize and automatically spell these words.

Because these words occur so often, children who read and write will encounter them in their reading and need to spell them as they write. Many teachers have found it effective to display high-frequency words in a highly visible spot in their classrooms and provide daily practice with these words. Teachers often refer to the place where the words are displayed as their *word wall* (Cunningham, 2013).

Doing a Word Wall

Doing a word wall is not the same thing as *having* a word wall. Having a word wall might mean putting all these words up somewhere in the room and telling your students to use them. In our experience, struggling readers cannot use these words because they do not know them or know which is which! To *do* a word wall, you have to:

- Be selective and "stingy" about which words to include, limiting the words to the most common words.

- Add words gradually—no more than five or six a week.

- Make the words very accessible by putting them where everyone can see them, writing them in big black letters, and using a variety of paper colors so that the constantly confused words (*went, want, what, with, will, that, them, they, this,* etc.) are on different colors.

- Practice the words by chanting and writing them, because struggling readers are not usually good visual learners and can't just look at and remember words.

- Do a variety of review activities to provide enough practice so that children can read and spell the words instantly and automatically.

Teachers who *do* word walls (rather than just *have* word walls) report that *all* their students learn these critical words.

Selecting Words for the Wall

How do you decide which words merit a place on your word wall? The selection of words varies from classroom to classroom, but the selection principle is the same: Include words your students need often in their reading and writing and that are often confused with other words. If you teach first grade and are using a commercial reading series, you may

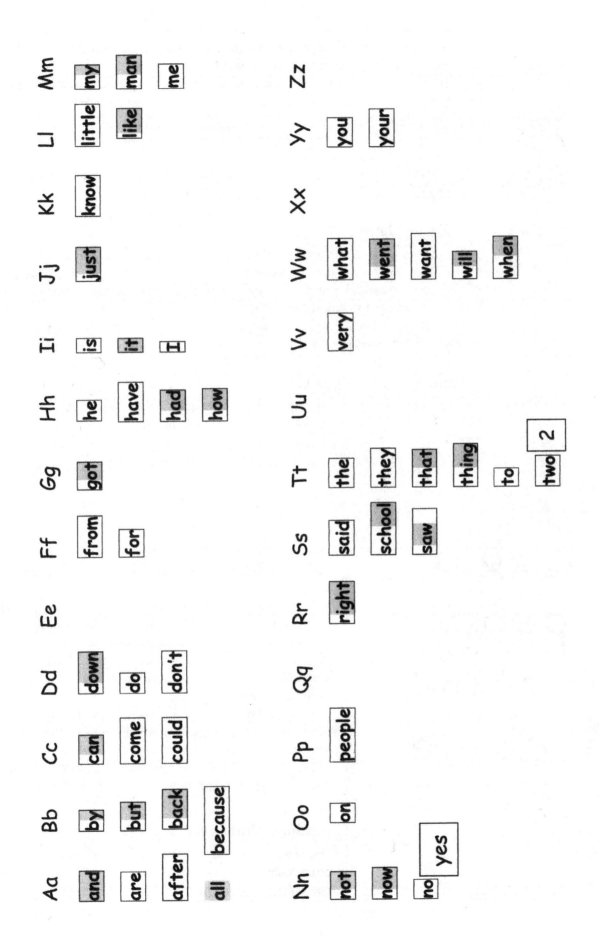

Aa and are after all

Bb by but back because

Cc can come could

Dd down do don't

Ee

Ff from for

Gg got

Hh he have had how

Ii is it I

Jj just

Kk know

Ll little like

Mm my man me

Nn not now no

Oo on

Pp people

Qq

Rr right

Ss said school saw

Tt the they that thing to two 2

Uu

Vv very

Ww what went want will when

Xx

Yy you your

Zz

yes

want to select the most common words taught in your reading program. Alternatively, you can select words from a high-frequency word list.

Beyond first grade, look for words commonly misspelled in your students' writing and add them to the wall. These common misspelled words often include homophones, and these should be added with a picture or phrase clue attached to all but one of the words. For example, add a card with the number 2 next to *two* and attach the word *also* and the phrase *too late* next to *too.* Your students can use this clue to correctly spell the homophone by thinking about whether they are writing the number *two,* the "too late *too,*" or "the other one."

Displaying the Words

Write the words with a thick, black, permanent marker on pieces of different-colored paper. Place the words on the wall above or below the letters they begin with. When confusable words are added, make sure they are on a different color of paper from the other words they are usually confused with. Highlight helpful rhyming patterns. Add five or six new words each week and do at least one daily activity in which your children find, chant, and write the spellings of the words.

Chanting and Writing the Words

Lead your students each day in a quick activity to practice the words on the wall by having them chant and write the words. Get your students out of their seats and lead them to chant (cheerleader style) the spelling of the words you are focusing on.

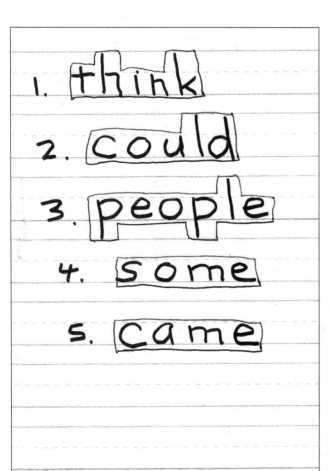

"what. w h a t what."
"they. t h e y they."

This chanting of the words provides your students with an auditory/rhythmic route to learning and remembering the words.

Next, have your students write each word after you model the correct writing. Many teachers tie this daily writing of five or six words into handwriting instruction and model for their students how to make each letter as the children write the words. When the words have been written, lead your students to check/fix their own papers.

On the day you add new words to the wall, make sure these are the words that get chanted and written. Review these same new words on the following day. During the rest of the week, however, choose five or six words, including old and new words, to chant and write.

Reading, Writing, and Word Walls

Once you have a word wall growing in your room, there will be no doubt that your students are using it as they are reading and writing. You will see their eyes quickly glance to the exact spot where a word that they want to write is displayed. Even when children are reading, they will sometimes glance over to the word wall to help them remember a particularly troublesome word.

Word walls provide children with an immediately accessible dictionary for the most troublesome words. Because the words are added gradually, stay in the same spots forever, are alphabetical by their first letters, are visually distinctive by different colors of paper, and are practiced daily though chanting and writing, all your students can learn to read and spell almost all of the word wall words. Because the words you selected are words the students need constantly in their reading and writing, their recognition of these words will become automatic and their attention can be devoted to less frequently occurring words and to constructing meaning as they read and write. When combined with easy reading, your modeling of expressive reading, repeated readings, and recognition of the most common words will result in more fluent reading for your students.

Summary

The research on fluency is wonderfully summarized and explained in a chapter in the 2011 *Handbook of Reading Research* (Rasinski, Reutzel, Chard, & Linan-Thompson, 2011). Fluency includes three components: accuracy, speed, and prosody (commonly called expression) (Rasinski, 2003). Developing fluency needs to be one of the major goals of reading instruction. When children are first starting to read, their reading is not apt to be fluent. They must stop at almost all the words and take a second or two to recognize the word or figure it out. As their word-identification skills develop and their reading vocabularies increase, their reading becomes more fluent.

Allington (2009) suggests three reasons some students struggle to become fluent readers. First, much of what struggling readers are given to read is too difficult. Second, struggling readers read much less than more capable readers. Finally, teachers often ask struggling readers to read aloud and then immediately interrupt that reading to correct reading errors. These struggling readers come to rely on the teacher to correct their errors and don't develop self-monitoring strategies.

Fluency develops when children do a lot of reading and writing—including a great deal of easy text. In addition to making sure that all students are reading some text that is easy for them, teachers can model fluent, expressive reading using echo and choral reading lesson formats.

Repeated reading helps children develop fluency because with each reading, their word identification becomes quicker and more automatic, freeing attention for expression, phrasing, and comprehension. Letting children choose books they want to read and practice reading those books along with a recording help build both fluency and confidence. Fluency Development Lessons have been demonstrated to help students become fluent readers. These lessons are especially important for struggling readers whose reading is well below grade level.

In English, words such as *of, said, the, have, they,* and many others occur in almost every text we read. These words are called "high-frequency words" because they occur so often in everything we read and write. In order to read and write fluently, children must be able to instantly and accurately identify these high-frequency words. Teachers can display these high-frequency words on a word wall and provide opportunities for students to practice these difficult words by chanting and writing them.

How Well Does Your Classroom Help All Children Become Fluent Readers?

1. Do I make sure that all my children do some easy reading and make the reading of easy books socially acceptable?

2. Do I model expressive reading in my read-alouds?

3. Do I include echo and choral reading of plays and poetry so that students practice expressive reading?

4. Do I provide opportunities for students to reread text in a way that students find enjoyable and satisfying?

5. Do I make sure that all my students can automatically read and spell the common words that make up half of all the words they read and write in my classroom and throughout their lives?

5

Teaching Phonics and
Spelling Patterns

WHEN YOU ARE READING OR WRITING, your brain is busy constructing meaning and simultaneously identifying or spelling words. Most of the time, you don't even know that you are identifying or spelling words because you have read or written these words so many times that their identification and spelling has become automatic. In the previous chapter, you learned that your students must develop fluency and be able to quickly and effortlessly identify most words.

Even when you can instantly recognize most words, you will occasionally come to a word you have never before seen. Imagine that while reading, you encounter the word *triremes.* When your eyes see the letters of a word you have never seen before, your brain cannot immediately identify that word. You must stop and figure it out. This figuring out may include determining the pronunciation for the word and the meaning for the word. In this case, you can probably pronounce *triremes,* but since no meaning is triggered by your pronunciation, this word can't join the others in your working memory and help them construct some meaning to shift to long-term memory. Your reading is stalled by the intrusion of this unknown word. You have to either figure out what it is and what it means or continue reading, hoping the other words—the *context*—will allow you to continue to construct meaning, in spite of the unfamiliar word *triremes.* Curious about the meaning of *triremes?* (It is true that "inquiring minds want to know!") Triremes were Greek war ships. The name derives from the sets of three oars on each side of the ship.

All proficient readers have the ability to look at regular words they have never seen before and assign probable pronunciations. Witness your ability to pronounce these made-up words:

cate   frow   perdap   midulition

Now, of course, you were not reading because having only pronounced these words, you would not construct any meaning. But if you were in the position of most young readers, who have many more words in their listening/meaning vocabularies than in their sight-reading vocabularies, you would often meet words familiar in speech but unfamiliar in print. Your ability to rapidly figure out the pronunciations of "unfamiliar-in-print" words enables you to make use of your huge store of "familiar-in-speech" words and thus create meaning.

Before we go on, how did you pronounce the made-up word *frow?* Did it rhyme with *cow* or with *snow?* Because English is not a one-sound, one-letter language, there are different ways to pronounce certain letter patterns. Even so, the number of different ways is limited, and with real words, unlike made-up words, your speaking vocabulary lets you know which pronunciation to assign.

Not only do readers use their phonics knowledge to read words they have not seen before, but this same knowledge also enables them to write. If the four made-up words had been dictated to you and you had to write them, you would have spelled them reasonably close to the way we spelled them.

All good readers and writers develop this ability to come up with pronunciations and spellings for words they have never read or written before. Many struggling readers do not. When good readers see a word they have never before seen in print, they stop briefly and study the word, looking at every letter in a left-to-right sequence. As they look at all the letters, they are not thinking of a sound for each letter, because good readers know that sounds are determined not by individual letters but by letter patterns. Good readers look for patterns of letters they have seen together before and then search their mental word banks, looking for words with similar letter patterns. If the new word is a big word, they "chunk" it—that is, they put letters together to make familiar chunks.

Based on their careful inspection of the letters and their search through their mental bank for words with the same letter patterns, good readers try out a pronunciation. If the first try does not result in a word they have heard, they will usually try another pronunciation. Finally, they produce a pronunciation that they recognize as sounding like a real word that they know. They then go back and reread the sentence that contained the unfamiliar-in-print word and see if their pronunciation makes sense, given the meaning they are getting from the context of surrounding words. If the pronunciation they came up with makes sense, they continue reading. If not, they look again at all the letters of the unfamiliar word and see what else would "look like this and make sense."

Imagine a young boy reading this sentence:

The dancer came out and took a bow.

Imagine that he pauses at the last word and then pronounces *bow* so that it rhymes with *show*. Since that is a real word that he remembers hearing, his eyes then glance back and he quickly rereads the sentence. He then realizes, "That doesn't make sense." He studies all the letters of *bow* again and searches for similar letter patterns in his mental word bank. Perhaps he now accesses words such as *how* and *now*. This gives him another possible pronunciation for this letter pattern, one that is also recognized as a previously heard word. He tries this pronunciation, quickly rereads, realizes his sentence now "sounds right," and continues reading.

From this scenario, we can infer the strategies this good reader used to successfully decode an unfamiliar-in-print word:

1. Recognize that this is an unfamiliar word, and look at all the letters in order.
2. Search your mental word bank for similar letter patterns and the sounds associated with them.
3. Produce a pronunciation that matches that of a real word that you know.
4. Reread the sentence to cross-check your possible pronunciation with meaning. If meaning confirms pronunciation, continue reading. If not, try again!

Had the unfamiliar word been a big word, the reader would have had to use a fifth strategy:

5. Look for familiar morphemes, and chunk the word by putting letters together that usually go together in the words you know.

To be a good reader, you must be able to automatically recognize most words and you must be able to quickly decode the words you do not immediately recognize. To be a good writer, you must be able to automatically spell most of the words and come up with reasonable spellings for the words you cannot automatically spell. While children are learning to read and spell high-frequency words and doing lots of easy and repeated reading to develop fluency, they also need to be learning to decode unfamiliar words. Once children know the common sounds for most letters, they need to start paying attention to the patterns in words so that they can use these patterns to decode and spell words. A variety of lesson frameworks you can use to help your students learn and pay attention to patterns in words will be described in the remainder of this chapter.

Guess the Covered Word

Many words can be figured out by thinking about what would make sense in a sentence and seeing if the consonants in the word match what you are thinking of. You must do two things simultaneously—think about what would make sense and think about letters and sounds. Struggling readers often prefer to do one or the other, but not both. Thus, they may guess something that is sensible but ignore the letter sounds they know, or they may guess something that is close to the sounds but makes no sense in the sentence! Doing a weekly Guess the Covered Word lesson will help your students combine these strategies effectively.

Before class begins, write four or five sentences on the board that start with your students' names, follow a similar word pattern, and end with words that vary in their initial sounds and word length.

Rasheed likes to play *soccer.*
Kate likes to play *softball.*
Rob likes to play *basketball.*
Juan likes to play *hockey.*

Cover the last word in each sentence with a sticky note, tearing or adjusting it to the length of the word.

Rasheed likes to play ▉▉▉▉
Kate likes to play ▉▉▉▉
Rob likes to play ▉▉▉▉
Juan likes to play ▉▉▉▉

Begin the activity by reading the first sentence and asking students to guess the covered word. Write four guesses on the board, next to the sentence.

Rasheed likes to play ▉▉▉▉
ball   games   monopoly   football

Next, uncover all the letters up to the vowel. Erase the guesses that do not begin with that group of letters. Have students continue offering guesses that make sense and begin with the correct letter. Write their responses on the board. Keep the students focused both on meaning and on beginning letters.

Rasheed likes to play s▉▉▉▉
soccer   softball

When the first letter is revealed, some students will guess anything that begins with that letter. For example, if the first letter is an *s,* they may guess *sand.* Respond with something like "*Sand* does begin with an *s,* but I can't write *sand* because people don't play *sand.*" Finally, uncover the whole word and see if any guesses were correct. Repeat the procedure on the remaining sentences.

Rasheed likes to play *soccer.*

Once students understand how Guess the Covered Word works, include some sentences in which the covered word begins with the digraphs *sh, ch, th,* and *wh.* Explain that the rules of this game require you to show your children all the letters up to the first vowel. Then show them some sentences that contain the digraphs *sh, ch, th,* and *wh* as well as single consonants. Include examples for both sounds of *c*. Vary your sentence pattern and where in the sentence the covered word is.

> Caroline likes to eat *ch*▪▪▪▪▪
> *W*▪▪▪▪▪ is Chad's favorite fruit.
> Jessica likes strawberries on her *c*▪▪▪▪
> Bo likes strawberry *sh*▪▪▪▪▪
> Melinda bakes pumpkin pies for *Th*▪▪▪▪▪▪
> I don't know *wh*▪▪ pie I like best.

(If you guessed *cherries, watermelon, cereal, shortcake, Thanksgiving* and *which*, you are a true word wizard!)

Guess the Covered Word works for teaching and reviewing *blends,* groups of letters in which you can hear the sounds blended together, such as *br, pl,* and *str.* As with digraphs, vary the sentence pattern and where in the sentence the covered word is.

> Justin likes to *sw*▪▪ in the *s*▪▪▪▪▪
> Curtis plays baseball in the *spr*▪▪▪
> *Sk*▪▪▪ is Jennifer's favorite sport in the winter.
> Andrew likes to *sk*▪▪▪ all year round.
> Val likes to play all kinds of *sp*▪▪▪.

Be sure that when you uncover the beginning letters, you uncover everything up to the vowel. If you have uncovered an *s* and one of your students guesses the word *snow,* tell him or her that that was good thinking for the *s.* Then, have everyone say *snow* slowly and hear the *n.* Say something like "My rule is I have to show you all the letters up to the vowel, so if the word were *snow,* I would have to show you not just the *s* but the *n,* too."

Sometimes, struggling readers get the idea that the only time you use reading strategies is during reading lessons! It is important to show them how cross-checking can help them figure out words when they are reading all kinds of things. You might write a paragraph, such as the following, that is related to the science or social studies topic you are studying. Cover the words in the usual way, and have the whole sentence read before going back to guess without any letters and then with all the letters up to the vowel.

> *M*▪▪▪▪▪ are warm-blooded animals. Their body
> *t*▪▪▪▪▪▪▪ stays the same regardless of the weather.
> All mammals at some time in their *l*▪▪▪ have hair.
> *Wh*▪▪ have hair only before they are born. Mammals
> nurse their babies and give them more *pr*▪▪▪▪▪ than
> other animals. Mammals also have larger *br*▪▪▪ than any
> other group of animals.

(Did you use the context, all the letters up to the vowel and word length to figure out the words *mammals, temperature, lives, whales, protection,* and *brains*?)

Common Core Connections: Guess the Covered Word

Reading: Foundational Standard 4 requires children in all elementary grades to use context to confirm or self-correct word recognition and understanding. The Guess the Covered Word lesson framework teaches children how to use context along with letter sounds to figure out words that make sense.

Using Words You Know

Using Words You Know is an activity designed to help students learn to use the words they already know to decode and spell lots of other words. Here are the steps of a Using Words You Know lesson:

1 Show students three to five words they know, and have these words pronounced and spelled. For our sample lesson, we will tell students that some of the ways they travel—including bikes, cars, vans, and trains—can help them spell other words.

2 Draw four columns, and head each column with one of these words: *bike, car, train,* or *van.* Have students set up the same columns on their own papers and write these four words.

bike	car	train	van

3 Tell students that words that rhyme usually have the same spelling pattern. The spelling pattern in a short word begins with the vowel and goes to the end of the word. Underline the spelling patterns *i-k-e, a-r, a-i-n,* and *a-n,* and have students underline them on their papers.

4 Tell students that you are going to show them some new words and that they should write each one under the word with the same spelling pattern. Show them words that you have written on index cards. Let a different student go to the board or chart and write each new word there as the other students write the word on their papers. Do not let the students pronounce a word aloud until it has been written on the board. Then help the students pronounce the words by making them rhyme. Use less common words that your students will have in their listening vocabularies but don't immediately recognize. When you have 10 to 12 words written, have the students read the rhyming words and identify the spelling pattern.

bike	car	train	van
hike	jar	pain	span
pike		chain	scan
spike		drain	
		Spain	
		sprain	

5 Explain to your students that thinking of rhyming words can help them spell. This time, do not show them the words but rather say the words. Have students decide which words they rhyme with and use the spelling pattern to spell them. Have these words added to the chart.

bike	car	train	van
hike	jar	pain	span
pike	scar	chain	scan
spike	mar	drain	plan
strike	spar	Spain	bran
		sprain	clan
		stain	
		strain	
		brain	
		grain	

6 End this first part of the lesson by helping students verbalize that in English, words that rhyme often have the same spelling pattern and that good readers and spellers do not sound out every letter but rather try to think of a rhyming word and read or spell the word using the pattern in the rhyming word.

For the second part of the lesson (probably on the next day), use the same procedures and same four key words again:

(1) Draw four columns on the board or chart and write the words from the previous lesson to head each column. Have students head four columns on their papers with these words and underline the spelling patterns. Explain to the students that using the rhyme to help read and spell words works with longer words, too.

(2) Show students some words written on index cards, and have them write each word under the appropriate word. Once the word has been written on the board or chart, have students pronounce the word, making the last syllable rhyme:

| guitar | caravan | Japan | maintain |
| cigar | unlike | entertain | hitchhike |

(3) Now say these words and have students decide which word the last syllable rhymes with and use that spelling pattern to spell it. Give help with the spelling of the first part, if needed:

| lifelike | restrain | streetcar | boxcar |
| dislike | caveman | trashcan | contain |

(4) Again, end the lesson by helping students notice how helpful it is to think of a rhyming word you know how to spell when trying to read or spell a strange word.

bike	car	train	van
hike	jar	pain	span
pike	scar	chain	scan
spike	mar	drain	plan
strike	spar	Spain	bran
hitchhike	cigar	sprain	clan
unlike	guitar	stain	caravan
lifelike	boxcar	strain	Japan
dislike	streetcar	brain	caveman
		grain	trashcan
		maintain	
		entertain	
		restrain	
		complain	

In Using Words You Know lessons, you should always choose the words you ask your students to read and spell. Do not ask students for rhyming words, because, especially for the long vowels, there is often another pattern. *Crane, Jane,* and *rein* also rhyme

Knowing 37 spelling patterns will allow children to read and spell over 500 words commonly used by young children (Wylie & Durrell, 1970). Many teachers display each pattern with a word and picture to help children learn the pattern that will help them spell many other words.

Here are the 37 high-frequency spelling patterns (with possible key words):

ack (black)	ail (pail)	ain (train)	ake (cake)	ale (whale)	ame (game)
an (pan)	ank (bank)	ap (cap)	ash (trash)	at (cat)	ate (skate)
aw (claw)	ay (tray)	eat (meat)	ell (shell)	est (nest)	ice (rice)
ide (bride)	ick (brick)	ight (night)	ill (hill)	in (pin)	ine (nine)
ing (king)	ink (pink)	ip (ship)	it (hit)	ock (sock)	oke (Coke)
op (mop)	ore (store)	ot (hot)	uck (truck)	ug (bug)	ump (jump)
unk (trunk)					

with *train,* but you should only use words that rhyme and have the same pattern. You can do Using Words You Know lessons with any words your students can already read and spell. To plan a lesson, select known words that have lots of rhyming words with the same spelling pattern. A rhyming dictionary, such as *The Scholastic Rhyming Dictionary* (Young, 1994), or an online dictionary is a great help in finding suitable rhyming words.

Making Words

Making Words is a popular activity with both teachers and children. Children love manipulating letters to make words and figuring out the secret word that can be made with all the letters. While your students are having fun making words, they are also learning important information about phonics and spelling. As they manipulate letters to make words, they learn how making small changes, such as changing just one letter or moving two letters around, results in completely new words. They also learn to stretch out words and listen for the sounds they hear and the order of those sounds. When you change the first letter, you also change the sound you hear at the beginning of the word. Likewise, when you change the last letter, you change the sound you hear at the end of the word. These ideas seem commonplace and obvious to those of us who have been reading and writing for almost as long as we can remember. But they are a revelation to many beginners—one that gives them tremendous independence in and power over the challenge of decoding and spelling words.

The Making Words activity is an example of a type of instruction called *guided discovery.* In order to truly learn and retain strategies, children must discover them. But some children do not make discoveries about words very easily on their own. In a Making Words lesson, you can guide your students to make these discoveries by carefully sequencing the words they are to make and giving them explicit guidance about how much change is needed.

Making Words lessons have three steps. In the first step, you make words. Begin with short, easy words and move to longer, more complex words. The last word is always the secret word—a word that can be made with all the letters. As the children make each word, a child who has made it successfully goes up to the pocket chart or chalk ledge and makes the word with big letters. Children who have not made the word correctly quickly fix their word to be ready for the next word. The small changes made between most words encourages even those children who have not made a word perfectly to fix it, because they soon realize that spelling the current word correctly increases their chances of spelling the next word correctly. In each lesson, have students make 10 to 15 words, including the secret word that can be made with all the letters.

In the second step of a Making Words lesson, sort the words into patterns. Many children discover patterns just through making the words in the carefully sequenced order, but some children need more explicit guidance. This guidance happens when all the words have been made and you guide the children to sort them into patterns. Depending on the sophistication of the children and the words available in the lesson, words might be sorted according to their beginning letters—all the letters up to the vowel. Alternatively, to focus on just one sound-letter combination, you may ask children to sort out all the words that begin with *sp* or *sn*. Once the words with these letters have been sorted, you and the children should pronounce the words and discover that most words that have the same letters also have the same sound.

Another pattern that children need to discover is that many words have the same root word. If they can pronounce and spell the root word and if they can recognize the root word with a prefix or suffix added, they can decode and spell many additional words. To some children, every new word they meet is a new experience! They fail to recognize how

Steps in Planning a Making Words Lesson

1. Choose your secret word, a word that can be made with all the letters. In choosing this word, consider child interest, the curriculum tie-ins you can make, and the letter-sound patterns to which you can draw children's attention through the sorting at the end.

2. Make a list of other words that can be made from these letters.

3. From all the words you could make, pick 12 to 15 words using these criteria:

   - Words that you can sort for the pattern you want to emphasize

   - Little words and big words to create a multilevel lesson (Making little words helps your struggling students; making big words challenges your highest-achieving students.)

   - Words that can be made with the same letters in different places (*barn/bran*) so children are reminded that ordering letters is crucial when spelling words

   - A proper name or two to remind the children that we use capital letters

   - Words that most students have in their listening vocabularies

4. Write all the words on index cards and order them from shortest to longest.

5. Once you have the two-letter words together, the three-letter words together, and so on, order them so you can emphasize letter patterns and how changing the position of the letters or changing/adding just one letter results in a different word.

6. Choose some letters or patterns to sort for.

7. Choose some transfer words—uncommon words you can read or spell based on the rhyming words.

8. Store the cards in an envelope. Write the words in order on the envelope, the patterns you will sort for, and the transfer words.

new words are related to already known words and thus are in the difficult, if not impossible, position of starting from "scratch" and trying to learn and remember every new word. To be fluent, fast, automatic decoders and spellers, children must learn that *play, playing, played, plays, player,* and *replay* all have *play* as their root and use their knowledge of how to decode and spell *play* to quickly transfer to these related words.

In every lesson, sort the rhyming words. Each lesson should contain several sets of rhyming words. Children need to recognize that words that have the same spelling pattern from the vowel to the end of the word usually rhyme. When you sort the words into rhyming words and point out that the words that rhyme have the same spelling pattern, children learn rhyming patterns and how to use words they know to decode and spell lots of other words.

The final step of a Making Words lesson is the transfer step. All the working and playing with words you do while making words will be worth nothing if children do not use what they know when they need to use it. Many children know letter sounds and patterns and do not apply this knowledge to decode unknown words they encounter during reading or to spell words they need while writing. All teachers know that it is much easier to teach children phonics than it is to actually get them to use it. This is the reason that you need to end every Making Words lesson with a transfer step. Once you have the words sorted according to rhyme, have your students use the sorted rhyming words to spell some new words with the same rhyming pattern.

Here is an example of how you might conduct a Making Words lesson and cue the children to the changes and words you want them to make.

Beginning the Lesson

The children all have the letters: **a e u c c k p s**

These same letters—big enough for all to see—are displayed in a pocket chart. The letter cards have lowercase letters on one side and capital letters on the other side. The vowels are in a different color.

Source: Patricia Cunningham

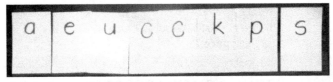

Source: Patricia Cunningham

The words the children are going to make are written on index cards. These words will be placed in the pocket chart as the words are made and will be used for the Sort and Transfer steps of the lesson.

The teacher begins the lesson by having the children hold up and name each letter as the teacher holds up the big letters in the pocket chart.

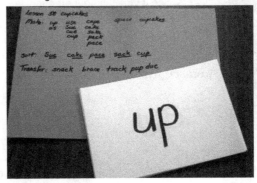

Source: Patricia Cunningham

"Hold up and name each letter as I hold up the big letter. Let's start with your vowels. Show me your **a**, your **u**, and your **e**. Now show me your two **c**'s, **k**, **p**, and **s**. Today you have 8 letters. In a few minutes, we will see if anyone can figure out the secret word that uses all 8 letters."

Part One: Making Words

"Use 2 letters to spell the word **up**. I got **up** at 6:30."

(Find someone with **up** spelled correctly and send that child to spell **up** with the big letters.)

"Change 1 letter to spell **us**. The fifth-graders put on a play for **us**."

"Add a letter you don't hear to spell **use**. We **use** our letters to make words."

"Move the same letters to spell the name **Sue**. Do you know anyone named **Sue**?"

(Find someone with **Sue** spelled with a capital **S** to spell **Sue** with the big letters.)

"Change 1 letter to spell **cue**. When you are an actor, you listen for your **cue**."

(Quickly send someone with the correct spelling to make the word with the big letters. Keep the pace brisk. Do not wait until everyone has **cue** spelled with their little letters. It is fine if some children are making **cue** as **cue** is being spelled with the big letters. Choose your struggling readers to go to the pocket chart when easy words are being spelled and your advanced readers when harder words are being made.)

"Change 1 letter in **cue** to spell **cup**. The baby drinks from a sippy **cup**."

"Change the vowel to spell **cap**. Do you ever wear a **cap**?"

"Add a silent letter to change **cap** into **cape**. Batman wore a **cape**."

"Change 1 letter to spell **cake**. Do you like chocolate **cake**?"

"Change 1 letter to spell **sake**. I hope for your **sake** that it doesn't rain during the game."

"Change the last 2 letters to spell **sack**. A **sack** is another name for a bag."

"Change 1 letter to spell **pack**. **Pack** your clothes for the sleepover."

"Change the last letter to spell another 4 letter word, **pace**. The racers ran at a very fast **pace**."

"Add 1 letter to spell **space**. When we write, we leave a **space** between words."

"I have just one word left. It is the secret word you can make with all your letters. See if you can figure it out."

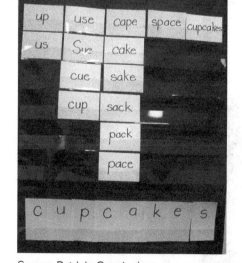

Source: Patricia Cunningham

(Give the children one minute to figure out the secret word. Then give clues if needed.) Let someone who figures it out go to the big letters and spell the secret word: **cupcakes**.

Source: Patricia Cunningham

Part Two: Sorting the Words into Patterns Using the index cards with words you made, place them in the pocket chart as the children pronounce and chorally spell each one. Give them a quick reminder of how they made these words:

> "First we spelled a 2 letter word, **up, u-p**."
> "We changed the last letter to spell **us, u-s**."
> "We added the silent e to spell **use, u-s-e**."
> "We used the same letters with a capital S to spell **Sue, S-u-e**."
> "We changed the first letter to spell **cue, c-u-e**."
> "We changed the last letter to spell **cup, c-u-p**."
> "We changed the vowel to spell **cap, c-a-p**."
> "We added the silent e to spell **cape, c-a-p-e**."
> "We changed 1 letter to spell **cake, c-a-k-e**."
> "We changed 1 letter to spell **sake, s-a-k-e**."
> "We changed the last 2 letters to spell **sack, s-a-c-k**."
> "We changed 1 letter to spell **pack, p-a-c-k**."
> "We changed the last letter to spell **pace, p-a-c-e**."
> "We added a letter to spell **space, s-p-a-c-e**."
> "Finally, we spelled the secret word using all our letters, **cupcakes, c-u-p-c-a-k-e-s**."

Next have the children sort the rhyming words. Take one of each set of rhyming words and place them in the pocket chart.

Sue   cake   pace   sack   cup

Ask three children to find the other words that rhyme and place them under the ones you pulled out.

Sue   cake   pace   sack   cup
cue   sake   space   pack   up

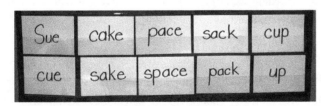

Source: Patricia Cunningham

Have the children chorally pronounce the sets of rhyming words.

Part Three: Transfer Tell the children to pretend it is writing time and they need to spell some words that rhyme with some of the words they made today. Have the children use whiteboards or half-sheets of paper to write the words. Say sentences that children might want to write that include a rhyming word. Work together to decide which words the target word rhymes with and to decide how to spell it.

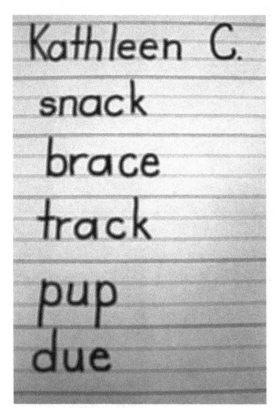

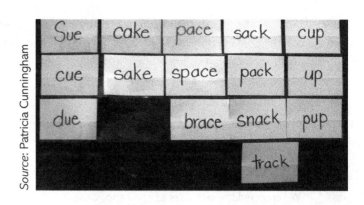

"Boys and girls, let's pretend it is writing time. Terry is writing about what he likes to eat for a **snack** and he is trying to spell the word **snack**. Let's all say **snack** and stretch out the beginning letters. What 2 letters do you hear at the beginning of **snack**?"

Have the children stretch out **snack** and listen for the beginning letters. When they tell you that **snack** begins with **sn**, write **sn** on an index card and have the children write **sn** on their papers or whiteboards.

Take the index card with **sn** on it to the pocket chart and hold it under each column of words as you lead the children to chorally pronounce the words and decide if **snack** rhymes with them:

"Sue, cue, snack." Children should show you "thumbs down."

"Cake, sake, snack." Children should again show you "thumbs down."

"Pace, space, snack." Children should again show you "thumbs down."

"Sack, pack, snack." Children should show you "thumbs up."

Finish writing **snack** on your index card by adding **ack** to **sn** and place **snack** in the pocket chart under **sack** and **pack**.

Make up sentences and use the same procedure to demonstrate how you use **pace** and **space** to spell **brace** and **sack** and **pack** to spell **track**.

We hope this sample lesson has helped you see how a Making Words lesson works and how Making Words lessons help children develop phonemic awareness, phonics, and spelling skills. Most important, we hope you see that in every lesson children will practice applying the patterns they are learning to reading and spelling new words.

One-Vowel Lessons

Vowels are the tricky part of English spelling, so the first lessons we do with students have only one vowel. Here are some one-vowel lessons you can use to launch your children into a successful start with making words.

Letters:	a d h n s		
Words to Make:	as an and has had sad sand hand hands		
Sort:	and	had	as
	sand	sad	has
	hand		

Transfer:	Use rhyming words to spell *bad*, *band*, *land*, and *mad*.
Letters:	e d n p s
Words to Make:	Ed Ned end den pen pens dens send spend

Sort:	Ed	end	pen	dens
	Ned	send	den	pens
		spend		

Transfer:	Use rhyming words to spell *bed*, *lend*, *ten*, and *hens*.
Letters:	i p r s t
Words to Make:	is it sit pit tip sip rip trip strip trips

Sort:	it	rip
	sit	sip
	pit	tip
	trip	
	strip	

Making Big Words

For older students, we choose a secret word that has some related words. We print the letters on a strip and copy them. The students tear the strips into letters and use them to make words.

a	e	e	b	c	c	l	l	r	y

Make:	all call ball bell cell real able cable cycle clear really caller/recall clearly recycle recyclable
Sort Related Words:	call, caller, recall; real, really; clear, clearly; cycle, recycle, recyclable (Use related words in sentences that show relationship.)

Sort Rhymes (with same spelling pattern):

all	bell	able
ball	cell	cable
call		

Transfer:	Have students use rhyming words to spell *table, stable, swell,* and *shell*.

a	e	i	d	h	h	r	s	s	w

Make:	ear hear dish wish wash wise rise herd heard arise dishes wishes washes radishes dishwasher
Sort homophones:	herd, heard (Put in a sentence to make meaning clear.)

Sort Related Words:	hear, heard; rise, arise; wish, wishes; dish, dishes, dishwasher, wash, washes (Use related words in sentences that show relationship.)

Sort Rhymes (with same spelling pattern):

ear	dish	wise	dishes
hear	wish	rise	wishes
		arise	

Transfer: Have students use rhyming words to spell *year, spear, revise,* and *franchise.*

e	e	i	g	h	l	s	s	t	w
_	_	_	_	_	_	_	_	_	_

Make: hit with wish heel tile while wheel sheet sleet sweet light sight wishes weight hitless whistle weightless

Sort Related Words: wish, wishes; hit, hitless; weight, weightless (Use related words in sentences that show relationship.)

Steps in Teaching a Making Words Lesson

1. Place the large letter cards needed in a pocket chart or along the chalk tray.

2. Have children pass out letters or pick up the letters needed.

3. Hold up and name the letters on the large letter cards, and have the children hold up their matching small letter cards.

4. Write the numeral 2 (or 3 if no two-letter words are in this lesson) on the board. Tell them to take two letters and make the first word. Have them say the word after you stretch out the word to hear all the sounds.

5. Have a child who makes the first word correctly make the same word with the large letter cards on the chalk tray or pocket chart. Do not wait for everyone to make the word before sending a child to make it with the big letters. Encourage anyone who did not make the word correctly at first to fix the word when he or she sees it made correctly.

6. Continue to make words, giving students clues, such as "Change the first letter only" or "Move the same letters around and you can make a different word" or "Take all your letters out and make another word." Send a child who has made the word correctly to make the word with the large letter cards. Cue students when they are to use more letters by erasing and changing the number on the board to indicate the number of letters needed.

7. Before telling students the last word, say, "Has anyone figured out the secret word—the word we can make with all our letters?" If someone has, offer congratulations and let him or her make it. If not, give students clues until someone figures out the secret word.

8. Once all the words have been made, take the index cards on which you wrote the words and place them one at a time (in the same order that children made them) along the chalk ledge or in the pocket chart. Have children say and spell the words with you as you do this. Ask children to sort these words for patterns—including beginning letters, rhymes, and related words.

9. To encourage transfer to reading and writing, show students how rhyming words can help them decode and spell other words. Say some words that rhyme and have students spell these new words by deciding which words they rhyme with.

Sort Rhymes (with same spelling pattern):

heel	tile	sheet	light
wheel	while	sleet	sight
		sweet	

Transfer: Have students use rhyming words to spell *mile, smile, slight,* and *parakeet.*

Modeling How to Decode Big Words

Big words present special decoding problems. Most of the words we read are one- and two-syllable words, but polysyllabic words often carry most of the content. Decoding and spelling polysyllabic words is based on patterns, but these patterns are more sophisticated and require students to understand how words change in their spelling, pronunciation, and meaning as suffixes and prefixes are added. The *g* in *sign* seems quite illogical until you realize that *sign* is related to *signal, signature,* and other words. Finding the *compose/ composition* and *compete/competition* relationship helps students understand why the second syllable of *composition* and *competition* sound alike but are spelled differently. To decode and spell big words, your students must (1) have a mental store of big words that contain the spelling patterns common to big words; (2) chunk big words into pronounce-able segments by comparing the parts of new big words to the big words they already know; and (3) recognize and use common prefixes and suffixes.

Modeling is the most direct way to demonstrate to your students what to do when they encounter a long, unfamiliar word. When you model, you show someone how to do something. In real life, we use modeling constantly to teach skills. We would not think of explaining how to ride a bike. Rather, we would demonstrate and talk about what we were doing as the learner watched and listened to our explanation. Vocabulary introduction is a good place to model how you figure out the pronunciation of a word for students. Here is an example of how you might model for students one way to decode the word *international.* Write a sentence containing the word on the board:

> The thinning of the ozone layer is an inter<u>nation</u>al problem.

> "Today, we are going to look at a big word that is really just a little word with a prefix added to the beginning and a suffix added to the end."

Underline *nation* in the sentence you have just written.

> The thinning of the ozone layer is an inter<u>nation</u>al problem.

> "Who can tell me this word? Yes, that is the word *nation.* Now, let's look at the prefix that comes before *nation.*"

Underline *inter.*

> The thinning of the ozone layer is an <u>inter</u>national problem.

> "This prefix is *inter.* You probably know *inter* from words such as *interrupt* and *internal.* Now, let's look at what follows *inter* and *nation.*"

Underline *al.*

> The thinning of the ozone layer is an internation<u>al</u> problem.

> "You know the suffix **al** from many words, such as **unusual** and **critical**."

Write *unusual* and *critical* and underline the *al.*

> unusu<u>al</u> critic<u>al</u>
>
> "Listen as I pronounce this part of the word."

Underline and pronounce *national.*

> The thinning of the ozone layer is an inter<u>national</u> problem.
>
> "Notice how the pronunciation of *nation* changes when we put *a-l* on it.
> Now let's put all the parts together and pronounce the word—*inter nation al.*
> Let's read the sentence and make sure *international* makes sense."

Have the sentence read and confirm that ozone thinning is indeed a problem for many nations to solve.

> "You can figure out the pronunciation of many big words if you look for common prefixes, such as *inter;* common root words, such as *nation;* and common suffixes, such as *al.*"

> "In addition to helping you figure out the pronunciation of a word, prefixes and suffixes sometimes help you know what the word means or where in a sentence we can use the word. The word *nation* names a thing. When we describe a nation, we add the suffix *al* and have *national.* The prefix *inter* often means between or among. Something that is *international* is between many nations. The Olympics are the best example of an *international* sporting event."

This sample lesson for introducing the word *international* demonstrates how you can help your students see and use morphemes—meaningful parts of words—to decode polysyllabic words. A similar procedure could be used to model how you would decode a word that did not contain suffixes or prefixes. For the word *resources,* for example, you could draw students' attention to the familiar first syllable *re* and then point out the known word *sources.* For *geologic,* you might write and underline the *geo* in the known word *geography* and then point out the known word *logic. Policies* might be compared to *politics* and *agencies.*

Modeling is simply thinking aloud about how you might go about figuring out an unfamiliar word. It takes just a few extra minutes to point out the morphemes in *international* and to show how *policies* is like *politics* and *agencies.* But taking these extra few minutes is quickly paid back as your students begin to develop some independence in figuring out those big words that carry so much of the content.

The Nifty-Thrifty-Fifty

English is the most morphologically complex language. Linguists estimate that for every word you know, you can figure out how to decode, spell, and build meanings for six or seven other words, if you recognize and use the morphemic patterns in words. Activities in this section teach students how to spell a Nifty-Thrifty-Fifty store of words to decode, spell, and build meaning for thousands of other words. These 50 words include examples for all the common prefixes and suffixes as well as common spelling changes. Because these 50 words help with so many other words, we have named them the Nifty-Thrifty-Fifty (Cunningham, 2013).

The Nifty-Thrifty-Fifty words should be introduced gradually, and students should practice chanting and writing them until their spelling and decoding become automatic. The procedures for working with these words and their important parts follow:

1 Display the words, arranged by first letter, someplace in the room. Add four or five each week. You may want to use a bulletin board or hang a banner above a bulletin board and attach the words to it. The words need to be big and bold so that they are seen easily from wherever the students are writing. Using different colors makes them more visible and attractive. Many teachers use large colored index cards or write them with different colors of thick, bold permanent markers.

2 Explain to students that in English, many big words are just smaller words with prefixes and suffixes added to the word. Good spellers do not memorize the spelling of every new word they come across. Rather, they notice the patterns in words and these patterns include prefixes, suffixes, and spelling changes that occur when these are added.

3 Tell students that one way to practice words is to say the letters in them aloud in a rhythmic, chanting fashion. Tell students that although this might seem silly, it really is not because the brain responds to sound and rhythm. (That is one of the reasons you can sing along with the words of a familiar song even though you could not say the words without singing the song and also why jingles and raps are easy to remember.) Point to each word and have students chant it (cheerleader style) with you. After "cheering" for each word, help students analyze the word, talking about its meaning and determining the root, prefix, and suffix, and noting any spelling changes. Here is an example of the kind of word introduction students find most helpful:

> **composer**—A composer is a person who composes something. Many other words, such as *writer, reporter,* and *teacher,* are made up of a root word and the suffix *er,* meaning a person or thing that does something. When *er* is added to a word that already has an *e,* the original *e* is dropped.
>
> **discovery**—A discovery is something you discover. The prefix *dis* often changes a word to an opposite form. To *cover* something can mean to hide it. When you *discover* it, it is no longer hidden. *Discovery* is the root word *cover* with the added prefix *dis* and suffix *y.* There are no spelling changes.
>
> **encouragement**—When you encourage someone, you give them encouragement. Many other words, such as *argue, argument* and *replace, replacement,* follow this same pattern. The root word for *encourage* is *courage.* So *encouragement* is made up of the prefix *en,* the root word *courage,* and the suffix *ment.*
>
> **hopeless**—Students should easily see the root word *hope* and the suffix *less.* Other similar words are *painless* and *homeless.*
>
> **impossible**—The root word is *possible* with the suffix *im.* In many words, including *impatient* and *immature,* the suffix *im* changes the word to an opposite.
>
> **musician**—A musician is a person who makes music. A *beautician* helps make you beautiful, and a *magician* makes magic. *Musician* has the root word *music* with the suffix *ian,* which sometimes indicates the person who does something. None of the spelling changes but the pronunciation changes. Have students say the words *music* and *musician, magic* and *magician,* and notice how the pronunciation changes.

④ Once you have noticed the composition for each word, helped students see other words that work in a similar way, and cheered for each word, have students write each word. Writing the word with careful attention to each letter and the sequence of each letter helps students use another mode to practice the word. (Do not, however, assign students to copy words five times each. They just do this "mechanically" and often do not focus on the letters.) Students enjoy writing the words more and focus better on them if you make it a riddle or game. You can do this simply by giving clues for the word you want them to write:

a. Number 1 is the opposite of *discouragement*.
b. Number 2 is the opposite of *hopeful*.
c. For number 3, write the word that tells what you are if you play the *guitar*.
d. For number 4, write what you are if you play the *guitar* but you also make up the songs you play.
e. Number 5 is the opposite of *possible*.
f. For number 6, write the word that has *cover* for the root word.

After writing the words, have students check their own papers, once more chanting the letters aloud and underlining each as they say it.

⑤ When you have a few minutes of "sponge" time, practice the words by chanting or writing. As you are cheering or writing each word, ask students to identify the root, prefix, and suffix and talk about how these affect the meaning of the root word. Also have them point out any spelling changes.

⑥ Once students can automatically, quickly, and correctly spell the words and explain to you how they are composed, it is time to help them see how these words can help them decode and spell other words. Remind students that good spellers do not memorize the spelling of each word. Rather, they use words they know and combine roots, suffixes, and prefixes to figure out how to spell lots of other words. Have the students spell words that are contained in the words and words you can make by combining parts of the words.

Have each word used in a sentence and talk about the meaning relationships when appropriate. Note spelling changes as needed. From just the eight words—*composer, discovery, encouragement, hopeless, impossible, musician, richest,* and *unfriendly*—students should be able to decode, spell, and discuss meanings for the following words:

compose	encourage	music	dispose	enrichment
pose	courage	rich	discourage	uncover
discover	hope	friend	discouragement	richly
cover	possible	friendly	enrich	hopelessly

⑦ Continue adding words gradually, going through the above procedures with all the words. Do not add words too quickly, and provide lots of practice with these words and the other words that can be decoded and spelled by combining parts of these words. Because this store of words provides patterns for so many other words, you want your students to "overlearn" these words so that they can be called up instantly and automatically when students meet similar words in their reading or need to spell similar words while writing.

Common Core Connections: Multisyllabic Words

Reading: Foundational Standard 3 in third, fourth, and fifth grades focuses on morphemes. Students are expected to know the meanings of common prefixes and suffixes and to use these to decode unfamiliar multisyllabic words. Language Standard 4 also focuses on morphology. Second- and third-grade students are expected to determine meanings for new words when common prefixes or suffixes are added to root words. Modeling how to decode big words students encounter in their reading and teaching them key words, such as those on the Nifty-Thrifty-Fifty list, teach students how to use morphemes—prefixes, suffixes, and roots—to decode, spell, and build meaning for big words.

Nifty-Thrifty-Fifty Words and Transferable Chunks

Key Word	Prefix	Suffix/Ending/Spelling Change
antifreeze	anti (against)	
beautiful		ful (y-i)
classify		ify
communities	com (with or together)	es (y-i)
community	com (with or together)	y
composer	com (with or together)	er
continuous	con (with or together)	ous (drop e)
conversation	con (with or together)	tion
deodorize	de (take away)	ize
different		ent
discovery	dis (not or reverse)	y
dishonest	dis (not or reverse)	
electricity	e	ity
employee	em	ee (person)
encouragement	en (make or give)	ment
expensive	ex	ive
governor		or (person)
happiness		ness (y-i)
hopeless		less (without)
illegal	il (not or opposite)	
impossible	im (not or opposite)	ible
impression	im (in)	ion
independence	in (not or opposite)	ence
international	inter (between)	al
invasion	in (in)	sion
irresponsible	ir (not or oppostite)	ible
midnight	mid (middle)	
misunderstand	mis (wrong or bad)	
musician		ian (person)
nonviolent	non (not)	
overpower	over (more than or too much)	

Key Word	Prefix	Suffix/Ending/Spelling Change
patiently		ly
performance	per	ance
prehistoric	pre (before)	ic
prettier		er (y-i)
promotion	pro (for or in favor of)	tion
rearrange	re (back or again)	
replacement	re (back or again)	ment
richest		est (most)
semifinal	semi (half or partly)	
signature		ture
submarine	sub (under or behind)	
supermarkets	super (really big)	s
swimming		ing (double m)
transportation	trans (across or through)	tion
underweight	under	
unfinished	un (not or opposite)	ed
unpleasant	un	ant (drop e)
valuable		able (drop e)
written		en (double t)

Summary

Reading is a complex process in which you have to identify words from which you construct meaning. Writing is equally (if not more!) complex. Both reading and writing require that the most common words be read and spelled automatically—without thought or mediation—so that the brain's attention can focus on meaning. When children are first starting to read and write, their word identification and spelling will not be automatic. Teaching them how to read and spell high-frequency words and providing a lot of varied practice reading will help children develop fluency.

As they are learning high-frequency words and developing fluency, children also need to learn patterns so that they can quickly decode and spell words they have not yet learned. The patterns in short words are the *onsets*—commonly called beginning letters—and the *rimes*—spelling patterns. In big words, *morphemes*—prefixes, suffixes, and roots—are the patterns that allow readers to quickly decode and spell longer words.

Few instructional studies have compared different types of phonics instruction. After reviewing the research on phonics instruction, Stahl, Duffy-Hester, and Stahl (1998) concluded that there are several types of good phonics instruction and that there is no research base to support the superiority of any one particular type. The National Reading Panel (NRP) (2000) reviewed the experimental research on teaching phonics and determined that explicit and systematic phonics is superior to nonsystematic or no phonics but that there is no significant difference in effectiveness among the kinds of systematic phonics instruction. The NRP also found no significant difference in effectiveness among tutoring, small-group, or whole-class phonics instruction.

A number of studies have supported integrating phonics and spelling instruction with young children (Ehri & Wilce, 1987; Ellis & Cataldo, 1990). Juel and Minden-Cupp (2000) noted that based on their observations, the most effective teachers of children who entered first grade with few literacy skills combined systematic letter-sound instruction with onset-rime, compare–contrast activities instruction, and taught these units with applications in both reading and writing.

Phonics and spelling instruction in the upper grades has not been investigated much, but some understanding about the new words encountered in these grades provides some instructional direction. In 1984, Nagy and Anderson published a landmark study in which they analyzed a sample of 7,260 words found in books commonly read in grades 3 through 9. They found that most of these words were polysyllabic words and that many of these big words were related semantically through their morphology. Some of these relationships are easily noticed. For instance, the words *hunter, redness, foglights,* and *stringy* are clearly related to the words *hunt, red, fog,* and *string.* Other more complex word relationships exist between words such as *planet/planetarium, vicious/vice,* and *apart/apartment.* Nagy and Anderson hypothesized that if children knew or learned how to interpret morphological relationships, they would know six or seven words for every basic word. To move children along in their decoding and spelling abilities in the upper grades, instruction needs to focus on morphemes—prefixes, suffixes, and roots—and how they help us decode, spell, and gain meaning for polysyllabic words.

How Well Does Your Classroom Help All Children Learn to Decode and Spell Words?

1. Am I teaching my students to figure out new words while reading by using both context and letter sounds to decode unknown words?

2. Do I include activities such as Using Words You Know and Making Words, which focus my students' attention on patterns and using those patterns to decode and spell new words?

3. Do I model how to decode big words by looking for familiar patterns during reading lessons and when introducing math, science, and social studies vocabulary?

4. Am I making sure that students have a bank of big words that they can read and spell so that they can use the patterns from these big words to read and spell other big words?

6

Meaning Vocabulary

READ EACH OF THESE THREE WORDS, and think about what comes immediately to mind:

plastic   purple   racket

What did you think of for *plastic*? Did you image the multitude of plastic objects that make up everyday life? Did you experience negative feelings, such as "I hate using plastic knives, forks, and spoons," while simultaneously realizing that our current world would be very different if it weren't for the omnipresence of plastic? Did you worry because most plastic biodegrades so slowly and is not good for the environment?

What did your brain do with the word *purple?* Did you picture something purple? Did you think "I hate purple" or "Purple is one of my favorite colors"? Did you imagine different shades of purple—orchid, lavender, lilac? Perhaps the word *purple* made you think immediately of someone you know who was in the military and earned a Purple Heart, and you wondered how this medal came to be associated with the color purple.

Did you picture a tennis or badminton racket for the word *racket?* Or did you think of all the racket being made by the construction across the street? Perhaps you were reminded about the shenanigans of your local government and thought, "It's all a racket!"

When we see or hear words, our brains make all kinds of connections with those words, depending on our past experiences. These connections include images and scenes from our own lives as well as from movies and television. We have emotional reactions to words. Words make us worry, celebrate, appreciate, and wonder.

What our minds don't do when they see or hear a word is think of a definition. Look up *plastic, purple,* and *racket* in any dictionary and you will find definitions such as these:

plastic—any of a large group of synthetic organic compounds molded by heat pressure into a variety of forms

purple—a color made by mixing red and blue

racket—a loud noise; a scheme for getting money illegally; an oval strung frame with a long handle used for hitting balls

When you see or hear words, your brain makes connections to those words. Your brain does not think of definitions.

Now think back to your elementary school days and recall your associations with the word *vocabulary.* Do you remember looking up words and copying their definitions? If a word had several definitions, did you copy the first one or the shortest one? Did you ever look up a word and still not know what it meant because you did not understand the meanings of the other words in the definition? Did you copy that definition and memorize it for the test, in spite of not understanding it? Do you remember weekly vocabulary tests, in which you had to write definitions for words and use those words in sentences?

Copying and memorizing definitions has been and remains the most common vocabulary activity in schools. It is done at all levels and in all subjects. This definition copying and memorizing continues in spite of research that shows definitional approaches to vocabulary instruction increase children's ability to define words but have no effect on reading comprehension (Baumann, Kame'enui, & Ash, 2003).

Vocabulary is critical to reading comprehension. If you are reading or listening to something in which you can instantly access the appropriate meanings for the words, you are well on your way to understanding. But when you are reading or listening to something and you don't have meanings for a lot of the words, your comprehension is severely impaired. Vocabulary is also crucial for writing. We all know that one of the challenges of writing well and clearly is "choosing just the right word." Vocabulary is one of the most valuable tools for literacy. In the next four chapters, we will describe specific strategies you can use to teach students to comprehend and to write clearly. A schoolwide, day-in-day-out vocabulary-building component in the curriculum provides the foundation on which specific comprehension and writing skills can be built.

How Do We Learn All the Words We Know?

How many words do you know?

> 5,000?
> 10,000?
> 20,000?
> 50,000?
> 100,000?

If you found it difficult to estimate the size of your vocabulary, you should be comforted to know that this seemingly simple question is a difficult one to answer. The first question is, of course, "What do you mean by *know?*" Is it enough to know that anthropoids are some kind of apes, or do you have to know the specific information that anthropoids are apes without tails, such as chimpanzees, gorillas, orangutans, and gibbons? The next question is, "How many meanings of the word do you have to know?" If you know the sports meaning of coach, do you also have to know the motorbus and "coach class" meanings to count this word in your meaning vocabulary? The other complication in counting the words you have meanings for is how to count the various forms of a single word. If *play, plays, playing, played, playful, replay,* and *player* count as separate words, your vocabulary is much larger than if these words count as one word, all related to the root word *play.* All these variables—word depth, multimeaning words, and how to count words with the same root—result in wide differences in the estimate of vocabulary size.

In spite of the difficulties of estimating vocabulary size, it is important for teachers to have an idea of what the meaning vocabulary development goal is. Biemiller (2004) estimates that entering kindergarteners have meanings for an average of 3,500 root words. They add approximately 1,000 root word meanings each school year. The average high school graduate knows about 15,000 root words.

Other vocabulary experts (Graves, 2006; Stahl & Nagy, 2006) argue that Biemiller's estimate is way too low. They believe that words with multiple meanings should be counted as separate words and that many children do not recognize words with common roots. Furthermore, they believe that proper nouns—Canada, Abraham Lincoln, the White House—should be included in the total word count. When counted in this way, these experts argue that the average child learns 2,000 to 3,000 word meanings each school year and that the average high school graduate has meanings for 40,000 to 50,000 words. Regardless of which estimates you believe, the number of new words children need to add to their vocabularies each year is staggering.

Children differ greatly, however, in the sizes of their meaning vocabularies at school entrance and as they continue through the grades. Children who enter school with small vocabularies tend to add fewer words each year than children who enter with larger vocabularies. Since vocabulary size is so closely related to children's comprehension as they move through school, there is a sense of urgency about intensifying efforts to build more and deeper word meaning stores for all children.

To help you understand how we add words to our meaning vocabulary stores, consider the analogy that learning word meanings is a lot like getting to know people. As with words, you know some people extremely well, you are well acquainted with others, you have only vague ideas of still others, and so on. Your knowledge of people depends on the experiences you have with them. You know some people, such as family members and close friends, extremely well because you have spent most of your life in their company. You have participated with them regularly in situations that have been intense and emotional as well as routine. At the other extreme, think of people that you have only heard about as well as historical figures, such as Charles Darwin and Amelia Earhart, and current public figures, such as politicians and entertainers. You have heard of them and seen pictures and videos of them, but these people are known to you only through the secondhand reports of others. Your knowledge of people that you know indirectly through secondhand information is limited in comparison to your knowledge of those you know directly through firsthand experience. Learning words—like coming to know people—varies according to how much time you spend with them and the types of experiences you share.

Now think of how you make new friends. Social gatherings, such as parties and meetings, are excellent opportunities for getting to know others. When you move through a gathering on your own, you strike up conversations and get to know new people, in part as a function of your motivation and your social skills. However, having a host, hostess, friend, or group of friends introduce you to people tends to expedite the process. And once you have made new contacts, you might get to know them better as you meet again in other settings. And don't forget the power of social networking: The more people you know, the more opportunities you have for helping each other out and meeting even more people.

The levels of knowledge about people and the dynamics of getting to know them are comparable in many ways to learning words. When given the opportunity, students learn new words on their own, depending on their motivation and literacy skills. Students also benefit from direct introductions to and intensive interactions with a few new words. As students learn new words, their opportunities for learning additional words increase exponentially.

Literacy experts all agree on the need for vocabulary building for all students at all grades. They disagree, however, about the best way to provide students with the valuable vocabulary tools they need. We know that you can teach specific vocabulary and that learning new words will improve the comprehension of text containing those words. But the teaching must be quite thorough and across several days and weeks, and thus, the number of words any teacher can directly teach is limited. Many of the words children add to their vocabularies each year are learned through reading. Thus, wide reading is often recommended for vocabulary development.

When you meet a word in your reading, you have two sources of information to help you figure out the meaning of that word. Consider the following sentence:

I wish I understood how they can colorize old movies.

If you had never heard the word *colorize* before, you probably figured out what it meant by using the context of the sentence and your morphemic knowledge about the root *color* and the suffix *ize*. Since you know that when you *modernize* something, you make it more modern; when you *categorize* things, you put them into categories; and when you *rationalize* something you have done, you make it rational (even if it really wasn't!), then you quickly realize that to *colorize* something is to make it have color. Of course, you know that old movies were black and white, and thus you can read the sentence, immediately understand the meaning of *colorize,* and wonder how they do that! Because we know that wide reading is associated with large vocabularies and that the clues available when you come to a new word in your reading are context and morphemes, some experts argue that the best way to help students build vocabulary is to promote wide reading and teach the use of context and morphemes.

Since we know that words can be directly taught and that wide reading—supported by context and morpheme detection—are both valuable ways of building vocabulary, the wise thing for most teachers to do is to "hedge their bets" and tackle the vocabulary challenge from "both fronts." In the remainder of this chapter, we will describe a variety of ways teachers can help all their students grow their vocabularies.

Teach Vocabulary with "Real Things"

We all learn best when we have real, direct experience with whatever we are learning. Most of the vocabulary learning children do before they come to school is based on real things and real experiences. Children first learn to name things—*table, chair, cat, dog.* Two-year-olds delight in pointing to the objects they can see and naming them. Put them in a new environment, such as the beach or the doctor's office, and they will almost immediately begin to point to things and ask, "What's that?" It is not only nouns that children learn through direct experience. Every young child knows the meanings of *run* and *walk* and has probably been told many times that you can't run in the parking lot! Children also learn emotion words through real experiences:

> "I know you feel sad that your friend moved away. I would be sad too if that happened."

The words we know best and remember longest are those we have had real, direct experience with. Teachers who want to build students' vocabularies are always looking for ways to introduce words with "real things."

Bring Real Things into the Classroom and Anchor Words to Them

Look around your house or apartment, and identify common objects your students might not know the names of—even if they have the same objects in their houses or apartments! Here are some of the objects one teacher brought to school for Show and Talk:

- Vases in assorted sizes, colors, and shapes
- Balls—tennis, baseball, basketball, football, golf, volleyball, beachball
- Art—watercolors, oils, photographs in frames of different colors, materials, and sizes
- Kitchen implements—turkey baster, strainer, spatula, whisk, zester
- Tools—hammer, screwdriver, nails, screws, drill, wrench

In addition to the names of objects, of course, many descriptive words are used in talking about the objects and many verbs are used in talking about what you do with the objects. You may want to teach children a simple version of the game 20 Questions, in which you think of one of the objects, and the children see how many questions they have to ask you to narrow down which one it is.

"Mine" Your School Environment for Real Things

In addition to gathering objects from home and carting them to school, look around your school environment and think about what objects your students might not know the names for. They probably know the words *door* and *window,* but can they tell you that what goes around the door and window is the *frame?* Can they tell you that the things that allow the door to open and close are the *hinges* and that the thing you grab to open and close the door is the *knob?* They can turn the water in the sink off and on, but do they know that they use *faucets* to do that? Is your playground covered with *asphalt? Gravel? Grass? Sand?* What kind of *equipment* do you have in your *gymnasium,* and what can you do with it?

Seize Unexpected Events as Opportunities for Vocabulary Development

Clever teachers seize every opportunity to turn classroom occurrences into opportunities for vocabulary development. The misfortune suffered by a child who breaks his leg and arrives at school with his leg in a cast and walking on crutches can be "mined" for vocabulary development opportunities. The clever teacher will encourage the children to ask questions and share their own experiences with broken bones. He or she might take a photo of the child with the broken leg and write a few sentences summarizing that experience:

> Michael slipped on the ice and broke his leg. He went to the hospital in the ambulance. The doctor set the bone and put a cast on his leg. He has to walk with crutches and can't move very quickly.

Look for Real-Thing Connections for New Vocabulary Words

When you are reading to or with children and new words occur, think first of how you might connect those new words with things in their environment. When reading about a mountain ledge, you might point out the window ledge and table ledge as examples of other kinds of ledges right there in your classroom. The word *pierce* can be connected with students' pierced ears. When encountering the word *unexpected,* you can remind your students of something unexpected that happened in the classroom.

Introduce Science and Social Studies Units with Real Things

As you are planning to introduce a new science or social studies topic, begin by collecting objects that are even vaguely related to that topic. Some museums, libraries, and school media centers have crates of objects related to commonly studied topics. In some schools, teachers take responsibility for gathering objects related to a particular topic and then teach those topics at different times so that everyone can use the same objects.

Send Students Looking for Real Things in Their Home Environments

Many of the objects you bring to school or identify in school to build vocabularies can also be found in the home environments of your students. Get in the habit of posing questions that will send students looking for and identifying similar objects in their homes:

> "Do you have tools (kitchen implements, balls, vases, picture frames, etc.) in your house? What do they look like? What do you use them for?"

> "How many faucets (hinges, knobs, ledges, door frames, etc.) do you have in your house? Count them and bring in the number tomorrow. We will add up all the numbers at the beginning of math."

"Is there gravel (asphalt, grass, sand, etc.) anywhere in your neighborhood?"

"Is there a playground or park near your house? What kind of equipment does it have?"

In addition to having children identify common objects in their home environments, encourage them to talk with family members about those objects. Children can tell them that they have the same things at school, too, and explain what they are for. Children can tell their families about how they are using batteries—like the ones they have at home—to learn about electricity in school.

Teachers are always looking for opportunities to make home-school connections. Having children take new vocabulary words they are learning into their home environments helps make school learning more relevant and extends each child's opportunities for vocabulary development.

Take Advantage of Media and Technology

Many young children have a concept for *mountain* even if they have never seen a real mountain. Most young children can recognize zebras, elephants, and monkeys even though they have never been to a zoo, circus, or other place with these animals. Many children who have never sailed or been in a canoe know what sailboats and canoes are. How did this learning occur? Did someone explain to them what a mountain was? Was the dictionary definition of the word *monkey* read to them? Did some adult attempt to explain or define a *canoe?* In most cases, when children have concepts for objects and realities they have never directly experienced, they have seen these objects or realities portrayed on television, in movies or videos, or in pictures or picture books.

The Internet makes providing visual images and simulated experiences a daily possibility in every classroom. Through the Internet, you can follow the progress of the latest space probe, find images of all the major deserts of the world, and see and hear Winston Churchill as he rallies the people of London during World War II. You and your children can take virtual field trips all over the world and back in time.

The saying "A picture is worth a thousand words" is definitely true when it comes to vocabulary. When you can't provide the real thing in your classroom, looking to the media for visual and auditory images is definitely the next best thing.

Talking Partners

To own a new word, you have to use that word. Incorporate the "Turn and Talk" routine into your vocabulary activities. Many teachers seat their students in talking partners so that they can quickly ask children to turn and talk.

"Tell your partner about something unexpected that happened to you."

"Share with your partner if you know anyone who has broken a bone and had to go to the hospital."

"Tell your partner where you think you might find ... in your house or neighborhood."

"Have you ever seen a ...? Tell your partner where you saw it and what it was like."

Simulate Real Experiences with Dramatization

Using word dramatizations is a powerful way to help students build vivid word meanings. Both skits and pantomimes can be used to help students "get into words." To prepare your students to do vocabulary skits, select six words and write them on index cards. Tell your students that in a few minutes, their group will plan a skit—a quick little play—to demonstrate the word they have been given. Choose a few students to work with you and model for them how to plan a skit. Talk with your group as the rest of the class listens in. Plan a scene in which you can use the word several times. When you have a plan, act out your skit using the target word as many times as possible. Have one member of your group hold up a sign containing the word every time it occurs in the skit.

Imagine, for example, that the word your group is acting out is *curious*. You decide that the skit will involve a dad and his 2-year-old son walking to the post office. The dad and the 2-year-old meet several people on their walk, and each time, the 2-year-old stops, points to the stranger, and asks these questions:

"What's your name?"

"Where are you going?"

"What's that?"

"What are you doing?"

"What's in the bag?"

"Why are you wearing that funny hat?"

The dad smiles each time and explains to the stranger that his son is curious about everything. The strangers answer the boy's questions and then remark, "He's the most curious kid I ever saw" as they walk on.

Perform the skit as the class watches. At the end of the skit, have the people in the skit ask the audience how the skit showed that the little boy was curious. Finally, you should ask if anyone in the audience has a story to share about a curious person.

Next, divide the class into five groups, putting one of the children who helped you in the skit in each of the groups. Give each group a card on which the word they will dramatize is written. Today, you are focusing on adjectives and give the groups the words *nervous, frantic, impatient, jubilant,* and *serene*. Help the groups plan their skits by circulating around and coaching them. Encourage the child in each group who helped in the original skit to take a leadership role and help boost the group's confidence that they can do this.

Each skit is acted out with one person in each group holding up the card each time the word is used. The group then asks the audience what they saw in the skit that made the word "come alive." You should ask if anyone in the class wants to share a personal experience with the target word. After the last skit, place the six word cards with others on a board labeled

GET YOUR ADJECTIVES HERE: COOL DESCRIBING
WORDS TO SPICE UP YOUR TALK AND WRITING

Pantomime is another form of dramatization that is particularly useful when the words you want to teach are emotions or actions. Imagine that you want to introduce the emotional adjectives *confused, disappointed, furious,* and *frightened*. Assign a pair of students to each word. Have the rest of the class watch the pairs pantomiming the words and try to guess which pair is acting out each word. The same kind of pantomime can be done with actions such as *swaggered, crept, sauntered,* and *scurried*. Adverbs are also fun to pantomime. Imagine four pairs of students walking to school: One pair walks *briskly*. One pair walks *cautiously*. One pair walks *proudly*. One pair walks *forlornly*.

For any kind of dramatization, it is important to conclude the activity by asking all the students to relate the word that was acted out to their own experience:

"When have you been *confused? Disappointed? Furious? Frantic?*"

"When have you *swaggered? Crept? Sauntered? Scurried?*"

"When would you walk *briskly? Cautiously? Proudly? Forlornly?*"

Acting out words in skits and pantomimes provides students with real experience with many words. They will remember these words because of this real experience and because they enjoyed acting and watching their friends act. Keep a list of words your class encounters that could be acted out in skits or pantomimes, and schedule 20 minutes for vocabulary drama each week. You will be amazed at how students' vocabularies and enthusiasm for words will grow.

Maximize Word Learning from Reading

Reading is one of the major opportunities for vocabulary learning. Many words occur much more frequently in written text than in spoken language. As children listen to text being read aloud by the teacher and read independently, they will have lots of opportunities to add words to their meaning vocabularies. Unfortunately, many children do not pay a lot of attention to the new words they meet while reading, and thus, they miss many opportunities to increase the sizes of their vocabularies. This section describes lesson frameworks you can use to teach your students how to figure out meanings for new words while reading.

Three Read-Aloud Words

Teacher read-aloud is one of the major opportunities for children to learn new word meanings. Several studies have demonstrated the power of focused read-alouds on fostering vocabulary growth (Beck, McKeown, & Kucan, 2002; Juel et al., 2003). In each of these studies, the teachers went beyond just reading books aloud to children. Before they read a book aloud, they selected a few words that they felt many children would not know the meanings of. After the book had been read aloud and discussed, the teachers returned to those selected words and focused student attention on them. To maximize

The Power of Wide Reading

Imagine that across the school day and at home, your students read for approximately 60 minutes, five days a week. At the end of a year they will have read more than 2,000,000 words. Mason, Stahl, Au, and Herman (2003) estimate that students who read 2,000,000 words each year will add more than 2,000 new word meanings to their meaning vocabulary each year!

vocabulary growth from reading, choose one short piece each week and use that book, magazine, or newspaper article to teach your students how to learn new words from their reading. This lesson framework is called "Three Read-Aloud Words" and here is how each lesson is carried out:

1. Identify three "Goldilocks" words from a piece you are going to read aloud.

   Any good book or article is going to have many words on which you could focus your attention. Narrowing the number of words you are going to teach to a reasonable number increases the chances that all your children will learn them. Beck, McKeown, and Kucan (2002) divided vocabulary into three tiers. The first tier includes words generally known by almost all children. *Boy, girl, jump, sad, laugh,* and *late* are examples of Tier 1 words. Many of your students will not know Tier 2 words but will need to know them. *Despair, exhausted, catastrophe,* and *proceeded* are Tier 2 words. Tier 3 words include less common, subject area specific, and technical words. *Languid, ratio, constitution,* and *igneous* are examples of Tier 3 words. Beck and other experts suggest that we focus our time and energy in vocabulary development in teaching Tier 2 words. Some people refer to the Tier 2 words as "Goldilocks" words because they are not too well known, not too obscure, but hopefully "just right" for your students.

   As you begin to select your three Goldilocks words from the piece you are going to read aloud to your students, you will probably find a lot more than three possibilities. Narrow it down to three by considering the usefulness and appeal of the words to your children and how well the words are defined by the context and pictures. You might also choose a word because it has a word part (prefix, suffix, or root) you want your students to notice and analyze.

   Once you have chosen the three words, write them on index cards. For this example lesson, we are going to imagine that you have chosen an article on sports from a student news magazine. The three Goldilocks words you chose to focus on are *overpowered, resurgent,* and *squandered.*

2. Read the text the first time, making no reference to the three chosen words.

   The first time you read anything aloud should always be for enjoyment and information. Read the piece aloud as you normally would, stopping from time to time to ask questions that will engage your students in the text but without doing anything particular about your chosen words.

3. Show the three words to your students.

   After reading and talking about the piece, show your students the words on index cards, one at a time. Have your students pronounce the words but do *not* let anyone share any meanings. This may feel quite counterintuitive. As teachers, we are used to giving students meanings for words or asking them for meanings they know. However, when doing Three Read-Aloud Words, you want your students to discover that they can learn new words from their reading by thinking about the context along with any pictures or known word parts. If you let anyone tell what a word means, you have defeated your purpose of demonstrating how the students can acquire new meanings from their reading. If one of your students responds to a word by saying, "I know what *overpowered* means," your response should be, "I am so glad you think you know but wait to tell us until we get to *overpowered* in the article!"

4. Reread the text and have the children stop you when you read each of the words.

Put the index cards with your three chosen words where your students can clearly see them. Now read the text to them again. On this second reading, do not stop to discuss pictures or engage the children with questions. When you come to one of the chosen words, some of your children are sure to notice and signal you. Tell students to stop you by shouting "STOP" and the word (for example, "Stop! *Overpowered!*"). No hand raising allowed in this activity!

When they signal you, stop reading and use the context, pictures, and word parts to explain each word. If words are repeated more than once, let the children stop you each time and see if any new information is added to their understanding of the word.

The word **resurgent** occurs in a sentence that explains that two batters scored four times and that the resurgent Yankees had won 9 of their last 11 games. This context, along with the meanings of word parts the children know—**re** and **surge**— lets you conclude that the word **resurgent** means "coming back."

The meaning of **overpowered** can also be figured out by using the context and the meanings of word parts—**over** and **power**—to determine that **overpowered** means won the game by being much stronger.

Squandered has no word parts to help, but the context tells you that the losing team was in the lead but gave it up by walking two batters and then letting the next players get hits. **Squandered** means wasted, lost, or gave up.

5. Help your students connect their own experience to the three words.

Once you have finished reading, stopping each time one of the chosen words occurs, focus again on each word and ask a question that helps children connect their own experience to the text. For these words, you might ask students the following:

> "Can you think of a time when a team you were on or a favorite team was **resurgent**?"
>
> "Have you or a favorite player ever **overpowered** someone or been **overpowered** by someone?"
>
> "What could you **squander** in addition to the lead in a game?"

Let students turn and talk with each other for a minute after you ask each question. Then let them share their connections with these three words.

6. Display the title and the three word cards somewhere in the room.

After you have introduced these three words and modeled for the children how context, pictures, and word parts are helpful in figuring out meanings for new words; assisted the children in connecting these words to their own experiences; and given them an opportunity to use these words to retell the text, display these words some-place in the room. You may want to copy the article or cover of the book and display the three index cards next to it. Tell your students that you and they are going to be on the lookout for these words in books and conversations and to try to use the words at school and at home. Every time someone hears, reads, or uses one of these words, he or she can put a tally mark next to the word. The word with the most tally marks at the end of one week is the winning word! (Kids love competitions, especially if they cannot possibly be the loser!) Once you do this, contrive to use these words in your conversations with the children over the next several days. Congratulate them when they notice the word and allow them to put a tally mark next to the word. Soon, you

Read-Aloud Words Posters

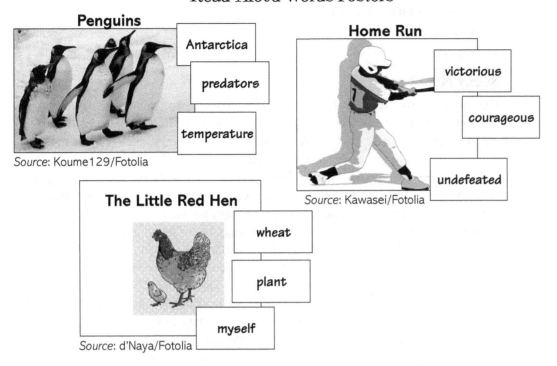

Penguins
- Antarctica
- predators
- temperature

Source: Koume129/Fotolia

Home Run
- victorious
- courageous
- undefeated

Source: Kawasei/Fotolia

The Little Red Hen
- wheat
- plant
- myself

Source: d'Naya/Fotolia

will notice that the students are trying to sneak these words into their talk—exactly what you are aiming for!

Word Detectives

Word Detectives is a lesson framework you can use to teach your students how to figure out meanings for words while reading. Here are the steps in a Word Detectives lesson:

1. From a text your students are going to read, choose 6 to 10 words your students are unlikely to have meanings for and for which meaning can be figured out using context, pictures, and morphology. Include a word or two that students are familiar with but that has a different meaning in this text.

2. Seat your students in trios—with an advanced, an average, and a struggling reader in each trio.

3. Show students the words and have them pronounce each one but do not let anyone suggest any meanings.

4. Have each person in the trio write two or three of the words on tiny sticky notes.

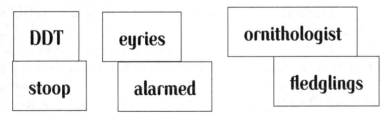

DDT eyries ornithologist

stoop alarmed fledglings

5. Give each trio one copy of the text and have the trio read the text together.

6. Their first job as detectives is to find each word and place their sticky note close to the word.

7. Each detective trio should then use the clues—context, pictures, or familiar word parts—to sleuth out the meaning of the mystery words.

8. Come together as a class and let detectives tell how they used the clues to solve the mystery.

Sticky Note Day

If you are using the Three Read-Aloud Words and Word Detectives lesson frameworks, you are teaching your students how to use pictures, context, and familiar word parts to clarify meanings for new words. Just because they know how to use these clues to figure out what unfamiliar words mean does not ensure they will use these strategies when they are reading independently. In fact, many struggling readers employ the "skip it" strategy when they come to a word they don't instantly recognize or have a meaning for. To get your students to use what they know about learning word meanings from their reading, designate one day each week as a "Sticky Note Day." At the beginning of their independent reading time, give each student one sticky note. Tell everyone to be on the lookout for one word that is new to them and that they can figure out the meaning of based on the pictures, context, and/or word parts. Explain to your students how you choose your Three Read-Aloud Words by looking for useful words that many of them don't know that they probably don't know the meaning of but that they can figure out. Ask your students to be on the lookout during their reading for a perfect word to teach to the class. They should write that word on a sticky note and place the sticky note on the sentence in which they first see the word.

When the time for independent reading is over, gather your students together and let four or five volunteers tell their word and read the context and/or share the picture or word parts that helped them with the meaning of that word. Do not let everyone share their words, because this would take more time than you have, and you want your students to be excited about finding new words—not bored with having to listen to 25 explanations! Assure your students that you will give them another sticky note next Thursday and that you will let other children share their findings with the class.

If you designate one day each week as "Sticky Note Day," your students will get in the habit of looking for interesting new words and using the pictures, context, and word parts to figure out the word. Soon, they will be doing this in all their reading—even when they don't have a blank sticky note staring at them—and they will be on their way to adding exponentially to their vocabularies every time they read!

Ten Important Words

Another clever vocabulary strategy created by Ruth and Hallie Yopp (2007) is called Ten Important Words. This lesson format is designed to help students learn to determine which words in a text are the most important words. In informational text, when your students have chosen the most important words, they have simultaneously identified the major concepts or main ideas.

Just as in Word Detectives, begin the lesson by arranging your students into groups of three, making sure to include a range of abilities in each trio and providing supportive peers for your English language learners or other students who need good peer role models. Give each group 10 small sticky notes and tell them that their job is to read the text together and place the sticky notes on what they think are the most important words. The piece they are reading should be relatively short, such as three or four pages of a textbook chapter or a two-page spread in a *Weekly Reader, Scholastic News,* or *Time for Kids* magazine. In this example, they are reading an informational piece on endangered sea turtles.

As they read, if the children decide other words are more important than the ones they have already designated with sticky notes, they may move the notes around. When the reading time is almost up, stop them and tell them that they must now make their final decisions and write these 10 words—one to a sticky note.

When the trios have made their choices, gather the students together and create a class tally. Ask each trio to tell you one of their 10 words and then have the other trios show you how many of them also included this word. Write that word and the number of trios that chose it on your list and then ask a second trio for one of their words and get a count of the number of trios that included that word. Continue going around to the different trios until all the words included by any trio are tallied. Look at the tally completed in one classroom after the class had read a selection on *Sea Turtles* (page 192). This class of 25 students was divided into seven trios and one quartet, so the largest number of votes a word could get was eight. The top 10 words from the article on endangered sea turtles are *sea turtles, endangered, ocean, shells, migrate, swim, nests, reptiles, flippers,* and *eggs*.

Once the top 10 list is compiled, you can engage the students in a variety of tasks that require them to talk about, write about, draw, or act out these words. Give two of the 10 important words to each trio and have them do two things that demonstrate each word. You might want to post a list of possibilities including:

- List synonyms and antonyms.
- Create three good sentences that use the word in different ways.
- Draw two pictures that illustrate the word.
- Act out the word.
- Return to the text and find sentences and pictures in the selection that further explain the word and put sticky notes on them.

sea turtles	‖‖‖ ‖‖	8
ocean	‖‖‖ ‖	7
migrate	‖‖‖ ‖	6
endangered	‖‖‖ ‖‖	8
shells	‖‖‖ ‖	7
swim	‖‖‖ ‖	6
plankton	‖‖‖‖	4
plastron	‖‖‖	3
carapace	‖‖‖	3
nests	‖‖‖ ‖	6
reptiles	‖‖‖ ‖	6
flippers	‖‖‖‖	5
eggs	‖‖‖‖	5
Hawksbill	‖	2
Loggerhead	‖	2
Leatherback	‖	2

Completing these two tasks for the two words will cause your students to talk with one another and further develop their meanings for the words. After 10 to 15 minutes, gather your students together and let them share their products.

Ten Important Words can be used with any informational text. Depending on the length of the text and the age of your students, you may want to adjust the number up or down a few words. In addition to providing your children multiple opportunities to actively engage these words, this strategy, if used regularly, will help your students with the important but difficult task of identifying key vocabulary in their own reading.

Teach Independent Word Learning Strategies

Morphemes

You learned in the previous chapter that *morphemes* are prefixes, roots, and suffixes, which are meaningful parts of words. Look again at the Nifty-Thrifty-Fifty list on pages 79 and 80. This list has an example word for each of the common prefixes and suffixes. You may want to teach students these words or help them collect other words from their reading that have these helpful parts.

Four prefixes—*un, re, in,* and *dis*—are the most common, and knowing them will help students figure out the meaning of over 1,500 words. Graves (2004) suggests teaching these four prefixes to all elementary students. You may want to focus on each of these for a few weeks. Begin a chart with some *un* words your students are familiar with, such as *unhappy, unlucky,* and *unlocked.* Help students notice the prefix *un* and that it changes the meaning of the root word to the opposite meaning. Encourage your students to be on the lookout for words in their reading in which *un* changes a word to the opposite meaning, and add these to the chart.

After a few weeks, make a chart for *re,* with the meaning of "back" or "again," and add such common words as *return, reboot,* and *replay.* The prefix *in,* which means "the opposite," can be spelled *in, im, il,* and *ir,* so you may want to start the *in* chart with the key words *insane, impossible, illegal,* and *irregular.* Your *dis* chart might begin with common words such as *dishonest* and *disagree.*

One problem with teaching students to look for prefixes and use them as clues to meaning is that many words start with *un*—such as *uncle, understand,* and *uniform*—but *un* is not the prefix and does not have the meaning of opposite. Graves (2004) provides the practical solution that for these simple prefixes, elementary children can be taught that a letter combination is not a prefix if removing it leaves a nonsense word. Thus, *un* is not the prefix in *uncle, understand,* and *uniform* because *cle, derstand,* and *iform* are not words.

When teaching morphemes to help students build meanings for words, it is probably best to begin with these four common prefixes because students will encounter many words in which these prefixes have these predictable meanings. Once students are comfortable with these prefixes, you may want to add some of the less common and less transparent ones from the Nifty-Thrifty-Fifty list.

Elementary students can also learn to notice base or root words and think about how words with the same roots are related. Again, you should start with the most common and predictable root or base words. The word *play* occurs in such related words as *replay, playground,* and *playoffs. Work* is part of many words, including *workers, workout,* and *workstation. Place* is another common base word, and students often know the meaning of *placemats, replace,* and *workplace.* Beginning a chart with common words and asking students to be on the lookout for other words containing those words will help them become attuned to root and base words in their reading.

Vocabulary experts disagree about teaching students Latin and Greek roots. Although it is true that these roots do contain clues to meaning, the meaning relationships are often hard to figure out, and students might get discouraged if they cannot "ferret out" the meaning of a word based on the meaning of the root. Perhaps the most sensible way for elementary teachers to approach Greek and Latin roots is to be aware of them and to point out relationships when they think these will be understandable to most of their children. When encountering the word *spectacle,* for example, you might remark that a *spectacle* is something you see that is quite striking or unusual. Furthermore, you might point out that the root *spect* means "to watch" and invite the students to think about how words they know, such as *inspection* and *spectators,* are related to this meaning. The word *constructive* might be explained as "helpful" or "building up," as opposed to *destructive,* which is "unhelpful" or "tearing down." Students might be told that the root *struct* means "build" and asked to think about how other words they know, such as *structure* and *reconstruction,* are related to this meaning.

Context

If you are doing Three Read-Aloud Words and Word Detectives lessons regularly and having students share how they figured out the meanings of sticky-note words in their own reading one day each week, then you are teaching them to use context, including pictures, to figure out the meanings of unfamiliar words. This regular attention to how context and pictures make word meanings clear is probably the best instruction you can do so that your students get in the habit of and know how to use pictures and context.

English Language Learners

Some words are similar in English and Spanish. Words derived from the same base or root word are called *cognates.* Here are some Spanish–English *cognates:*

piloto	pilot
exactamente	exactly
clima	climate
curioso	curious
familia	family
decidir	decide
hospital	hospital

Instruction in Spanish–English cognates should follow the suggestions given for teaching morphemes described in this chapter and the preceding chapter. Help your students become sensitive to the meaningful parts of words and get in the habit of deciding if two similar-looking words share meaning as well.

One caution you may need to point out to students is that context does not always directly reveal the meaning of an unfamiliar word and can sometimes be misleading. Imagine that the only reference in the text to the word *incredulously* is in this sentence:

> Her dad listened incredulously.

This context does not provide much of a clue to the meaning of this new word. On the other hand, the text might continue with a much richer context:

> Her dad listened incredulously. "I find what you are telling me really hard to believe," he admitted when she had finished explaining how the accident had happened.

How much context helps with meaning varies greatly. If a word is important and the context is slim, students need to use the dictionary to figure out the meaning that might make sense in the context of what they are reading.

Context can sometimes be misleading in trying to determine a word's meaning. One student had put a sticky note on the word *grimaced* and explained that the word meant "yelled." The sentence in which the student had read the word was:

> The waiter in the crowded restaurant grimaced as the tray slid to the floor.

The teacher explained to the student that "yelled" would make sense here but that the waiter could have done many things and there really wasn't enough context to decide exactly what the waiter did. The child quickly looked up the word *grimaced* in the dictionary and shared its meaning with the class. The teacher had the whole class twist their faces into the grimaces they might make if they had just dropped a whole tray of food in a crowded restaurant.

As children are sharing their sticky-note words, you will have many opportunities to show them both how the context can be extremely helpful and how it can lead them astray. You can also model how a dictionary is best used—to clarify meaning and let you know if the meaning you inferred from the context is indeed the right one.

Common Core Connections: Meaning Vocabulary

Strategies for acquiring new vocabulary and using vocabulary in all subject areas pervade these standards. Reading: Standard 4 and Language Standards 4, 5, and 6 are all about students learning how to figure out word meanings, including the academic vocabulary of science and social studies. The anchor standard for all grade levels for Language Standard 4 requires students to determine or clarify the meanings of unknown and multiple-meaning words by using context clues and meaningful word parts, and consulting dictionaries as needed.

Dictionaries

This chapter began with a discussion of unproductive dictionary use—looking up words and copying and memorizing definitions. There are, however, a variety of ways to promote active use of the dictionary to help students broaden their concepts and also teach them what a valuable resource the dictionary is. Students should learn to turn to the dictionary to find out about an unfamiliar word on a scavenger hunt list. The teacher should regularly ask one child to consult the dictionary when a new word occurs and the meaning of that word is unclear. A teacher who regularly says, "Let's see what the dictionary can tell us about this word" and sends one child to look it up is modeling the way adults who use the dictionary actually use it. (Did you ever see an adult look up a word to copy and memorize the definition? Maybe the reason so few adults use the dictionary is because that is the only way they have ever seen anyone use it!) If you have a dictionary on your classroom computers, model how useful this is by saying to a child, "See what our computer dictionary has to say about this word."

In many classrooms, helpers are appointed to jobs each week. Someone greets visitors, someone collects papers, someone waters the plants, and so on. Why not appoint a weekly "Dictionary Disciple"? This person gets possession of the dictionary and is always ready to be dispatched to the farthest corners of the wide world of words to seek and share facts about them.

Promote Word Wonder

Enthusiasm is contagious! Teachers who are enthusiastic about words project that enthusiasm by conveying their eagerness to learn unfamiliar words and by sharing fascinating words they encounter outside the classroom. Young children are usually enthusiastic about new words, repeating them over and over, enjoying the sound of language, and marveling at the meanings being expressed. Encourage the continuation of this natural enthusiasm. Open your class to wondering about words, to asking spontaneous questions about unfamiliar words, and to making judgments about the sounds and values of words.

We hope this chapter has increased your "word wonder" and that you see that the activities described are all intended to transmit the "Words are wonderful" message. In addition to the ideas already described, here are a few more "tricks of the trade" for turning all your students into "word wizards."

Display Words in Various Ways

Displaying words enhances learning by calling attention to particular terms and signaling the importance of learning them. We have already suggested some ways of displaying words in your classroom. The Three Read-Aloud Words can be displayed along with the cover of the book, and the children can add tally marks as they hear, read, or sneak these words into conversations at school and at home. Words that are dramatized can be added to lists of other words dramatized in the past. Class books can be made both for general words and for specific science and social studies words. Vocabulary boards are effective tools for calling attention to words and their meanings. Words can be displayed on a word wall or bulletin board so that all students can see them. Once the words are up, students can visit and revisit them to learn their meanings.

Many teachers like students to keep vocabulary notebooks. If you do this, make sure your students see themselves as word collectors rather than definition copiers. In fact, most teachers do not allow students to copy any definitions into their notebooks. Rather, the students include the sentences in which they found the words and note their personal connections with the words. Students often enjoy illustrating the words in their collections with pictures and diagrams. Some older word sleuths like to include information about the words' origins.

Read Books about Words to Your Students

Some books for children call special attention to words by presenting them in humorous or unusual ways. Countless children have delighted in Amelia Bedelia's literal attempts to dress a chicken and draw the drapes. Sharing books with children that celebrate and play with words is just one more way to show your students you are a serious word lover.

Designate a Weekly "Words Are Wonderful Day"

Choose a day of the week and designate it as "Words Are Wonderful Day." Do a variety of things to celebrate words that day. Read a wonderful word play book during your teacher read-aloud. Share a new word that you have come across in the last week. Find a crossword puzzle your children would enjoy, and let them work in teams to complete it.

Culminate this day by picking "One Wonderful Word." Let students nominate various words that have been highlighted throughout the past week, and let everyone vote for the most wonderful word. Display this word on some kind of trophy chart along with all the other wonderful words chosen in previous weeks.

Summary

As we try to close the achievement gap and make high levels of literacy possible for all children, we must pay renewed attention to the issue of meaning vocabulary. In 1977, Becker identified the lack of vocabulary as a crucial factor underlying the failure of many economically disadvantaged students. In 1995, Hart and Risley described a relationship between growing up in poverty and having a restricted vocabulary. In 2001, Biemiller and Slonim cited evidence that the lack of vocabulary is a key component underlying school failure for disadvantaged students. More and more of the children in U.S. schools are English language learners. The limited English vocabulary of many of these children is one of the major factors impeding their literacy development.

Researchers now agree that most meaning vocabulary is learned indirectly, probably through teacher read-aloud and independent reading. Research supports both the direct teaching of some words and the teaching of vocabulary learning strategies (Baumann, Kame'enui, & Ash, 2003; Blachowicz & Fisher, 2015; Graves & Watts-Taffe, 2002; NRP, 2000). The activities that have been described in this chapter are designed to teach children some vocabulary directly and to teach children how context, pictures, and morphemes give them clues to words and how to use dictionaries to clarify the meanings of words. Teaching them these strategies for independent word learning will maximize their learning of words from teacher read-aloud and their own independent reading.

How Well Does Your Classroom Help All Children Build Rich Meanings for New Words?

1. Do I provide many opportunities for my students to build word meanings by associating words with real objects and experiences?

2. Do I use lots of visuals—including the world available on the Internet—to help students build meanings for words they cannot have real experiences with?

3. Do I include some acting and pantomiming activities to simulate real experiences and build vocabulary?

4. Do I help students build meaning vocabulary when we encounter new words or old words with different meanings during my teacher read-aloud?

5. Do I help students become independent word learners by teaching them how to use context, picture, and morphemic clues to figure out the meanings of new words they encounter in their reading?

6. Do I create a classroom climate of "word wonder" so that my students are curious and enthusiastic when encountering new words?

7

Comprehension

A MYTH ABOUT CHILDREN who have difficulty with reading comprehension is that they "just can't think!" In reality, everybody thinks all the time, and some struggling readers who must take care of themselves (and often younger brothers and sisters) are especially good thinkers and problem solvers. If children can "predict" that the ball game will be canceled when they see the sky darkening up and can "conclude" that the coach is mad about something when he walks in with a scowl on his face, then they can and do engage in higher-level thinking processes. The real problem is not that they cannot think but that they do not think while they read. Why don't they think while they read?

Some children do not think while they read because they do not really know that they should! Imagine an extreme case of a child who had never been read to and had never heard people talking about what they read. Imagine that this child goes to a school in which beginning reading is taught in a "learn the letters and sounds" and "read the words aloud perfectly" way. This child would learn to read words just as you would read this nonsensical sentence:

He bocked the piffle with a gid daft.

You can read all the "words" correctly, and you can even read with expression, but you get no meaning. In your case, of course, you get no meaning because there is no meaning there to get.

For children who have limited literacy experience and who are taught to read in a rigid, phonics-first method, with texts written to include only decodable words (*Tad has a tan hat*), the real danger is that they will not learn that thinking is the goal. The goal, to them, is sounding out all the words, which is what they try to do. Ask them what reading is, and they are apt to look at you as if you are a complete fool and tell you that reading is saying all the words right! The ability to decode is critical, but when we overemphasize accurate word pronunciation and only provide beginning reading materials in which all the words are "decodable," we can create readers who not only misread the purpose of reading but also do not comprehend what they are reading.

Some struggling readers are unaware that they should be thinking while they are reading, and many have inadequate background knowledge for understanding what they are reading. Read the next two sentences and think about the implications for your teaching:

Current models do not allow expectancy-based processing to influence feature extraction from words. Indeed, most current models largely restrict expectancy-based processing and hypothesis-testing mechanisms to the postlexical level. (Stanovich, 1991, p. 419)

You are probably wondering why we would waste book space (and your time) on these two nonsensical sentences. In reality, these sentences are not nonsensical. They actually have meaning, and if you are a research psychologist, you can think and talk intelligently about them! For most of us, however, we can say these words, but we cannot really read them because we are unable to think as we say them. Background knowledge, which includes topically related vocabulary, is one of the major determinants of reading comprehension.

In addition to specific knowledge about the topic, knowledge about the type of text about to be read is called up as well. When you begin to read a story or a novel, a whole set of expectations based on other stories that have been heard or read are called up. You do not know who the characters are but you do expect to find characters. You also know that the story takes place in a particular time and place (setting) and that goals will be achieved or problems will be resolved. In short, you have a story structure in your head that allows you to fit what is read into an overall organization.

Imagine that you are going to read a *Consumer Guide* article on the newest car models. Again, you do not know what specific information you will learn, but you do have expectations about the type of information and how it will be related. You expect to find charts comparing the cars on different features and to find judgments about which cars appear to be the best buys.

Imagine that you are about to read a travel magazine article about North Carolina. You have never been there and do not know anyone who has, so you do not know too many specifics. However, you do have expectations about what you will learn and about how that information will be organized. You expect to learn some facts about the history of North Carolina, along with some descriptions of historical regions and locations in the state. You also expect to find information about places tourists like to visit, such as the coast and the mountains. You would not be surprised to find a summary of the cultural and sporting events that are unique to North Carolina. Information about the climate and the best times to visit different parts of the state, as well as some information on how to get there and places to stay, would also be expected. As you begin to read, you may create a mental outline, or web, that helps you understand and organize topic and subtopic information.

The different ways in which various reading materials are organized are referred to as *text structures* and *genres*. To comprehend what we are reading, we must be familiar with the way in which the information is organized. The fact that most children can understand and remember stories much better than informational text is probably because they have listened to and have read many more stories and thus know what to expect and how to organize the story information. To create readers who think about what they read, we must help them become familiar with a variety of ways that authors organize ideas in their writing.

Even with a clear understanding that reading is primarily thinking, sufficient background knowledge, and a familiarity with the kind of text structure being read, you cannot think about what you read unless you can identify a majority of the words. Try to make sense of this next sentence, in which all words of three or more syllables have been replaced by blanks:

The _____ _____ fresh ideas for action and _____ new

_____ that will help the _____ _____ and the _____

meet the challenge of _____ adult and _____ _____

worldwide.

Now read the same sentence but put the words *conference, provided, generated, partnerships, literacy, community, association, promoting, adolescent,* and *literacy* in the blanks. To learn to think while you read, you must

- Be able to quickly identify almost all the words.
- Have sufficient background knowledge that you can connect to the new information.
- Be familiar with the type of text and be able to see how the author has organized the ideas.
- Have a mindset that reading is thinking and know how to apply your thinking in comprehension strategies.

Comprehension Strategies

The different kinds of thinking that we do as we read are referred to as *comprehension strategies*. As you read, your brain uses these thinking strategies:

- Calling up and connecting relevant prior knowledge
- Predicting, questioning, and wondering about what will be learned and what will happen

- Visualizing or imagining what the experience would look, feel, sound, taste, and smell like
- Monitoring comprehension and using fix-up strategies such as rereading, pictures, and asking for help when you cannot make sense of what you read
- Determining the most important ideas and events and summarizing what you have read
- Drawing conclusions and making inferences based on what was read
- Evaluating and making judgments about what you think: Did you like it? Did you agree? Was it funny? Could it really happen?

In teaching all these strategies, your big goal is for your students to use them not just during the lessons, but to become automatic at thinking strategically whenever and wherever they are reading. To do this, you will want to provide lots of modeling in initial lessons and then gradually turn over the responsibility for thinking to your students. This gradual release of responsibility model of instruction suggests that for any learning task, responsibility should shift slowly and purposefully from teacher-as-model, to joint responsibility, to independent practice and application by the learner (Pearson & Gallagher, 1983). The teacher moves from assuming all the responsibility to having the students assume all the responsibility. Depending on the complexity of the task, this gradual release may occur over a day, a week, a month, or even a year. It may help you to conceptualize this by thinking about this sequence.

1. I do and you watch. (Teacher models.)
2. I do and you help. (Teacher models and invites suggestions from students.)
3. You do it together and I help. (Students apply strategy in small groups with teacher support as needed.)
4. You do and I watch. (Students apply strategy independently; teacher observes and assesses.)

Think-Alouds to Teach Comprehension Strategies

Think-alouds are a way of modeling or "making public" the thinking that goes on inside your head as you read. To explain *Think-alouds* to your students, tell them that two voices are really speaking as you read. The voice you can usually hear is your voice reading the words but inside your brain is another voice telling you what it thinks about what you are reading. In *Think-alouds* you can demonstrate for your students how we think as we read.

Across your lessons, try to include all the thinking strategies. Show your students you are making connections by starting sentences like these:

> "This reminds me of ..."
> "I remember something like this happened to me when ..."
> "I read another book where the character ..."
> "This is like in our school when ..."
> "Our country doesn't have that holiday, but we have ..."

Demonstrate how your brain predicts, questions, and wonders:

> "I wonder if …"
> "I think I know what is coming next …"
> "He will be in trouble if …"
> "I think we will learn how …"

Stop periodically and summarize the most important ideas or events:

> "So far in our story …"
> "So far I have learned that …"

Share the conclusions and inferences you are making based on the facts you have read:

> "It didn't say why she did that, but I bet …"
> "I know he must be feeling …"

Demonstrate how you monitor meanings and use fix-up strategies:

> "I wonder what it means when it says …"
> "I don't understand …"
> "It didn't make sense when …"
> "I'm going to reread that because it didn't make sense that …"

Share the images, pictures, and visualizations your brain creates:

> "Even though it isn't in the picture, I can see the …"
> "Mmm, I can almost taste the …"
> "That sent chills down my spine when it said …"
> "For a minute I thought I could smell …"
> "I could hear the …"
> "I can imagine what it is like to …"
> "I can picture the …"

Share your opinions, judgments, and evaluations:

> "My favorite part in this chapter was …"
> "I really liked how the author …"
> "What I don't like about this part is …"
> "It was really interesting to learn that …"
> "If I were her, I would …"

Teachers use *Think-alouds* in a variety of ways, but the most efficient and effective use of time is probably to read and think-aloud the first quarter or third of a selection your students are about to read. In addition to hearing you think your way through the text, children get introduced to the selection, including characters, setting, type of writing, and important vocabulary. After listening to you think-aloud your way through the first part of the text, children collaborate in small groups, finish reading the selection, and share the thinking voices inside their brains.

The following example of a *Think-aloud* is based on the first part of *Missing: One Stuffed Rabbit* by Maryann Cocca-Leffler (1999). The *Think-aloud* begins with the cover of the book. The teacher reads aloud the title, *Missing: One Stuffed Rabbit,* and looks at the picture, saying something like what follows:

> "This is an intriguing illustration on the cover of the book. A girl is reading from a notebook labeled Coco, and she looks very unhappy. The two children listening look surprised and upset. Because the title of the book is *Missing: One Stuffed Rabbit,* I bet the unhappy and surprised looks have something to do with the lost rabbit. I wonder who lost the rabbit and who the rabbit is and what the notebook has to do with it?"

The teacher turns the page and thinks aloud about the picture on the first two pages:

> "I see a teacher holding a stuffed rabbit and reaching into a fishbowl to pull out a slip of paper. The children in the class are all watching her. They all look happy and excited. In the other picture is the stuffed rabbit and the notebook labeled Coco. I bet Coco is the name of the stuffed rabbit."

The teacher then reads aloud the text on these two pages, which explains that Coco is indeed the stuffed rabbit and that the teacher is pulling the name of one student who will get to take Coco home for the weekend. She pulls out a slip of paper and the lucky winner is Janine!

> "I bet Janine is the girl in the front in the glasses. She is also the unhappy-looking girl on the cover, reading from Coco's notebook."

The teacher turns the page and thinks aloud first about the pictures.

> "There's Janine looking very happy and hugging Coco and his notebook."

The teacher reads the text aloud and we discover that the notebook is Coco's diary. Each student gets to take Coco home overnight and write Coco's thoughts about the adventure in his diary.

> "I used to have a diary when I was younger. I wrote in it every night."

The next two pages have some of the diary entries written by children who have already taken Coco home and helped him write about his adventures. We learn that Coco fell off the monkey bars while playing with Danny, went to Matthew's soccer game and cheered when Matthew got a goal, and went to the skating rink with Christina. The teacher makes these comments:

> "I love how the author showed the diary pages. I can tell different children wrote them because you can see the different handwriting. I can't wait to see what Janine does with Coco and what she writes in the diary."

The pictures and text on the next two pages show Janine and Coco being picked up by Janine's mom and heading home. They stop to visit with Janine's Nana. On this page, the teacher models self-monitoring:

> "It says Nana cut some carrots for Coco. Nana is a funny name. I wonder who she is?"

The following pages show Janine and Coco having a good time together. Janine reads Coco a bedtime story and gives him a ride on the back of her bike. After reading these four pages, the teacher comments:

> "They seem to be having such a good time. But I am worried. I remember how unhappy Janine looked on the cover, and the title of the book says a stuffed rabbit is missing. I hope Janine is not going to let Coco get lost!"

The next four pages show the family shopping at the mall and, sure enough, as they are having lunch, Janine realizes that she cannot find Coco! She thought she put him in one of the bags, but he is not there. Coco is missing!

> "I can just imagine how Janine must be feeling. She looks like she is going to cry, and I feel like crying too! How could she have lost him? Will she find him? What will the other kids—and the teacher!—say if she doesn't find him?"

At this point in the book, the teacher stops reading and thinking aloud and turns to the children, asking them what they think will happen. They share some ideas and the looks on their faces show how concerned they are. The teacher quickly reviews the pages read and reminds the children that she shared her thinking with them about the pictures and the words. Next, the teacher puts the students in trios and tells them that it is now their turn to read and share their thinking. She chooses one group to model for the others what they will do, and, with the teacher's help, this group shares their thinking about the pictures and words on the next two-page spread. The teacher tells them that when they read, little voices inside their heads tell them what their brains are thinking. "When we do *Think-alouds*," says the teacher, "we let that little voice talk out loud so that we can hear what all our different brains are thinking."

The trios eagerly begin reading. The teacher circulates to the various groups and encourages them to verbalize their thinking. She also writes down some of the most interesting thoughts to share with the whole group when they reconvene after reading to react to the story and "debrief" their thinking.

English Language Learners

Modeling and having students engage in *Think-alouds* are important for all your students. Think about how much more important they are for your students who are learning English as they learn to comprehend. When you are modeling and inviting children to join in the modeling, your English language learners can watch, listen, and learn without being required to produce any language. Of course they do need to learn how to produce language but much of this production (talk) is done within the "safe" context of a small group, rather than in front of the whole class.

Many teachers, when they first hear about *Think-alouds*, are hesitant to do them because they do not know exactly what they are supposed to think! We hope that our example shows you that your brain is thinking as you read, and if you tune into that thinking and learn how to communicate your thinking to children, *Think-alouds* are not difficult to do. It is important to read the selection and plan what you are going to say as you think aloud. Many teachers find it helpful to attach sticky notes with reminders to the appropriate pages. We try to use as many different ways of expressing our thinking as we can and try to have it match as closely as we can the thinking actually engendered by the text.

Although we normally invite participation, it is important not to let the children "chime in" as you are thinking. If you use the procedure of beginning the selection by sharing your thinking and finishing the selection with the children sharing their thinking, they are usually willing to let you have your turn! Some teachers tell the children that they are to pretend to be invisible while the teacher is reading and thinking. They get to hear the teacher thinking, but they are invisible and should not let the teacher know they are there! You want to signal the children when you are reading and when you are thinking. Many teachers look at the book when they are reading and then look away from the book—perhaps up toward the ceiling—when they are thinking. Other teachers use a different voice to signal their thinking. They read in their "reading voice" and think in their "thinking voice."

Common Core Connections: Think-Alouds

The goal of comprehension instruction is that children learn how to think as they read on their own. *Think-alouds* help children see what good comprehenders do. Many of the Common Core standards can be easily modeled during a *Think-aloud*. When you monitor, you are demonstrating what is required in Reading Foundation Standard 4, which includes using context to confirm or self-correct word recognition and rereading as necessary. When you stop and summarize what has happened so far, you are demonstrating the thinking required by Reading Standard 2, which included summarizing the key ideas and supporting details. When you share conclusions and inferences you are making based on the facts, you are demonstrating the thinking required in Reading Standard 1. When you compare what you are reading to something else you have read, you are doing the compare–contrast thinking required by Reading Standard 9. *Think-alouds* allow you to share your thinking and model all the different strategies your brain uses to make sense of what you are reading. Two wonderful sources just full of examples to teach children to think and share their thinking are *Strategies That Work* (Hillocks & Goudvis, 2000) and *Mosaic of Thought* (Keene & Zimmerman, 1997).

Steps in Planning and Teaching a Think-Aloud Lesson

1. Choose a selection that truly causes you to think.
2. Decide how much of that selection you will read aloud.
3. Look at the pictures and read the selection before you do the *Think-aloud*. Look for places where you actually use different thinking strategies. Think about how you will explain your thinking to your children. Write your thoughts on sticky notes and attach them to the pages.
4. Do the *Think-aloud* as the "invisible" children watch and listen. Comment on pictures first; then read the text, stopping at appropriate places and sharing your thoughts.
5. Put your students in trios to share their thinking as they finish the reading. Circulate and encourage children to share what their "thinking voice is telling them."
6. Gather your students and have everyone look again at the pages they read and share some of their thoughts on each page.

Lesson Frameworks for Comprehending Narrative Text

In the introduction to this chapter, we contrasted story text and informational text and suggested that most children are better at understanding stories because they have had so much experience reading and listening to them. The Common Core recognizes that comprehending narratives—stories, plays, and poetry—is very different from comprehending informational text and lists different standards for these two very different kinds of text. Furthermore, the Core recognizes that our students need more experience and instruction reading informational texts and states that, by fourth grade, at least half of what students read should be informational text. Because of the importance of teaching students how to read informational text, the next chapter will be devoted entirely to lesson frameworks to teach students how to read informational text. The remainder of this chapter will describe lesson frameworks that teach children to comprehend narratives.

Story Maps

Story maps are popular and effective devices to guide students' thinking when they are reading a story. There are many different ways of creating story maps, but all help children follow the story by drawing their attention to the elements that all good stories share. Stories have characters and happen in a particular place and time, which we call the *setting*. In most stories, the characters have some goal they want to achieve or some problem they need to resolve. The events in the story lead to some kind of solution or resolution. Sometimes stories have implicit morals or themes from which we hope children learn. The story map here is based on a model created by Isabel Beck (Macon, Bewell, & Vogt, 1991). Here is the story map frame and an example based on *The Three Little Pigs:*

Story M
Main Characters:
Setting (Time and Place):
Problem or Goals:
Event 1:
Event 2:
Event 3:
Event 4:
Event 5:
Solution:
Story Theme or Moral:

Story Map
Main Characters: Mother Pig, three little pigs, Big Bad Wolf
Setting (Time and Place): Woods, make-believe time and place
Problem or Goals: Pigs wanted to be independent and have their own houses.
Event 1: Mother Pig sends three little pigs out to build their own houses.
Event 2: First little pig gets some straw and builds a straw house. Big Bad Wolf blows the straw house down.
Event 3: Second little pig gets some sticks and builds a stick house. Big Bad Wolf blows the stick house down.
Event 4: Third little pig gets some bricks and builds a brick house. Big Bad Wolf cannot blow the brick house down.
Event 5: Big Bad Wolf runs off into woods (or gets scalded coming down the chimney, depending on how violent the version of the story is).
Solution: Pigs live happily ever after in strong brick house.
Story Theme or Moral: Hard work pays off in the end!

When using story maps to develop a sense of story structure, follow the gradual release of responsibility model. Model how you complete a story map based on a familiar story. As you complete the map, think aloud about your thought processes to make them visible to your students. Let your students share the responsibility by helping you complete a story map based on another familiar story.

Once your students understand the story map elements, have them work in trios to complete story maps. Once the story maps are completed, let students retell the story using the completed map as their guide.

The Beach Ball

You can also use a beach ball to help your students develop their ability to understand and retell stories. Write these questions in black permanent marker on each colored segment of the ball:

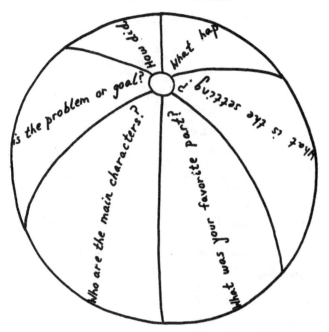

Who are the main characters?

What is the setting?

What happened in the beginning?

What happened in the middle?

How did it end?

What was your favorite part?

After reading a story, form yourself and your students into a large circle. Toss the ball to one of your students. That student catches the ball and can answer any question on the ball. Have each student toss the ball back to you and then you toss the ball to another student. The next student can add to the answer given by the first student or answer another question. The ball continues to be thrown to various students until all the questions have been thoroughly answered. Some questions, such as, "What happened in the story?" and "What was your favorite part?" have many different answers.

The Beach Ball is a favorite lesson framework for children in all classrooms, including children in intermediate grades. As children read a story, they begin to anticipate the answers they will give to the questions on the various colored segments. If you use *The Beach Ball* lesson framework every week or two, your students will develop a clear sense of story structure, and their comprehension (and memory) for important story elements will increase.

English Language Learners

Toss the beach ball to your English language learners first. They may not have enough English to be able to elaborate about the story events but they can surely tell you who some of the main characters are and they love telling you their favorite part.

Common Core Connections: Story Maps and Beach Balls

The *Story Map* and *The Beach Ball* lesson frameworks help your students focus on key details and make inferences when reading stories. In these lessons, students learn to describe characters and settings and retell stories including events that occurred at the beginning, middle, and end of the story. These lesson frameworks help students achieve the goals of Reading Standards 1, 2, and Standard 3 for literature.

Story Map Lesson Steps

1. Decide on a story map skeleton that will work best for your students.
2. Choose a familiar story and model how to complete a story map. Share your thinking as you complete it.
3. Choose another familiar story and let students help you complete a second story map.
4. Assign your students to trios, making sure to have a strong reader and a child who struggles in each trio. Have the trios read the story together and complete the story map.
5. Gather your students and let them retell the story, using the maps as guides.
6. When all students understand how to complete a story map, let students choose a story and compete the story map independently.

Beach Ball Lesson Steps

1. Model answering the beach ball questions using a familiar story.
2. Choose another familiar story and let students help you answer the questions for the colored segments of the ball.
3. Form small groups of students and have them read a story and decide together what answers they will give for the questions on the beach ball.
4. When all students understand the questions and how to answer them, let them choose a story and then use the beach ball segments to guide their retelling of that story to the class or a small group.

Themes, Morals, and Lessons Learned

When reading narratives—stories, plays, and poems-——what we tend to remember are the characters and major events in the plot. Often, we also remember some big ideas we constructed about life. After reading Dickens's *A Tale of Two Cities*, you might conclude that the huge wealth difference between the few rich aristocracy and the many poor workers was not only unfair but immoral. Frost's "The Road Not Taken" may have led you to conclude that conformity is not always the best route. Our "take-away" after reading a narrative is often a lesson that we apply to our own lives. Reading Standard 2 for narrative text focuses on these themes, morals, or lessons learned. Third-graders are expected to recount stories, including fables, folktales, and myths from diverse cultures and determine the central message, lesson, or moral and explain how it is conveyed through key details in the text. Fifth-graders are expected to determine a theme of a story, drama, or poem from details in the text, including how characters in a story or drama respond to challenges or how the speaker in a poem reflects upon a topic, and to summarize the text. These are lofty goals for children who are eight to ten years old! Yet, it is this very kind of critical thinking that adults do when they read.

Before you can think about what you can learn from a story, you have to have a clear understanding of what happened. As we read narratives, we ask ourselves "WHO did WHAT to WHOM, and WHEN and WHERE did these events occur?" In other words, we keep up with characters, settings, and plot. Before doing a *Themes, Morals, and Lessons Learned* lesson, we have students read the story and use the *Story Map* or *Beach Ball* lesson framework to focus students on characters, settings, and events. Next students reread the text to decide what the "take-away" is. What can you learn from this story that you can apply to your own life?

In this sample lesson the class has read a biography of Wilma Rudolph and completed this story map by noting main characters, settings, and major events. They will focus on the question of what "take-away"—theme, moral, or lesson learned—is in the second part of the lesson.

Story Map

Main Characters: Wilma Rudolph
Tennessee State track and field coach

Setting (Time and Place): Tennessee, 1940
Rome, 1960

Major Events:

Wilma gets polio and there is no cure for it.

Wilma does leg exercises and gets a leg brace.

Wilma goes to school but can't play basketball with the other kids.

Wilma keeps doing exercise and when she is 12, she can walk without the brace.

Wilma becomes a basketball star and her team goes to the state finals. They lose the last game.

Wilma goes to college on a track and field scholarship.

Wilma goes to the Olympics and wins three gold medals.

Theme, Moral, Lesson Learned:

In the second part of the lesson, the teacher shifts student attention from what happened in Wilma's life to what we can learn from Wilma's life. She focuses her students' attention on the character traits of determination and perseverance. She chooses "The Little Engine that Could," a story with which her children are all familiar with and which demonstrates these character traits. After leading the children to retell *The Little Engine That Could*, she writes the words *determination* and *perseverance* on index cards, has everyone pronounce these two big words, and says:

> "You show determination and perseverance when you continue to work at something even when it is hard. It was hard for the little blue engine to pull the toy train over the mountain, but he was determined to do it and eventually he succeeded. Can you think of anything that was hard for you but you kept working at it until you succeeded?"

The students eagerly share personal memories of learning to ride without training wheels, earning the different color belts in karate, learning to swim, and earning badges in various scout groups. As each child shares the experiences, the teacher points to the words *determination* and *perseverance* and says, "Even though it was hard, you didn't give up. You were showing determination and perseverance."

Next she asks them if they thought Wilma Rudolph had shown determination and perseverance. Everyone agrees that she had and the teacher tells them that she agrees, too, but that they need to find evidence to support their opinions.

> "I have marked the Wilma biography with some sticky notes where I think there are clear examples of Wilma showing determination and perseverance. I am going to read until I get to the first sticky note and then tell you what evidence I found in this part that Wilma was determined and wouldn't give up."

She reads until she gets to the first sticky note and then she stops and thinks aloud about Wilma and determination and perseverance.

> "I can tell Wilma was determined to learn to walk because she practiced her leg exercises constantly even when it really hurt."

Next, the teacher reads until she comes to the second sticky note and asks the class how Wilma's action let us infer that she is a determined person who doesn't give up when things get hard. The students eagerly explain that in this part of the story, Wilma took off her leg brace and walked without it down the church aisle even though her leg was trembling and it really hurt.

> "Now it's your turn to find examples of Wilma's determination and perseverance and mark them with sticky notes. Get into your trios and read the rest of the biography together. Mark examples of Wilma's determination and perseverance. Talk to one another about how the event you marked shows determination and perseverance so that when the class gathers together you can explain how you concluded this and what the evidence is for your conclusions."

Two (or Three) Heads ARE Better Than One!

No matter how hard you try or how fast you move, if you are the only person in your classroom who is teaching, there is not enough of you to go around! The most obvious and available resource you have to provide more "just right" instruction to each of your students is your other students. In the most effective classrooms, teachers use a variety of collaborative groupings to help their students accomplish a variety of tasks. Many teachers would like to include more small group work in their classrooms but observe that their children spend a lot of time vying for position and bickering about who does what. Often, one or two children sit on the sidelines and let a few children do all the work. These teachers often lament, "This class just can't work in groups!" In our opinion, the problem does not lie with the class but the size and composition of the groups. Whenever you have a group of five or six children, one or two of them is very apt to be sitting on the sidelines. It is very hard for five or six children (or adults!) to share a task. Three children, on the other hand, will often collaborate well—particularly if you consider who to group with whom. When we form trios to work together in reading, we spread our students who struggle with reading out among all the groups. We also include in each group a good reader and one of our most agreeable students. We assign the trios and watch them interact and make a few changes after the first couple of groups' work sessions. Once we observe that the trios work together pretty well, we leave them as permanent "teams." As the year goes on, they learn how to work with one another and build on each other's strengths. If you would like to incorporate more productive small group work in your class, try thoughtfully assigning your students to trios (with a duet or quartet or two if your numbers don't divide equally by three). Make some adjustments after the first couple of group work sessions. Then leave the teams to work out their dynamics. You will probably be pleasantly surprised to discover that your class can indeed work in groups!

The class quickly get into their trios and begin rereading their biographies. As the students read and talk and place sticky notes, the teacher circulates among the groups, coaching students as necessary to explain how what Wilma did was a good example of determination and perseverance.

When the class reconvenes, the teacher asks different groups to share their examples and explain their thinking. Next, the teacher goes to the board and says,

> "I want us to construct some statements showing what we learned about determination and perseverance from reading all about Wilma."

The first student responds,

> "Wilma showed determination because she didn't give up trying to walk even when no one thought she could."

The teacher agrees that this was true about Wilma and then crafts a statement that is not specific to Wilma and writes it on the board.

> "You can do things no one thinks you can do if you don't give up and show determination and perseverance."

The discussion continues and as students share specific examples related to Wilma, the teacher helps them craft statements that are not Wilma-specific. It is difficult for many to move to this abstract level of thinking but the teacher leads them with determination and perseveres until the class had constructed three more statements of lessons learned.

> "Sometimes, you don't succeed the first time, but if you keep trying and don't give up, you can eventually do it."
> "Determination means you really want to do something and perseverance means you keep trying until you do."
> "Most famous people have problems and failures but they show determination and persevere until they succeed."

Suddenly, a student has an "aha" moment and says, "I know what my dad would say about this. He would say, 'If at first you don't succeed, try, try, again.' My dad is always saying corny things like that!" The teacher declares his dad a very wise man and adds this to the other statements. Later in the day, she posts the five statements along with a picture of Wilma Rudolph on a board labeled "Determination and Perseverance." In the coming days, she refers to these statements to encourage students when they encounter a difficult task or give up after failing at something the first time.

Common Core Connections: Themes, Morals, and Lessons Learned

Reading Literature Standard 2 requires that students from grades one through five be able to figure out the theme, moral, or lesson you can learn from a story. This is a very abstract task and the *Themes, Morals, and Lessons Learned* framework was designed to provide enough modeling and scaffolding so that students could achieve this lofty goal. Students will need lots of practice with this across the year but the lessons also help you focus on character traits that are part of many elementary social studies curriculums.

The key to success with a *Themes, Morals, and Lessons Learned* lesson is to choose stories in which one or more of the characters clearly demonstrates the trait you are focusing on.

1. Have students read the story the first time to focus on characters, setting, and events. You may want to use the *Story Map* or *Beach Ball* lesson framework to focus their attention on these details.

2. When students have determined what happened in the story, shift their attention to what can be learned from what they read. Build the concept being focused on by having students share personal experiences and connect the words to those experiences. (Who is the bravest person you know? What have they done to demonstrate their bravery? When have you been brave? Does being brave mean you aren't afraid? Courage is a lot like bravery. When have you shown courage? When has someone you know shown courage? Which characters in books and videos have been especially brave and courageous? What did they do to let you know that?)

3. Mark the first two events that show that the character demonstrated the concept you are working on with sticky notes. Read the text and stop at the first sticky note and explain your thinking. ("I think Branch Rickey was very courageous when he hired Jackie Robinson to be the first black baseball player in the major leagues. He knew many people were going to think he should never have put a black baseball player on the team but he did it anyway because it was the right thing to do.")

4. Have students listen as you read to the second sticky note and then have the class explain why this second event was a good example of how the character's action demonstrated the concept.

5. Have students get back into their trios. Give them sticky notes and ask them to read until they find a clear example of the concept. Have them place a sticky note to mark each example and discuss what the character does to demonstrate the concept. Circulate and be sure each trio is supporting their decisions with evidence from the text.

6. Gather your students and have the trios share examples of characters demonstrating the concept. Help them share their thinking by asking, "How does … show that he/she was … … ?"

7. Conclude the lesson by helping students craft statements about the trait without using the characters' names. "What is the lesson we can learn about … from this book?" Record several examples so that students see there is not just one right answer.

Doing the Book

Children who "do" the book become more active readers. Characters, setting, events, dialogue, conclusions, mood, and motivation become important, and children pay more attention to them when they have to interpret and re-create the drama. This activity greatly increases story comprehension. The *Doing the Book* lesson framework can take a variety of forms, from performing a play, to acting out stories, to concentrating on re-creating a single scene of a play.

Do a Play Children of all ages enjoy being in a play, and some wonderful stories for children are already written in play format. Recasting a story as a play can also be a powerful reading/writing activity, especially if your older students create the script and stage directions from the original story.

When having your struggling readers do a play, remember that doing repeated readings is a powerful way to help children develop oral reading fluency and an understanding of characters. It helps their reading more if they do not memorize lines but rather read and reread their parts until they can read them fluently.

Some teachers do not do plays because there are not enough parts for everyone, or they do not know what to do with the children who are not in the play while the players are preparing. Most children enjoy preparing to do the play and then watching each other do it. For example, if you have a play that requires seven actors and you have twenty-four children in your class, divide your class into three groups of eight, putting a director and seven actors in each group. Let all three groups prepare and practice the play simultaneously. Then let each "cast" put on the play for the others.

If you have children do plays, remember that the purpose of this activity is for them to become more active readers, to visualize characters, to do some repeated readings, and to transfer their enjoyment from being in the play to reading. "Doing it" is what matters, not how professionally it is done. Props, costumes, and scenery should be nonexistent or very simple. Some teachers find that letting children make a simple mask to hide behind (using a paper plate and Popsicle stick) can help diminish shyness and stage fright.

Act Out a Story Acting out a story is another way to help children think actively and to visualize as they read. The best stories for acting out are the ones that you can visualize as plays. Everyone should have a part, as they did in the plays. Many teachers write down on little slips of paper the characters' names along with a number to designate acting cast:

First Little Pig 1	First Little Pig 2	First Little Pig 3
Second Little Pig 1	Second Little Pig 2	Second Little Pig 3
Third Little Pig 1	Third Little Pig 2	Third Little Pig 3
Mama Pig 1	Mama Pig 2	Mama Pig 3
Wolf 1	Wolf 2	Wolf 3
Man with sticks 1	Man with sticks 2	Man with sticks 3
Man with straw 1	Man with straw 2	Man with straw 3
Man with bricks 1	Man with bricks 2	Man with bricks 3
Director 1	Director 2	Director 3

The teacher then explains to the students that three groups will be acting out the story and that they will all have parts. She explains what the parts are and that she will pass out the slips after the story is read to determine which parts they will have. She encourages them to think about what all the characters do and feel because they might end up with any of the parts.

After the story is read and discussed, the teacher hands a slip of paper to each child randomly. (This procedure of letting chance determine who gets starring roles and who gets bit parts is readily accepted by the children and easier on the teacher, who will not have to try to decide who should and could do what. Sometimes, the most unlikely children are cast into starring roles and astonish everyone—including themselves!) The children then form three groups, and whoever gets the director slip in each group helps the others act out the story. The teacher circulates among the groups, giving help and

English Language Learners

English language learners, particularly, seem less self-conscious and more comfortable speaking when they have something to hide behind.

encouragement as needed. After 10 to 15 minutes of practice, each group performs its act while the other groups watch. Just as they enjoy doing a play, children generally enjoy acting out a story. Teachers who keep their focus on the process the children go through as they read and act out stories enjoy this activity and do not worry too much about the product. Acting out stories is designed to turn the children into active readers, not accomplished actors.

Make a Scene! Whereas full-blown plays may seem a bit daunting for children and teachers (and take time), a variation on this theme is often easier for children and can be quickly incorporated into many lessons. Rather than acting out a full play, have your students re-create a single scene. Scenes can be done by individuals, pairs, or small groups. They simply require the readers to select a scene, transform it into a script (not necessarily written out), briefly rehearse it, and then present it—no props, no costumes, just reenactment! The scene can be as short as a single exchange between characters or can even be a single sentence delivered in the appropriate voice. Children who can literally become Richard Best from *The Beast in Ms. Rooney's Room* or the sassy little brother in *Island of the Blue Dolphins* demonstrate an understanding of the story and the characters.

Compare/Contrast Bubbles

One of the basic thinking strategies we all use is making connections to things we already know. When we meet a new person, we may compare them to people we already know.

> "She looks a lot like my cousin."
> "He is a sports nut just like my dad."

We also notice how new people are different from people we know.

> "She doesn't talk like my cousin."
> "My dad is a Red Sox fan but he likes the Yankees."

Comparing and contrasting is also a thinking strategy we use to make sense of what we read.

> "She had a terrible disease when she was young just like Wilma Rudolph but she was not able to overcome it."
> "This book reminds me of another mystery I read but it is much more complicated."

The similarities and differences between two things can be demonstrated and organized in a Venn diagram, which we call a double bubble. This graphic organizer is very versatile and can be used to teach students to compare and contrast two things—settings, characters, themes, versions of the same tale, mysteries, poems, and other traits. Here is the double bubble created by a class of students who were comparing and contrasting two Magic Tree House books, *Buffalo Before Breakfast* and *Polar Bears Past Bedtime*.

Common Core Connections: Doing the Book

Language Standards 4 and 6 are the "speaking standards." Children are expected to speak clearly and in complete sentences when appropriate. All the *Doing the Book* lesson frameworks give children comfortable practice in speaking in an enjoyable, low-stress environment. *Doing the Book* lessons also help students achieve Reading Literature Standards 1, 2, and 3, which focus on key details about characters, settings, and events, and 5, which focuses on the differences between poems, plays, and stories.

1. Include plays in your reading repertoire. Have children read and do plays, and have older children turn stories into plays by writing scripts for them.

2. Have children do some impromptu acting out of stories—no scripts, props, or costumes needed. Children should read the story several times, parts should be chosen, and children should "do their thing." To include more children, have several casts performing the same story.

3. Have children act out scenes from longer stories. Let small groups choose different scenes; then have each group perform in order of scenes. All the groups not in a particular scene become the audience for that scene.

Polar Bears Past Bedtime

Buffalo Before Breakfast

Polar bear
Seal Hunter

The Arctic
present time
Jack and Annie
play with cubs
on ice, Ice
cracks, Polar
bear saves cubs
Jack and Annie.

People can learn
things from
watching animals.

Magic Tree
House
Jack Annie
Annie understands
animal talk
Jack writes facts
in note book
Theme/Moral

You can be brave
even if you are
afraid. People who
depend on animals
for survival respect
those animals.

Blackhawk
Blackhawk's
grandmother
Great Plains
200 years ago
Blackhawk take,
Jack and Annie to
see buffalo, Black-
hawk gets too close
to buffalo. Jack
saves Blackhawk.
Each group of
people have their
own ways of
living.

Common Core Connections: Compare/Contrast Bubbles

Reading Standard 9 requires students to be able to compare and contrast. At different grade levels, students learn to compare and contrast themes, settings, characters, and plots in a variety of genres, including folktales, myths, mysteries, adventures, and books in a series. *Compare/Contrast Bubbles* is a lesson framework that uses a Venn diagram graphic organizer to help students record the similarities and differences.

1. Choose two narratives that are in the same genre.

2. Have students read both or read one aloud to them and have them read the other one.

3. Have students draw two large circles that intersect in the center and label them with the title of the stories being compared and contrasted.

4. Have students discuss the story elements you want them to compare and contrast and record similarities in the intersection of the circles and differences on the appropriate side.

Summary

Comprehension—thinking about and responding to what you are reading—is "what it's all about!" Comprehension is the reason and prime motivator for engaging in reading. What comprehension is, how comprehension occurs, and how comprehension should be taught have driven hundreds of research studies in the last 30 years. Reading comprehension—and how to teach it—is probably the area of literacy about which we have the most knowledge and the most consensus. It is also probably the area that gets the least attention in the classroom.

In 1979, Dolores Durkin published a landmark study demonstrating that little, if any, reading comprehension instruction happened in most classrooms and that the little bit that did occur was "mentioning," rather than teaching. Having children answer comprehension questions to assess their reading comprehension was the activity most often seen. This finding shocked the reading community and probably propelled much of the reading comprehension research that has occurred since. Unfortunately, more recent research (Beck, McKeown, & Gromoll, 1989; Pressley & Wharton-McDonald, 1998) has indicated that reading comprehension instruction is still rare in most elementary classrooms.

Duke and Pearson (2002) reviewed the research and summarized what good readers do as they comprehend text. Good readers:

- Are active and have clear goals in mind.
- Preview text before reading, make predictions, and read selectively to meet their goals.
- Construct, revise, and question the meanings they are making as they read.
- Try to determine the meanings of unfamiliar words and concepts.
- Draw from, compare, and integrate their prior knowledge with what they are reading.
- Monitor their understanding and make adjustments as needed.
- Think about the author of the text and evaluate the text's quality and value.
- Read different kinds of text differently, paying attention to characters and settings when reading narratives, and constructing and revising summaries in their minds when reading expository text.

Previous chapters of this book described a variety of activities for building word identification, fluency, and vocabulary, all of which are required for comprehension. This chapter describes lesson frameworks designed to teach children how to think as they read narratives. *Think-Alouds; Story Maps; the Beach Ball; Themes, Morals, and Lessons Learned; Doing the Book;* and *Compare/Contrast Bubbles* all help children learn to do the varied kinds of thinking we do when we read narratives.In the following chapter, you will find lesson frameworks for teaching your students how to read informational text.

How Well Does Your Instruction Help All Children Learn How to Think as they Read and Comprehend Narrative Text?

1. Do I do *Think-alouds* to model the thinking strategies—connect, predict, visualize, monitor, summarize, infer, and evaluate?

2. Do I use the I do and you watch, I do and you help, You do it together and I help, and You do and I watch procedures to gradually release responsibility for thinking to my students?

3. Do I teach my students to be aware of how stories are structured and to retell stories, including main characters and settings and major events?

4. Do I teach my students to think about what the take-away from a story is—what theme, moral, or lesson they can learn when they read a story, play, or poem?

5. Do I teach my students how to compare and contrast stories and the elements of those stories?

6. Do I include some "doing the book" activities so that students can "bring the stories to life"?

8

Reading
Informational Text

HOW MANY MINUTES ACROSS THE DAY are your students actually reading and writing? Do your good readers read and write more than your struggling readers? Regardless of what grade you teach, your good readers almost surely read much more than your struggling readers. Good readers don't waste a minute of their independent reading time. They quickly grab a book when they finish an assignment in your classroom and they spend some time reading at home. Your good writers write more than your struggling writers (who are often the ones asking you how many sentences they have to write). If asked about the relationship between how much students read and write and their attitude toward reading and writing, most of us would explain that good readers and writers read and write more because they *like* to read and write, and struggling students read and write less because they *don't like* to read and write.

Consider the possibility that the cause/effect relationship between how much students enjoy literacy activities and how much time they spend in these activities might also flow in the opposite direction. Students who read and write more become more fluent in their reading and writing. Reading and writing are "easier" for them and so they feel more successful and enjoy reading and writing. Struggling students, on the other hand, don't read and write enough to become fluent, and every reading and writing encounter is a challenge for them. If we accept the fact that some students just don't like to read and write and will engage in these literacy activities only when forced to, then students who are behind in their literacy development will stay behind. So accepting the "they don't like to do it and so they will do less of it" idea will doom our efforts to help all our students achieve their highest literacy potential.

So, how can you get your students—*all* your students—to increase the volume of reading and writing they do every day in your classroom? The answer is to view every subject you teach as an opportunity to add reading and writing. This reading and writing time does not need to be lengthy or to occupy all the time you allocate to teaching these subjects. Imagine that your students are engaged in a reading or writing activity for 30 minutes twice each week during science and social studies. At the end of the week, you have added two hours of literacy engagement. Get all your students reading more, and all your students will read better than they would without this additional time.

Another compelling reason for increasing the amount of reading and writing that students do in science and social studies can be found in the Common Core Standards. Half the reading standards relate to informational text. By fourth grade, students are expected to be doing at least 50 percent of their reading in informational text. Reading informational text requires many of the same strategies required in reading stories. Students must accurately and fluently identify the words and access meanings for key vocabulary words and phrases. Reading informational text requires the same comprehension strategies we use as we read stories. When we read informational text, we

- Call up and connect relevant prior knowledge
- Predict, question, and wonder about what will be learned
- Visualize and imagine
- Monitor and use fix-up strategies
- Summarize the most important ideas
- Draw conclusions and make inferences
- Evaluate and make judgments

Reading informational text requires all these strategies—and more. When we read informational text, we need to do close reading so that we learn not only the big ideas but the facts and details that support those big ideas. Informational text has three common text structures—descriptive, sequential, and comparative—which we need to learn how to recognize and follow in order to organize the information we are learning. Finally, informational text has special features—maps, photos, charts, graphs, headings, bold words, and others—which require special reading strategies. The remainder of this chapter will describe lesson frameworks that teach children how to read and comprehend informational text.

Lesson Frameworks for Close Reading and Making Inferences

Reading Standard 1 of the Common Core is often called the "close reading" standard. Students are expected to be able to explain what the text says explicitly and to draw inferences from the text. *Guess Yes or No* and *Find It or Figure It Out* are lesson frameworks that teach students to pay attention to details and to make logical inferences.

Guess Yes or No

The *Guess Yes or No* lesson framework focuses your students' attention on important details in informational text by having them predict, before they read, which statements are true and which are false. Some of the statements require them to make logical inferences. Here is a sample *Guess Yes or No* lesson.

The class is about to read an article on Japan found in a student news magazine. The teacher wants her students to read the article closely and pay attention to the facts they learn about Japan. To plan the *Guess Yes or No* lesson, she reads the article and constructs 10 statements, some of which are true and some are false. She writes the false statements so that they can be turned into true statements by changing a word or two. She includes some statements that require students to make logical inferences to decide whether they are true or false. She also includes in the statements key vocabulary words students need to be able to pronounce and understand in order to fluently read the text. Here is the *Guess Yes or No* sheet she constructed for the article on Japan.

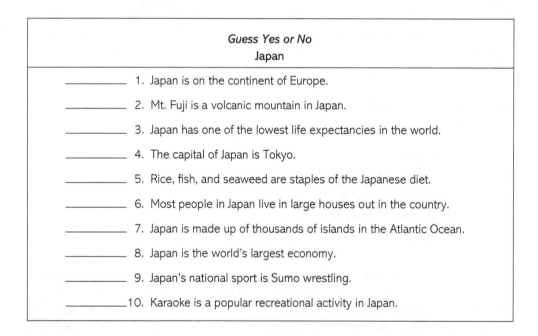

Guess Yes or No
Japan

_____ 1. Japan is on the continent of Europe.

_____ 2. Mt. Fuji is a volcanic mountain in Japan.

_____ 3. Japan has one of the lowest life expectancies in the world.

_____ 4. The capital of Japan is Tokyo.

_____ 5. Rice, fish, and seaweed are staples of the Japanese diet.

_____ 6. Most people in Japan live in large houses out in the country.

_____ 7. Japan is made up of thousands of islands in the Atlantic Ocean.

_____ 8. Japan is the world's largest economy.

_____ 9. Japan's national sport is Sumo wrestling.

_____10. Karaoke is a popular recreational activity in Japan.

The teacher follows the "gradual release of responsibility model" when teaching comprehension lessons. The class will watch and listen as she models how to figure out whether the first two statements are true or false. They will help her figure out the next two. Then the students will work together in trios to complete the final six statements. She has assigned students to trios so that there is at least one good reader and one struggling reader in each trio. The lesson begins with the whole class working together. The student assistant for the day hands out the *Guess Yes or No Japan* sheet to everyone so that each student has a copy. The teacher then sets the purpose for the lesson:

> "Today we are going to be learning about Japan. I have written 10 statements here about Japan, but some of them are not true. Before you read, you are going to guess whether each statement is true or false. You are going to write your guesses in pencil so that you can change them based on what you read in the article. It doesn't matter how many you guess right before you read. What matters is that you use your 'close reading' skills to figure out what the true facts are and change your guesses if they were wrong. Before we read the article, however, we need to read all 10 statements together and make sure we know how to pronounce all the words and what they mean. Everyone read #1 with me."

The class all reads the first statement.

> 1. Japan is on the continent of Europe.

Once the first statement is read, the teacher asks vocabulary-building questions:

> "Who knows how many continents there are in the world?"
> "Can we name them all?"
> "What continent do we live on?"
> "Has anyone ever been to another continent?"

The students share their accumulated knowledge about continents and then the teacher asks them to write "yes" or "no" to show whether they think Japan is on the continent of Europe. Some students are hesitant to guess and protest that they don't know the answer. The teacher assures them that they aren't supposed to know and that that is why the lesson is called "Guess Yes or No." She waits until everyone has written "yes" or "no" on the line before going to the next sentence. When everyone has committed themselves to a guess, they read the second sentence together.

> 2. Mt. Fuji is a volcanic mountain in Japan.

Again the teacher asks vocabulary-building questions.

> "What is a volcanic mountain?"
> "Do we have any volcanic mountains nearby us?"

She writes the words *volcano* and *volcanic* on the board and asks if anyone has even seen a volcano, and helps students understand how *volcano* and *volcanic* are related.

> "A volcanic mountain is a mountain that was formed by a volcano."

She then waits for everyone to write their guess before having students read the next sentence.

> 3. Japan has one of the lowest life expectancies in the world.

The teacher leads the students to determine the meaning of "life expectancy" by pointing out the related word, *expect*. She then asks them what they think the current life expectancy is for them and their parents. The students have varied answers and are clearly intrigued by this question. The teacher tells them that since they are going to read about Japan, the article probably won't tell them about life expectancies in the United States. One student quickly interjects that "We can google it!" The students write their "yes" or "no" guess next to #3 and everyone reads the next sentence.

4. The capital of Japan is Tokyo.

The teacher asks students what the capital of the United States is and what the capital of their state is, and to explain that the capital is the place where government happens. She writes the words *capital* and *capitol* on the board and help students distinguish between the meanings of these words that sound alike but have different meanings. Students record their guesses and read the next sentence together.

5. Rice, fish, and seaweed are staples of the Japanese diet.

The teacher asks them to name some staples of their diet. Students express amazement that anyone might eat seaweed but several students think that Japanese people probably eat a lot of rice and fish. As they are making their guess, they want to know if all three have to be staples of the Japanese diet if they guess "yes." She assures them that a "yes" guess has to include all three. It is clear from their response that they are eager to get the magazine article and see if Japanese people eat a lot of seaweed!

Before proceeding to the next sentence, the teacher picks up the stapler from her desk and helps the students realize that they know another meaning for *staples*. One student chimes in that it can also be the store, *Staples*. The lesson continues as the teacher leads her students to read each sentence chorally and builds meaning vocabulary, and students guess "yes" or "no" for each of the remaining statements.

When all the statements have been read and all the key vocabulary developed, the students gather in their assigned trios and the teacher hands the magazine to one student in each trio who quickly sits in the middle between the other two students. (The teacher has noticed that her students work together more and interact more when they have only one copy of the text to share so, even though she has enough copies of the magazine for everyone, they will only use one per trio for this lesson.)

When the students are positioned in their trios, she has everyone turn to the page where the article begins and draws their attention to the map at the beginning of the article. She models how to determine if the first statement is true by thinking aloud about the map and letting them listen in on her thinking.

"Here is a map and I find Japan here. I see that Japan is in Asia so the first statement must be false. Japan is not on the continent of Europe. It is in Asia. I will change the first statement to make it true."

1. Japan is on the continent of ~~Europe~~ **Asia**.

She asks everyone to change the first statement on their sheets to turn #1 into a true statement.

"Now, I will read this paragraph and see what I can find out about any of the other statements."

She reads the paragraph aloud and then explains her thinking.

> "This paragraph tells us that there are many volcanoes in Japan and that Mt. Fuji is the tallest mountain and has not erupted in hundreds of years, but scientists think it could erupt at any time. I conclude that Mt. Fuji is a volcanic mountain so I don't need to change the second statement because it is true."

After modeling how to determine the truth of the first two statements, she invites students to help her with the next two.

> "Let's read the next paragraph together. After we read it, we will figure out what it tells us about any of the remaining statements."

The teacher and students read the paragraph and decide to make the third sentence true by changing *lowest* to *highest*.

> 3. Japan has one of the ~~lowest~~ **highest** life expectancies in the world.

They look at the country map of Japan and conclude that the * symbol next to Tokyo means that Tokyo is the capital and so sentence #4 is true and doesn't need changing.

> "Now that you understand what to do, work together to complete the remaining statements. Read the paragraphs together and talk about any visuals and decide together which statements are true and how to turn the false statements into true statements."

The students get to work and the teacher circulates among the groups, making sure that students explain their thinking to justify whether a sentence is true or false. She notices one group of students changing a false sentence by simply inserting the word *not*.

> Japan is ^**not** the world's largest economy.

She helps them change the sentence without using the word *not*.

> Japan is the world's ^**third** largest economy.

She then makes a new rule that she announces to the class.

> "When making a false sentence true, the word **not** is **NOT** allowed!"

It doesn't take long for students to finish reading the short article and verify/change the remaining six statements. The lesson finishes with the class gathered together once more and focusing on the last six statements. For statements they believe are true, she has them locate and read aloud the evidence in the text that confirms these statements. They also read aloud portions of the text that let them decide that statements are false and share their thinking to determine that.

> "You can see on the map that Japan is lots of islands in the Pacific Ocean—not the Atlantic Ocean!"

One Student's Completed *Guess Yes or No* Sheet

    No   1. Japan is on the continent of ~~Europe~~. **Asia**

    Yes   2. Mt. Fuji is a volcanic mountain in Japan.

    No   3. Japan has one of the ^highest ~~lowest~~ life expectancies in the world.

    Yes   4. The capital of Japan is Tokyo.

    Yes   5. Rice, fish, and seaweed are staples of the Japanese diet.

    No   6. Most people in Japan live in ^apartments ~~large houses~~ out in the ~~country~~. **city**

    No   7. Japan is made up of thousands of islands in the ^Pacific ~~Atlantic~~ Ocean.

    No   8. Japan is the world's ^third largest economy.

    Yes   9. Japan's national sport is Sumo wrestling.

    Yes   10. Karaoke is a popular activity in Japan.

              11. Japan has the lowest homicide rate in the world.

The students express amazement that seaweed is indeed eaten almost every day and point out that it didn't tell us about life expectancies in the United States and they intend to find out.

To conclude the lesson, the teacher asks students to look back at the article and write one more statement that is true or that can be easily turned into a true statement. She asks students to do this individually and not to tell anyone whether their statement is true or false. When students have had 2 minutes to write this new statement, she lets several students read theirs to the class and call on other students to guess whether it is true or false and turn false statements into true statements.

Find It or Figure It Out

Have you ever asked your students a question and heard someone respond, "I don't know. It didn't say." Many children are quite literal when they read. They expect to find all the answers to questions right in the text. In reality, most of the thinking you do as you read is not literal. Your brain puts information you read together with information you know and figures out many things that are not directly stated. If you read the weather forecast and the chances of rain are 100 percent, you figure out that you probably need to rethink your plans for a barbecue this weekend. Figuring out something based on information from the text is called inferring. *Find It or Figure It Out* is a lesson framework you can use to teach your students how to use the information in the text and their prior knowledge to figure things out. Here is a sample lesson from a science class.

This science teacher decides to use the *Find It or Figure It Out* lesson framework to teach his students how to make and support inferences as they read a section in their science texts about tropical rain forests. He reads the text and constructs questions for each two-page spread. He makes sure that the answers to the "find it" questions are quite literal and can be found "right there" in a sentence or two. He constructs the "Figure it out" questions so that they require his students to make logical inferences. The answers are not right there but there are clues that let you figure out what the answers are.

Find It or Figure It Out
Tropical Rain Forests

1. (p. 4–5) Figure out if there are any rain forests in Africa and Australia.
2. (p. 6–7) Find out what high and low temperatures in tropical rain forests usually are and how much rain they get.
3. (p. 8–9) Figure out how a forest is like a cake.
4. (p. 10–11) Figure out which layer of the forest is as tall as many adults.
5. (p. 12–13) Figure out which part of a rain forest is hard to walk through.
6. (p. 14–15) Find out what epiphytes are and how they help trees.

With the whole class assembled, the teacher establishes the purpose for the lesson, builds meanings for important vocabulary, and models how to answer one question. He then asks the whole class to help him answer the second question. Next the class works in trios to answer the remaining questions. He has organized the trios so that each trio has a range of reading levels and has also tried to put students together who like to work with one another.

The lesson begins with the students seated in their assigned trios. The teacher hands one copy of the *Find It or Figure It Out Tropical Rain Forest* question sheet to each trio and the person who gets the sheet quickly sits between the other two. He gives the other two students tiny sticky notes in two different colors. Next he establishes the lesson purpose.

"Shortly, I am going to give you a piece to read about tropical rain forests. As you read, you are going to find the answers to some questions and figure out the answers to others. The answers to the 'find it' questions will be right there on the page. When you find these answers, you will put a green sticky note on them to show where you found them. The answers to the 'figure it out' questions will not be right there on the page but there will be clues in the text that you can use to figure them out. You are going to use the yellow sticky notes to mark the details from the text that are clues you used to answer the 'figure out' questions. Before we start reading about tropical rain forests, however, we need to use our collective class knowledge to build meanings for some key words. Read #1 with me and tell me what you think the key vocabulary words are."

1. (p. 4–5) Figure out if there are any rain forests in Africa and Australia.

The class reads the first sentence chorally and decides that *rain forests*, *Africa*, and *Australia* are important vocabulary words. The teacher directs the students' attention to the world map and they identify Africa and Australia. He then tells them that a rain forest is a forest that gets a lot of rain. When asked if anyone has ever seen a rain forest, one student describes the movie *Fern Gully: The Last Rain Forest*. Other students report having seen programs on the Discovery Channel about rain forests. Some suggest that you can probably find lots of cool videos about rain forests on YouTube and the teacher says that is a good idea and he will investigate that. Next, everyone reads the second sentence.

2. (p. 6–7) Find out what high and low temperatures in tropical rain forests usually are and how much rain they get.

The students decide that *high* and *low temperatures* and *tropical* are important vocabulary. The teacher leads them to talk about the high and low temperatures where they live and then writes the words *tropics* and *tropical* on the board. He asks students to tell how these words are related. Students volunteer that they think the tropics are a place where it gets very hot and that tropical would describe a rain forest that was in the tropics and probably very hot.

Together, the students read the remaining sentences. They jointly decide what key vocabulary words are and share their collective knowledge. No one knows what epiphytes are and the teacher says that is one thing they will find out when they get to that page. He has the students pronounce the word *epiphytes* several times and points out that *ph* has the sound they know from words such as *phone* and *elephant*.

When all the sentences have been read and meanings and pronunciations for vocabulary built, the teacher hands the text to the middle person in each trio. He then models how he figures out the answer to the first question.

1. (p. 4–5) Figure out if there are any rain forests in Africa and Australia.

He reads the page aloud and then thinks aloud.

"It doesn't say anywhere if there are tropical rain forests in Africa and Australia. But I can use the information in the sentences and the map to figure it out. When I look at the map on this page, I see that Africa and Australia are between the Tropic of Cancer and the Tropic of Capricorn. When I put that map information together with what I read in this sentence—*The most important rain forests are near the equator, in the area between the Tropic of Cancer and Tropic of Capricorn*—I can figure out that there are tropical rain forests in both Africa and Australia. I will put a yellow sticky note on this sentence and another on the map to mark the clues I used to figure out the answer. You should also mark these places with yellow sticky notes."

When the trios have marked the clues with yellow sticky notes, the teacher draws their attention to the second question.

2. (p. 6–7) Find out what high and low temperatures in tropical rain forests usually are and how much rain they get.

"Question #2 is a 'find it' question. We need to find two facts, what high and low temperatures in tropical rain forests usually are and how much rain they get. Read these two pages with me and help me find these facts."

The students and teacher read these two pages chorally and students eagerly volunteer the answers to both questions. They mark these two sentences with green sticky notes.

The temperature rarely goes above 93 degrees or drops below 68 degrees.
At least 80 inches of rain falls each year.

Before letting the trios read and work together to answer the remaining questions, the teacher makes sure that they identify questions #3, #4, and #5 as "figure it out" questions and question #6 as a "find it" question.

> "Begin by writing the answers to the first two questions that we did together on your *Find It or Figure It Out* sheet. Then read each question and find or figure out the answer. For the 'figure it out' questions, explain to each other which sentence and pictures have clues and how these clues help you figure it out. Mark them with yellow sticky notes and write the answer on your sheet. For question #6, you will need to find the sentences that tell you what epiphytes are and how epiphytes help trees. Use your green sticky notes to mark the places where you found these answers."

As the students work together, the teacher circulates and reminds students to explain to each other where they found answers and which sentences in the text provided clues that let them figure out answers not right there on the page.

The class gathers together and shares their answers to the questions and where they placed their sticky notes. For the "figure it out" questions, the teacher leads students to share their thinking and explain how they used the text evidence to figure out the answers. The teacher ends the lesson by reminding students that sometimes facts and details that you learn from reading are right there on the page. Other times, you have to be detectives and use the clues and your prior knowledge to figure things out.

Common Core Connections: Guess Yes or No, Find It or Figure It Out

Reading Standard 1 requires students to read closely to determine what the text says explicitly and to make logical inferences. It also requires students to cite specific evidence from the text to support their conclusions. *Guess Yes or No* and *Find It or Figure It Out* are lesson frameworks that teach students how to do close reading, make inferences, and support their answers with evidence from the text.

Guess Yes or No

The key to a successful *Guess Yes or No* lesson lies in the statements you create. As you create these statements, be sure to include key vocabulary so that you can build that vocabulary before students read. Include false statements that can easily be turned into true statements and some statements that require students to make logical inferences. (The chart shows the gross national product of several countries and Japan is listed third on the list behind the United States and China, so it must be the world's third-largest economy.)

To teach this lesson using the *Gradual Release of Responsibility* framework, follow these steps.

1. Have students read each statement with you and ask students questions to build meaning for vocabulary. Point out morphemic connections students should understand (*volcano, volcanic; expect, expectancy*). Help students use the context of the sentence to determine the appropriate meaning of multi-meaning words (*staples*) and help them clarify the meaning of homophones, the meaning of which they may confuse (*capital; capitol*).

2. Have students use pencils to write a *yes* or *no* next to each statement to indicate their guesses. Assure them that they can erase incorrect guesses and change them as they read.

3. Model (I Do and You Watch) and then have students work with you (I Do and You Help) to complete the first several statements. Be sure to locate evidence in the text to verify your answers.

4. Have students work in trios to read and decide whether each remaining statement is true or not. Have them turn the false statements into true statements without using the word "not." Observe their interactions and intervene and coach as necessary as the students work together. (You Do It Together and I Help)

5. Gather your students and have them read each statement and share how their trios turned false statements into true statements. Have them read evidence from the text that proves whether a statement is true or false.

6. Have each student write one or two new sentences that are true or false. Let a few students share their sentences and call on other students to tell if they are true or false and turn false statements into true statements.

Find It or Figure It Out

The *Find It or Figure It Out* lesson framework teaches students that not all the information is right there on the page but you can use clues to figure out information that is not directly stated. To help students understand the difference between literal and inferential thinking, make the "find it" questions very literal. The answer should be right there in a single sentence. The "figure it out" questions should require students to put together information from several parts of the text or to use their prior knowledge. Be sure to have them explain how they figured out the answers so that they can learn how you make inferences while you read. To teach the lesson using the gradual release of responsibility model, take the students through the "I do and you watch," "I do and you help" and "You do it together and I help" lesson steps. Before reading, have students read all the questions with you and build meanings for key words. Have them use two different colors of sticky notes to mark the places where they found answers or clues.

Lesson Frameworks for Text Structures

Comprehending informational text requires all the strategies required for comprehending stories. In addition, readers must be able to follow the three different text structures commonly found in informational text and use the special features of informational text. Many informational texts follow a descriptive text structure. These texts focus on a single topic and usually contain several main ideas about that topic. This abbreviated text about snakes is an example of descriptive text.

Snakes

Snakes have long, narrow bodies with a head on one end and tail on the other end. Their skin is covered in overlapping scales that can feel vibrations in the ground. Snakes don't have eyelids or ears like we do.
      Snakes vary greatly in size. The biggest snake is the Python. It can grow up to 33 feet long! The thickest snake is the Anaconda. The biggest one ever found measured 44 inches around. The Thread snake is the smallest snake …
      Snakes are reptiles. Like most reptiles, snakes are cold-blooded, which means they rely on the environment to control their body heat. Other common reptiles …
      Snakes shed their entire skin two or three times a year. The new skin grows underneath the old skin and …
      Some snakes are venomous but most are not dangerous. In fact, snakes can be very helpful … .

Other informational texts, such as this text about frogs and toads, compare and contrast various members of a category.

Frogs and Toads

What is the difference between frogs and toads? Actually, toads are a type of frog. There are several differences, however, between North American frogs and toads.

Frogs have smooth, wet skin that looks slimy. Toads have drier, rough skin that looks really bumpy, like warts. …

Frogs have skinnier bodies than toads do. Toads are kind of wide and fat. Frogs have longer legs and webbed hind feet, but toads …

Frogs and toads both lay their eggs in water because both frog and toad babies start off as tadpoles. The difference is that …

The third common informational text structure organizes ideas or events according to the sequence in which they occur. Sometimes, one event causes another event and there is not only a sequential relationship between events but also a cause/effect relationship. The text on space exploration is an example of a sequence/cause-effect text structure.

Space Exploration

In 1947, the first animals were launched into space. Fruit flies were used to study the effects of space travel on animals. They were chosen because fruit flies are quite similar to humans…

Albert II, a Rhesus monkey, was the first monkey in space. Albert went into space on June 14th 1949 …

On October 4th, 1957, Russia launched the first satellite, Sputnik 1, into space. The space race had begun! …

Students can learn to organize and summarize information following the three text structures by creating graphic organizers that show the relationships between the ideas. *Main Idea Trees* depict descriptive text. *Time Lines* and *Compare/Contrast Bubbles* depict text that has a sequential or comparative structure.

Main Idea Trees

We often talk about main ideas as if there is only one. This is sometimes true when we are reading stories, but informational text often includes several main ideas about a single topic. A tree can help children visualize and organize information. The topic you are learning about is the trunk of the tree. The main ideas about that topic are the large main branches and the details that relate to each main idea are the small branches that go off the large branches. Here is a sample lesson using the *Main Idea Trees* lesson framework.

The class is going to read an informational article about snakes. The teacher realizes that this piece of descriptive text has several main ideas with details to support each idea. He decides to help students visualize the main ideas and details by having them draw a tree and put main ideas on the main branches of the tree and details on small branches going off each main branch. He follows the gradual release of responsibility model in teaching this lesson.

The lesson begins with the teacher putting a large sheet of paper on the board and drawing a large tree with six big branches. He labels the trunk with the word *topic* and the branches with *main idea*.

> "Often when we are reading informational text, we are learning a lot of big ideas about one topic. We call these main ideas. Today, we are going to be reading about snakes. We are going to create trees and write the big ideas we learn about snakes on the big branches. Then we are going to draw some smaller branches and write details that tell more about the main ideas."

The teacher gives everyone a large piece of drawing paper.

> "Put your paper the tall way and use the whole paper to draw a tree with six large branches. Use the whole paper so that you will have lots of space to draw smaller branches and write the details on them. Instead of the word *topic*, write *snakes* on the trunk."

Students eagerly draw their trees and it is apparent they are intrigued with the idea of creating "snake trees." (Have students draw their trees rather than handing out a copy with

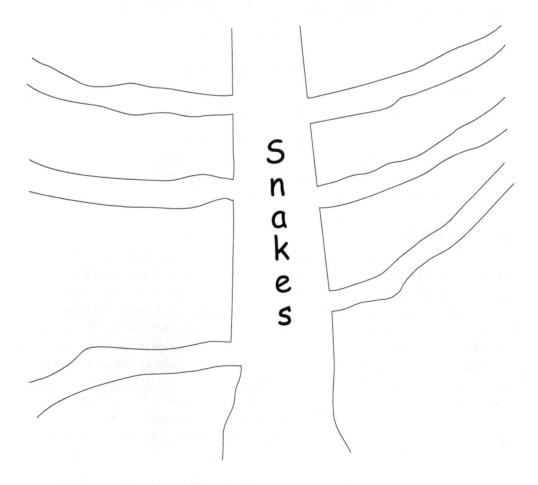

an already drawn tree. Your goal is that when students are reading descriptive text with several main ideas about one topic they construct this tree in their minds.) When students all have their trees drawn and have written the word *snakes* on the trunk, the teacher reads to them the first section of the text, which describes snakes' bodies. When he finishes reading this section, he thinks aloud:

> "I learned a lot of facts about snakes on this page. I learned that they don't have any arms or legs. They have eyes on the sides of their heads and really long bellies. Their skin is scaly and dry. I think this section is all about snakes' bodies so I am going to write that on one of my tree branches. Then I am going to draw some smaller branches off the main branch and write the details I learned about their bodies."

He writes this main idea and its details on one branch of the tree. His students copy this information on one of their tree branches.

> "Now we are going to read the next section together. Get in your trios and I will give you one copy of the article. Remember that the person I hand the article to sits in the middle and holds the text so that everyone can read it. After we read it, we will talk about what we learned and come up with a main idea that relates to all the details."

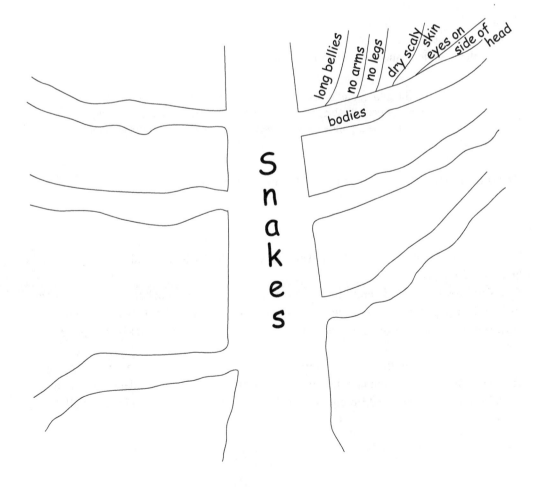

The teacher and students read the section. When they finish, he asks them what they learned and they respond:

> "Snakes shed their skins two or three times every year."
> "The old skin wears out and just peels off."
> "There is a new skin that grew under the old skin."

When they have shared the details, he leads them to determine the main idea of this section.

> "So these details are all about one idea. Who can tell us what all these details are about? What is the main idea of this section?"

The class decides that this section is all about how snakes shed their skins. The teacher and students all write this on a branch and then draw smaller branches to write the details about how snakes shed their skins.

> "Now it is time for you to work with your friends and finish your snake trees. You will start reading on this page where we left off. I have put these small sticky notes at each stopping point. When you get to the sticky note, stop and tell each other what you learned. Then come up with a main idea that all the details relate to. Write the main idea and details on your tree before going on to the next section."

As his students work together, the teacher circulates and observes the interactions of the groups. The students are all able to tell the details but some groups have difficulty coming up with the main idea and the teacher helps them to formulate this.

> "You learned that a thread snake is the size of worm and an anaconda can be as long as a bus, cobras can be 8–18 feet and garter snakes are usually 1–4 feet. What's the big idea about snakes that we learn from thinking about those sizes?"

One student smiles and respond in a questioning tone of voice:

> "Snakes are different sizes?"

The teacher responds, "Exactly," and everyone writes this main idea and the details on a branch of their tree.

The trios finish at different times. As students finish, the teacher encourages them to turn their papers over and draw some of what they learned about snakes. When the slower groups see the others drawing, they pick up the pace and quickly complete their trees.

The lesson ends with the class assembled together and using their trees to make suggestions to the teacher about how he can complete his tree. He helps students see that the main ideas can be stated in different ways as long as they capture the big idea that all the details relate to.

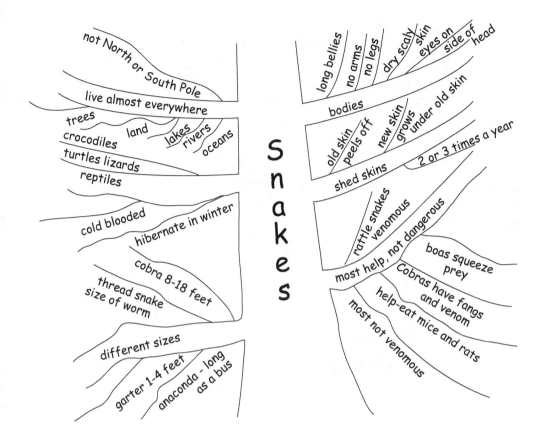

Time Lines

Time lines help us organize information in which the sequence of events is what is important. Here is the partially completed time line students constructed when reading about the history of space exploration.

Time Line Space Exploration

1947	1949	1957	1961	1962						
∧	∧	∧	∧	∧	∧	∧	∧	∧	∧	∧
fruit flies launched into space	Albert, a monkey, launched into space	Russia launched Sputnik 1 and Sputnik 2	Russian astronaut first human orbits Earth	JFK says America will get to the moon first and space race begins						

Compare/Contrast Bubbles

Chapter 7 described a sample lesson in which students compared two Magic Treehouse books and organized their information in a *Compare/Contrast Bubble*. Here is the compare/contrast bubble created by students who were reading about China and Japan.

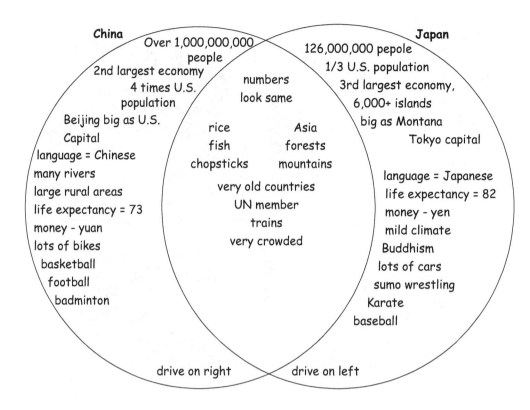

China — Japan

China:
Over 1,000,000,000 people
2nd largest economy
4 times U.S. population
Beijing big as U.S. Capital
language = Chinese
many rivers
large rural areas
life expectancy = 73
money - yuan
lots of bikes
basketball
football
badminton
drive on right

Both:
numbers look same
rice
fish
chopsticks
Asia
forests
mountains
very old countries
UN member
trains
very crowded

Japan:
126,000,000 pepole
1/3 U.S. population
3rd largest economy,
6,000+ islands
big as Montana
Tokyo capital
language = Japanese
life expectancy = 82
money - yen
mild climate
Buddhism
lots of cars
sumo wrestling
Karate
baseball
drive on left

Common Core Connections: Main Idea Trees, Time Lines, Compare/Contrast Bubbles

The Common Core recognizes the importance of students comprehending informational texts that follow the three common text structures. Reading Information Standard 2 requires students to determine main ideas of a text and explain how they are supported by key details. Standard 3 states that students should be able to describe the relationships between events using language that relates to time, sequence, and cause/effect. Standard 5 requires students to describe the overall structure of events, ideas, concepts, or information in a text. Standard 9 requires students to compare and contrast the most important details or events from two texts. The ability to understand text structure and use it to help organize ideas and information can be seen throughout the Informational Text Standards at all grade levels. Having students create *Main Idea Trees*, *Time Lines*, and *Compare/Contrast Bubbles* will teach them the abstract concept of text structure and help them learn to organize the ideas and facts that make up informational text.

Teaching a Main Idea Tree, Time Line, or Compare/Contrast Bubble Lesson

Choose text for these lessons that clearly have the text structure you want to focus on. Have your students use large paper and draw the main idea tree, time line, or compare/contrast bubbles. Use the "I do and you watch" step to model for your students how to complete the first few ideas or events. Let students help you complete one or two more. Have students work in trios to complete the tree, time line, or double bubble. Share the completed trees, time lines, and double bubbles and help students see that the wording of the information can vary as long as they have the important events, details, etc. in the correct place.

Teaching Informational Text Features

Look at any piece of informational text—a magazine article, a textbook chapter, a Gail Gibbons book— and you will see many features you don't see in stories, poems, or plays. The most noticeable feature of informational text is a variety of visuals—drawings, photos, maps, charts, graphs, and diagrams are common features of informational text. The next things you will probably find are headings that signal the main ideas of each section and, sometimes, sub-headings. Within the text, you will notice some bold or highlighted words. These are important vocabulary terms that are often defined in the text and sometimes further clarified in a glossary. Most informational text contains many words students may not know how to pronounce and in parenthesis next to some words, there is a handy guide to that word's pronunciation (pro-NUN-see-a-shun). If the text is divided into chapters, you can probably find a table of contents in the beginning and an index at the end, which will let you quickly locate specific information in that text.

With all these helpful features, students should be more successful at reading informational text than they are at reading stories. Most of us know the opposite is true. Most elementary students comprehend stories better than they comprehend information text. How can that be? Most likely, the explanation is simple. Most children don't know what all these helpful features are for or how to use them.

This section will describe two lesson frameworks designed specifically to teach students how to use all the special features of informational text. *Preview-Predict-Confirm* teaches students to build vocabulary by focusing on the visuals in a text. *Text Feature Scavenger Hunts* teach students to use visuals along with all the other special features of informational text.

Preview-Predict-Confirm

Preview-Predict-Confirm (Yopp & Yopp, 2004) is a lesson framework that teaches students to use the visuals in an informational text to build vocabulary and to predict what they will read. The lesson begins with students seated in their trios and talking about 10–15 visuals from a text they will read. Students have 20 seconds to look at each visual, talk about it, and try to predict words they will read connected to the visual. Next students have 8 minutes to write as many words as they can that they think will occur. At the end of 8 minutes, students look at their words and choose one word they think all the other groups will also have, one word they think is unique to their group, and one word they are most interested in. Next, the trios read the text together. They put a check on each word they listed that actually occurred and add five words they wish they had thought of. The class reconvenes and shares their discoveries. At the end of the lesson, students write a short paragraph using as many of their words as they can to tell what they learned. Here is a sample lesson using the book *Penguins* by Gail Gibbons.

The teacher sets the purpose for the lesson by showing a few of the visuals students will soon be looking at and having students talk about what is going on in the visuals and name things they see. She also asks them to predict what they think the text on the page will be about based on the visuals.

> "I can tell that you already know a lot about penguins and the pictures help remind you of what you know. When we study the visuals before we read, our brains make connections to what we already know and we can predict what the text might tell us. The visuals also make us think of

questions—things we want to know--and when we read, we find out if what we read answers those questions. Today, we are going to work on connecting what we know to visuals and predicting which words the author will use to tell us more about penguins."

Next the teacher seats her students in trios. She has arranged the trios to have a strong reader/writer in each group and has divided her English learners among the trios.

"I am going to show you some visuals from the text and you will have 20 seconds to talk about each one. Try to name everything you see in the visual and talk about what you think the text on this page—which I have covered—will tell you. I will show you what I want you to do on this first visual."

She displays the first visual for 20 seconds and talks aloud about what she sees and what she might learn from the text on this page.

"I see lots of penguins and it looks like they are climbing up the ice and then sliding down. Are those icebergs they're sliding on? I wonder where those penguins are?"

She removes this visual and then shows them a sheet with the word *Penguins* in the middle box and lots of empty boxes.

	Penguins	

"After you have talked about all the visuals, I am going to give your trio a sheet that looks like this. Your trio will have 8 minutes to write words in the boxes that you think you will find in the book based on what you saw in the visuals. I am going to begin by putting in the words *climbing, sliding,* and *iceberg* because I think those words will be in the book."

climbing		
sliding		
iceberg		
	Penguins	

> "Now, I am going to show you the second visual. Talk with your trio for 20 seconds about what you see. Name everything you can and try to think of questions the text might answer."

She shows the second visual and the trios talk animatedly for 20 seconds. After 20 seconds, she asks them to help her list words they think they will see and they suggest she add *diving, swimming,* and *ocean.* She writes these words in boxes on the penguin sheet.

> "Now I am going to show you the rest of the visuals for 20 seconds each. Talk about each and try to come up with words that you can add to the sheet that I will give you when you have seen all the visuals."

She shows them the remaining 10 visuals, which include a map, chart, and diagram in addition to pictures. She has covered all the words—except for any labels or captions that go with the visuals. The children talk excitedly about each visual. Here are some of the comments she overhears as students view the visuals.

> "Those are seals and walruses and whales. I bet whales eat penguins."
>
> "What is that funny looking little thing? It looks like a bug or maybe a shrimp."
>
> "There's an egg. Those must be the mother and father penguins."
>
> "The mother penguin is feeding the baby. I think she chews the food and then regurgitates it." "What does regurgitate mean?" "It's like when you throw up." "Oh, gross!"
>
> "Those penguins are all together. They look like they are in a huddle like at a football game. I think that helps they stay warm."
>
> "That's a map that shows the world and where different penguins live. That map has a lot of words that will for sure be in the book. Antarctica, Australia, South Pole, Pacific Ocean. We need more time to look at that map!"

"What's happening? I think it must be an oil spill. Look at that brown stuff in the water. I bet penguins are going to get covered in oil. Someone will need to rescue them."

"That's a penguin caught in that fishing net. How is he going to get out?"

When they have had 20 seconds to talk about each visual, the teacher gives them the penguin sheet. She hands the sheet to the fastest writer in each group and asks that person to be the recorder. She lets them copy the six words predicted based on the first two visuals, and then gives them 8 minutes to write words they think will occur in the text based on the other visuals. Here are the words one trio came up with.

climbing	diving	white
sliding	swimming	cold
iceberg	ocean	waddle
fins	emperor	beak
shrimp	**Penguins**	South Pole
frozen	net	oil
birds	trapped	predators
regurgitate	endangered	eggs
fish	Australia	tuxedos
ice	huddle	Antarctica

When the 8 minutes is up, she hands each trio three different-colored strips of paper and then explains their next task.

"On the red strip, I want you to decide on a word that you think is so obvious all the other trios also have this word. We call this word a common word because it is probably common to all the groups. I am going to write a C on this red strip to remind you what goes on the red strip."

C

"On the green strip, I want you to write a word your trio thought of but you don't think any of the other trios thought of. We call this a unique word because it might be unique to your group."

"On the blue strip, write the word your trio thinks is the most interesting word. You have 2 minutes to talk about your words and decide on your common, unique, and most interesting words."

After 2 minutes, she gathers the class together and has each trio show the words they have chosen as common, as unique, and as interesting. Here are one trio's words.

C ice	U regurgitate	I endangered

"Now I am giving your trio one copy of *Penguins*. The person I hand the book to needs to sit in the middle and you all need to read the pages together and decide which of the words you thought would be in this book are there. Put a "star" on each word that you find in the book."

The students read the book and are delighted to find that many of the words they guessed are actually in the book. As trios finish reading, the teacher asks them to turn their sheets over and go back through the book and list five words they wish they had thought of.

```
1.
2.
3.
4.
5.
```

When the groups have finished reading the book and checking the words that occurred, the teacher gathers the class together and lets volunteers share some words that occurred and some that didn't. The group that thought of *regurgitate* is disappointed to find that this word was not used in the book. The teacher sympathizes with them and tells them that perhaps the author thought they couldn't understand the word *regurgitate,* but she didn't know how smart they were. The three trios that finished first and had time to list the words they wished they had thought of shared their words and why they realized they should have thought of those words. The teacher ends the lesson by reminding students that they can learn a lot by studying the visuals before they read an informational text and that the visuals will help them read some of the words they may not have seen before.

Text Feature Scavenger Hunts

Learning how to read visuals—pictures, maps, charts, and graphs—and how headings, highlighted words, and other informational text features help us is not something most elementary children get excited about. You can make it fun and engaging, however, by organizing your class into teams and sending them on a scavenger hunt. When we began using this lesson framework in classroom, we discovered that most of our students didn't know what a scavenger hunt was! If your students are inexperienced with scavenger hunts, send them on a quick hunt in your classroom for objects. Give them just 5 minutes to find and record these items and then tally up points to declare the winner. Here is the classroom scavenger hunt one teacher used to introduce his class to a scavenger hunt.

Classroom Scavenger Hunt

You have 5 minutes to find and write the name of an object that matches the description.

something green	something opaque	something made of cloth
something rectangular	something oval	something taller than Mr. H
something you can see through	something that can move	something white
something made of glass	something growing	something breakable
something alive	something brown	something you can put things in
something made of wood	something liquid	something you can't move
something red	something you can read	something you can eat
something you can write on	something smaller than your thumb	something that can talk
something made of plastic	something rough	something you can turn off
something 8 inches long	something shiny	something you can't reach

Here is a sample Text Features Scavenger Hunt lesson using a chapter from a social studies book. The questions on the scavenger hunt directed the students' attention to all the special features of that chapter and book.

Great Depression Scavenger Hunt

Use the visuals and other special text features to answer these questions. Indicate where you found the answers. You have 20 minutes to find as many answers as you can. Your team will get one point for every correct answer and another point for writing where you found the answer.

Question	Your answer	Where did you find answer?
What instrument did Louis Armstrong play?		
What was the name of the dog on RCA's label?		
What was the name of a Charlie Chaplin movie?		
How many Ford cars were sold in 1920? In 1929? (2 pts.)		
What type of new buildings were built in New York City in the 1920s?		
Which year had the most business failures?		
About how many people lost their jobs in 1933?		
Which 5 states were in the Dust Bowl region? (5 pts.)		
Which president began the New Deal programs?		
In what year did Charles Lindbergh fly across the Atlantic?		
What is the 5th step in assembling a car in Henry Ford's factory?		
What is the first major heading in this chapter?		
What is the last major heading in this chapter?		
Use the index to decide on what page you will find information about:		

Question	Your answer	Where did you find answer?
Herbert Hoover		
Clarence Birdseye		
Henry Ford		
Find 3 bold words and write their glossary definitions.		
Here are the pronunciations for three words. Write the word and the page on which you found it.		
ur-buh-nuh-ZAY-shun		
in-dus-tree-uh-luh- ZAY-shun		
byu-RAH-kruh-see		

The teacher begins the lesson by showing students several pages of a chapter book they have recently read and several pages from the social studies book.

> "I know you haven't had time to read these pages but which one do you think is a story and which one is information?"

The class quickly decides that the one with no pictures is the story and the one with "all the pictures" is information. The teacher then flips through the pages of the social studies text and asks them besides pictures, what else is different about the informational text. She leads her students to notice that the social studies text contains maps, charts, bold words, and headings.

> "We call these special things that informational text has but story text doesn't usually have informational text features. Today we are going to look at this chapter in our social studies book and see how much we can learn from these special text features. We are going to go on a scavenger hunt in our book and see how much information we can find just by focusing on pictures, captions, graphs, charts, bold words, and other special features of informational text."

The teacher hands out one copy of the social studies book to each trio and asks them to turn to page 541.

> "Now we are going to go on a scavenger hunt in our social studies books. We are going to use the visuals and other features of the book to find answers to questions. Just as in our classroom scavenger hunt, you will have a limited amount of time and probably won't be able to find everything. At

the end of 20 minutes, we will come together and see what you found and determine the winner. I am going to do a few for you to get you started and then the 20 minutes will start."

She hands the Great Depression Scavenger Hunt to the student who is the most fluent writer in each trio. She reads the first question aloud and then says:

"I see a picture of Louis Armstrong at the top of page 542 and he has a trumpet. I will write *trumpet* in this box and p. 542 in the next box."

Question	Your answer	Where did you find answer?
What instrument did Louis Armstrong play?	trumpet	photo, p. 542

"You don't have to go in order on a scavenger hunt and I see the answer to another question right here so I will fill that one in."

What is the first major heading in this chapter?	New Forms of Expression	p. 542

"The writer in each trio should fill in these two answers on your sheet. Now, help me do two more and then I will turn you loose to find the rest of the answers. Who can find the answer to the second question?"

Someone quickly locates the photo of the dog and reads the caption that accompanies the photo. The teacher and the writer in each trio fill in this answer.

What was the name of the dog on RCA's label?	Nipper	caption, p. 543

"Good, now go to the very bottom or the sheet. The word is written the way it is pronounced. We need to find that word and figure out what it is. Help me find it. The word and page are quickly found and everyone records this answer."

byu-RAH-kruh-see	bureaucracy	p. 549

The class now understands what to do and is eager to get started. The teacher says, "You have 20 minutes to find as many answers as you can. The time begins now!" and starts a timer. The students quickly and eagerly get busy finding answers and writing them down. The teacher circulates and reminds one trio that they also need to include the page number where they found the information. For 20 minutes, the classroom is filled with "good noise" as students work to beat the clock.

The timer sounds and the teacher lets students finish the one they are writing and then demands that all pencils be put down. Together, the class checks the answer to each question, looking at the visual or special feature that provided the answer. As they look at each feature, they discuss it and the teacher gets students to explain how each special feature—maps, bar graphs, highlighted words, etc.—provides them with the answers they were seeking. Each team totals their points and after those points are double-checked by the teacher, there is a three-way tie. All three teams cheer and enjoy their bragging rights!

Great Depression Scavenger Hunt
Completed Sheet

Use the visuals and other special text features to answer these questions. Indicate where you found the answers. You have 20 minutes to find as many answers as you can. Your team will get one point for every correct answer and another point for telling where you found the answer.

Question	Your answer	Where did you find answer?
What instrument did Louis Armstrong play?	trumpet	photo, p. 542
What was the name of the dog on RCA's label?	Nipper	caption, p. 543
What was the name of a Charlie Chaplin movie?	The Kid	poster, p. 543
How many Ford cars were sold in 1920? In 1929? (2 pts.)	2,000,000 in 1920 4,500,000 in 1929	picture graph, p. 545
What type of new buildings were built in New York City in the 1920s?	skyscrapers	photo, caption, p. 546
Which year had the most business failures?	1931	bar graph, p. 547
About how many people lost their jobs in 1933?	13,000,000	line graph, p. 547
Which 5 states were in the Dust Bowl region? (5 pts.)	Colorado, Texas, Kansas, Oklahoma, New Mexico	map, p. 548
Which president began the New Deal programs?	Franklin Roosevelt	photo, caption, p. 549
In what year did Charles Lindbergh fly across the Atlantic?	1927	time line, p. 549
What is the 5th step in assembling a car in Henry Ford's factory?	Wheels and radiators are attached	diagram, p. 544
What is the first major heading in this chapter?	New Forms of Expression	p. 542
What is the last major heading in this chapter?	The New Deal	p. 548

Question	Your answer	Where did you find answer?
Use the index to decide on what page you will find information about:		
Herbert Hoover		p. 548
Clarence Birdseye		p. 546
Henry Ford		p. 544, 545
Find 3 bold words and write their glossary definition.	stock market: a place where people can buy and sell shares in a business	R 73
	depression: a time of little economic growth when there are few jobs and people have little money	R 66
	consumer goods: products made for personal use	R 65
Here are the pronunciations for three words. Write the word and the page on which you found it.		
ur-buh-nuh-ZAY-shun	urbanization	p. 546
in-dus-tree-uh-luh-ZAY-shun	industrialization	p. 545
byu-RAH-kruh-see	bureaucracy	p. 549

English Language Learners

All your students will benefit from learning to mine the graphics for everything they can learn from all the visuals. If you have children who are learning English, the visuals are a gold mine. The photos and illustrations accompanied by captions and labels will allow them to add multiple words to their English vocabularies. Once they learn how to interpret maps, graphs, diagrams, and charts, they can gain a huge amount of information from a very small number of words. All your students will comprehend what they read better if they always study the visuals first. English language learners may not yet be able to read the connected text in science and social studies texts but they can learn from these texts if you show them how huge amounts of information are portrayed by the visuals.

Common Core Connections: Preview-Predict-Confirm, Text Feature Scavenger Hunts

Common Core recognizes the importance of students using the special features of informational text as aides to comprehension. Reading Standard 5 specifies that elementary students should know and use special features, including headings, tables of contents, bold print, glossaries, and indexes. Reading Standard 7 specifies that students be able to use and interpret illustrations, charts, graphs, diagrams, and other visuals. The *Preview-Predict-Confirm* and *Text Features Scavenger Hunts* lesson frameworks also help students meet Reading Standard 4, which requires students to be able to determine the meaning of general academic and domain-specific words.

Teaching Preview-Predict-Confirm Lessons

- Select 12–15 visuals from a text, including any maps, charts, and diagrams. Scan these into a presentation or cover the words (except for labels, captions, etc. included in visuals). Assign your students to trios, making sure to have a strong reader/writer in each trio. Write the topic word in the center of the 30-box sheet and tear paper of three different colors into thirds on which they can write their common, unique, and most interesting word.
- Tell students the purpose for the lesson. Point out that by studying the visuals before you read informational text, you can make connections to what you already know and predict some words that you might see and some questions the text will answer.
- Use the "I Do and You Watch" and "I Do and You Help" procedures for the first visuals so that students will understand what they are expected to do. Show the remaining visuals and give trios 20 seconds to talk about each.
- Give trios a sheet with 30 boxes and the topic in the middle box. Hand the sheet to the fastest writer in the group and ask that student to be the recorder. Tell them that they have 8 minutes to try to fill up the boxes with words they think will be in the text.
- After 8 minutes, give each trio three different colored strips of paper. Give trios 2 minutes to choose a common word, a word they think all the other groups will also have; a unique word,

a word they don't think any other group will have; and the word they are most interested in learning more about. Have them write the words with a marker on the designated color strip, big enough so that everyone can see them when the class reconvenes. After 2 minutes, gather the class together. Have everyone hold up their paper with the word they think is common and see how many other trios did indeed include that word on their list. Next have groups hold up their unique word and determine if that word is truly unique to that group. If students ask, "What does regurgitate mean?" let the group with that word define the word. Finally, have each group display the word they are most interested in.

- Give trios one copy of the text and ask them to read it together. Have them put a "star" on each word on their sheet that actually occurred. When groups finish before others, have them look back through the text and choose five words they wish they had thought of and write these five words on the back of their sheets.
- Convene the class and discuss which words occurred in the text and their reasoning for choosing words they should have thought of.

Teaching Text Feature Scavenger Hunt Lessons

- Create scavenger hunt questions that focus your students' attention on all the special features of the text you have chosen.
- Use the "I Do and You Watch" step to model for your students how to talk about the visuals and choose words or find answers to the scavenger hunt questions. Let students help you complete one or two more. Have students meet in trios and give them 20 minutes to search for answers to the scavenger hunt questions.
- When the timer sounds, gather your students and have children share answers and where they found them. As their attention is directed to each special feature, have them explain how that special feature works and how it helps them comprehend the text.
- Tally up the points for each trio and cheer for the winners!

Summary

This common-sense notion that "more" results in better reading, writing, and content learning is supported by numerous research studies. Many studies have found that using effective instructional strategies in vocabulary or comprehension can improve student learning of subject matter (Hattie, 2009).

Comprehending informational text requires the same word identification accuracy and fluency, meanings for key words, and comprehension strategies required for comprehending stories. In addition, students need to do close reading and draw inferences so that they can learn the facts and details that make up informational text. They need to be able to follow information presented in the three common text structures and use the special features of informational text. *Guess Yes or No* and *Find It or Figure It Out* are lesson frameworks designed to teach students to do the close reading and inference making required to learn the facts and details that comprise informational text. Students can learn to follow and organize information presented in the descriptive, sequential, and comparative text structures by constructing *Main Idea Trees, Time Lines,* and *Compare/Contrast Bubbles*. *Preview-Predict-Confirm* and *Text Features Scavenger Hunts* teach students to use the visuals and other special features of informational text.

How Well Does Your Instruction Help All Children Learn to Comprehend Informational Text?

1. Do I teach my students how to make inferences when reading informational text and support these inferences with evidence?
2. Do I teach my students how to organize information when reading descriptive text that has several main ideas about one topic?
3. Do I teach my students how to organize information when reading text in which the sequence of events is important?
4. Do I teach my students how to organize information when two ideas or topics are being compared and contrasted?
5. Do I provide lessons that focus my students' attention on how to use the visuals and other special features of informational text?
6. Do I use the gradual release of responsibility procedures to provide scaffolding for my students in the initial stages of learning and move them toward independence?

9

Writing

IMAGINE that you come upon someone who is sitting, pen in hand or fingertips poised over a keyboard, staring at a blank page or blank screen. When you ask, "What are you doing?" the person will often respond, "I'm *thinking!*" Continue to observe, and you will see the person move into the writing phase eventually, but this writing will not be continuous. There will be constant pauses. If you are rude enough to interrupt during one of these pauses to ask "What are you doing?" the writer will again probably respond, "I'm *thinking!*"

Eventually, the writer will finish the writing, or rather the first draft of the writing. The writer may put the writing away for a while or may ask someone, "Would you take a look at this and tell me what you think?" Later, the writer will return to the writing to revise and edit. Words will be changed, and paragraphs will be added, moved, or deleted. Again, the writer will pause from time to time during this after-writing phase. If you ask what the writer is doing during this phase, you will get the familiar response: "I'm *thinking!*"

We offer this common scenario as proof that the essence of writing is thinking and that even the most naive writer knows this basic truth. Because writing is thinking and because learning requires thinking, students who write as they learn will think more and thus will learn more.

In addition to the fact that writing is thinking, writing is hard! It is complex. There are many things to think about at the same time. There are such big issues as:

- What do I want to say?
- How can I say it so that people will believe it?
- How can I say it so that people will want to read it?

In addition to these big issues, there are a host of smaller but still important issues:

- How can I begin my writing in a way that sets up my ideas and grabs the reader's attention?
- Which words will best communicate these feelings and thoughts?
- What examples can I use?
- Do I need to clarify here or include more details?
- How can I end it?
- Now, I have to think of a good title!

As if these grand and less grand issues are not enough, there are also a number of small details to worry about. Sometimes, these are taken care of during the after-writing phase, but often writers think about them as they write. Some examples include:

- I wonder if this sentence should begin a new paragraph?
- Do I capitalize the word *state* when it refers to North Carolina?
- How do you spell *Beijing?*
- Does the comma go inside or outside the quotation mark?

We do not offer this sampling of a few of the "balls" writers have to keep in the air as they perform the difficult juggling act of writing in order to discourage you. Rather, we offer them to convince you that students need instruction, guidance, support, encouragement, and acceptance if they are going to be willing and able participants in writing.

To become the very best writers, children need two kinds of writing instruction. First, all children need to engage in some writing in which they select the topics and decide how they will write about those topics. Most teachers organize their classrooms in a Writer's Workshop fashion to provide children with opportunities to write on their self-selected topics and help them learn how to write, edit, revise, and publish. Second, children need to engage in focused writing lessons in which they learn to do specific types of writing. The Common Core Writing Standards require elementary students to write narratives, informative/explanatory texts, and opinion pieces. Writing Standards 6, 7, and 8 require elementary students to conduct research projects that require them to integrate their informational reading and writing skills. This chapter will describe instruction during the Writer's Workshop time and a lesson framework for focused writing.

Writer's Workshop

Writer's Workshop (Calkins, 1994; Graves, 1995) is the term most commonly used to describe the process of children choosing their own topics and then writing, revising, editing, and publishing. In Writer's Workshop, you try to simulate as closely as possible the atmosphere in which real writers write and to help children see themselves as "real authors."

Usually, Writer's Workshop begins with a mini-lesson during which you model writing. Next, the children write. As the children write, you conference with them and coach them on how to revise, edit, and publish. Writer's Workshop usually concludes with an Author's Chair, in which children read their writing and get responses from the other "writers" in the room.

Writer's Workshop can be done in all elementary grades. Although the basic principles are the same, the focus for the mini-lessons and the amount of revising, editing, and publishing will be quite different. Regardless of grade, if you want to create willing writers, you must begin the year by emphasizing meaning and de-emphasizing mechanics and perfection. Because writing is hard and complex, children who see the goal as producing a certain number of perfect sentences will not write willingly and will only do the bare minimum needed to get by.

You want to establish in the first few weeks of school that the most important thing about writing in your classroom is *what* the writing says—not how perfectly it says it. To demonstrate this, teachers begin each school year by doing mini-lessons in which they focus on how you choose a topic and how you write the first draft as best you can. After the 8- to 10-minute mini-lesson in which the teacher writes what he or she "wants to tell," the teacher asks the students to write what *they* want to tell. As the children write, the teacher circulates and encourages them by making comments such as:

> "Did you really go to camp this summer? I went to camp every summer when I was your age. I think I will write about that one day soon."
>
> "Oh, you are interested in dinosaurs. I bet lots of the other students like dinosaurs, too. They will be eager to hear what you have learned about them."
>
> "I watched that TV program last night, too. It is one of my favorites."

When a child writes one sentence and has an "I wrote a sentence—that's all I know" attitude, the teacher barrages him or her with questions related to the sentence. Imagine that Tommy is sitting there with an "all done" expression on his face and has written:

> I got a dog.

English Language Learners

If you have ever tried to learn a second language, you know that learning to read a different language is hard and learning to write it is even harder. Knowing that you care more about their ideas than about the correctness with which they can write them frees up all your children to write. Your students who are learning English will attempt writing if you respond with enthusiasm to their ideas. Being willing to write in your classroom is especially important for these children because writing is one more avenue for them to learn and become literate in English.

The teacher asks Tommy lots of questions about his dog:

> "Do you really have a dog?"
>
> "Is your dog a male or a female?"
>
> "What's her name?"
>
> "Is she a big dog or a little dog?"
>
> "What color is she?"
>
> "Do you take her for walks?"
>
> "Where did you get her?"

Tommy eagerly answers the questions and volunteers more information about his dog. When the teacher and Tommy have had an animated discussion about the dog, the teacher moves on to another student after prodding Tommy to write more about his dog:

> "You sure have a lot to tell about your dog. I bet other kids will wish they had thought of writing about their dog when you share what you are writing about your dog."

As you circulate, remember the message you are trying to convey to your students:

> "The most important thing about writing in this classroom is *what* you write. I am eager to hear what you are telling me in your writing. Your classmates will also want to know about what you are writing."

Inevitably, as you circulate, someone will ask you to spell a word. How you respond to this request will determine the progress you can make in your Writer's Workshop for the rest of the year. If you spell words for children now, you will never be able to pull away from them and use the time while they are writing to hold conferences with individuals and groups about their writing. Consider the following responses to the "Can you spell *dinosaurs?*" request:

> "Yes, I can now, but I couldn't when I was your age and I don't want you to get too hung up on spelling when you're doing your first-draft writing. I want you to write what you want to tell—not just what you can spell. Let's stretch out *dinosaurs* together and put down the letters you think are there. You will be able to read it, and that's all that matters now. In a few weeks, we will start publishing some of our best pieces, and then we will fix up all the spelling to make them easy for everyone to read."
>
> "I'm sorry, but teachers aren't allowed to spell words for kids when they are first drafting, but I can help you stretch it out."
>
> "Dinosaurs—hmmm … I think I see the word *dinosaurs* in the title of that book over there."

However you accomplish it, make it clear to your students that you will help them stretch out words and point them to places in the room where they can find words, but on first draft, you cannot spell words for them. At the same time, assure them that if these are pieces they choose to publish, you will enthusiastically help them "fix" the spelling.

Limit the amount of time your children write for the first few weeks of school. Eventually, you want them writing for 15 to 20 minutes, but it is better to start with a smaller amount of time, perhaps 6 or 7 minutes, so that they do not get too discouraged and bored if they are not particularly good writers. Some teachers use a timer and increase the amount of time in one-minute intervals as the children become more able to sustain their writing.

When the time is up, circle your students and ask who wants to read or tell about what they have written. You may want to single out some of the children with affirming statements such as:

> "Carl has a big dog named Tammy. Carl, tell us more about Tammy."
>
> "Josh is a big dinosaur fan. He hasn't finished writing all he wants to about dinosaurs, but perhaps he will tell or read what he has written so far."
>
> "Jamal and I like the same TV show. I wonder how many of you like it, too."

Be sure you let your students read or tell what they are writing. Some children do not like to write but they almost all like to "tell," and soon they will be writing eagerly so they have a chance to tell during the sharing time. Again, keep in mind your goal for getting Writer's Workshop off to a successful start. You want the children to look forward to the writing time and you want them to see writing as a way of telling about themselves and the things that are important to them.

Make a point of asking some of your students to share writing they have not finished yet. Tell them that during Writer's Workshop, we do not usually start writing a new piece every day and that sometimes it takes a week or more to finish a piece if we are writing about something we really care about or know a lot about.

Tips for a Successful Launch of Your Writer's Workshop

The Mini-Lesson

Begin each Writer's Workshop with an 8- to 10-minute mini-lesson in which you write and the children watch. Include mini-lessons in which you model and think aloud about how you decide what to write about:

- "When I saw Carl writing about his dog Tammy, it reminded me of the dog I had when I was your age. I think I will write about Serena today."
- "Yesterday, we were reading about the pioneers. I am going to write what I think it would have been like to be a pioneer."
- "In science yesterday, we did that experiment with balloons. I think I will write about that."
- "Just before the buses came yesterday, we had that huge thunderstorm. My cat hates thunderstorms. I will tell you what my cat does when it thunders."
- "I went to the football game at Wake this weekend. I saw several of you there. I am going to tell you what I liked best about the game."
- "I have a lot of things I want to tell you about, and I think I might forget some of them. Today, instead of writing about one thing, I am going to make a list of all the things I might want to write about." (Refer to your "Things I want to write about list" over the next several weeks before you write, and add to it when you get good ideas from what your students are writing. Encourage your students to make their own lists, if they want to.)

Also, model for students what you do about spelling:

- Look up at your word wall periodically, and model how using it helps you spell.

  "*Because* is a tricky word. I am glad we have *because* on the word wall."

  "*Brook* rhymes with *look,* so I can use *look* to help me spell it."

  "*Talked* is our word wall word *talk* with *ed* on the end."

- Use other print in the room to spell words.

  "I can spell *Wednesday* by looking at the calendar."
  "*Hydrogen* is on our science board."
  "*Pioneers* is on the cover of the book I read to you this morning."

- Stop and stretch out a word, putting down the letters you think are there.

  "I can spell *ridiculous* now, but let me show you how I would have stretched it out when I was your age."

- Model for students how you add on to a piece you have not finished:

  "Yesterday, I was telling you about my two grandmothers, and I only had time to describe my mama's mother. I am going to reread what I wrote yesterday to get my thoughts back and then tell you about my dad's mother."

- "This is the third day I have been writing about our trip to the museum. I am going to reread what I wrote the first two days and hope I can finish this up today."

The Students Write

- Increase the time gradually, starting with a small amount of time that all your students can handle. Many teachers use a timer and increase writing one minute at a time.
- Circulate and encourage your writers by "oohing" and "ahing" about their topics. Ask questions of students who have just written a sentence or two. Comment regularly that they have "given you a good idea for your writing." If you are keeping a writing topics list, go right over and add it to your list.
- Do not spell words for students but help them stretch them out, and use the word wall and other print in the room to find words.

The Students Share

- Let volunteers tell or read what they have written.
- Spotlight some children whom you interacted with as they were writing.
- Let children ask questions of their fellow writers.
- Point out children who are going to be "adding on" to their writing tomorrow.
- Encourage children to find writing topics during this sharing by asking questions of one another. How many of them have dogs? Grandmas? Went to the football game? Ever broke a bone?
- Add topics to your writing list, inspired by what they share.

Adding Editing to Writer's Workshop

Early in the year at every grade level, we have three major writing goals we want to accomplish. We want children to get in the habit of writing each day and coming up with their own topics, based on what they want to tell. We want them to learn to use the supports for spelling words displayed in the classroom and how to stretch out the big words they need to be able to write what they really want to tell. Finally, we want them to realize that they can take several days to write a piece if they have a lot to tell and that in order to add on, they need to read what they have already written.

When all the children are writing willingly, if not well, we begin teaching them how to edit their writing. Here is how one teacher described the first editing lesson.

One Teacher's First Editing Lesson

As I was getting ready to write one morning, I told the children that soon we would be publishing some of their best pieces and, before we did so, we needed to know how to edit. I then wrote on a sheet of chart paper:

Our Editor's Checklist
1. Do all my sentences make sense?

I explained to the children that one thing editors always read for is to make sure that all the sentences make sense. Sometimes, writers leave out words or forget to finish a sentence, and then the sentences don't make sense. I told the children, "Each day, after I write my piece, you can be my editors and help me decide if all my sentences make sense." I then wrote a piece and purposely left out a word. The children who were, as always, reading along as I wrote and often anticipating my next word, noticed my mistake immediately. When I finished writing, I said, "Now let's read my piece together and see if all my sentences make sense. Give me a 'thumbs up' if my sentence makes sense." The children and I read one sentence at a time, and when we got to the sentence where I had left out a word, we decided that the sentence didn't make sense because my mind had gotten ahead of my marker and I had left out a word. I wrote the word in with a different-colored marker and thanked the children for their good editing help.

After I wrote my piece, the children all went off to do their own writing. As they wrote, I circulated around and encouraged them. When the writing time was up, I pointed to the editor's checklist we had just begun. I said, "Be your own editor now. Read your paper and give yourself a 'thumbs up' if each sentence makes sense. If you didn't finish a sentence or left a word out, take your red pen and fix it." I watched as the children did their best to see if their sentences made sense and noticed a few children writing things with their red pens.

Every day after that when I wrote, I left a word out or didn't finish a sentence. The children delighted in being my editor and helping me make all my sentences make sense. Every day when their writing time was up, I pointed to the checklist and they read their own sentences for sense. They didn't find every problem, but they all knew what they were trying to do. After a few weeks, I noticed almost everyone picking up their red pens and glancing up at the checklist as soon as the writing time ended.

Now, I am about to add to our checklist a second thing to read for. I will add:

2. Do all my sentences have ending punc?

From now on, the children will read my sentences and give me a thumbs up if the sentence makes sense and another thumbs up if it has punc (more fun to say than punctuation!) at the end. When the writing time is up, I will remind them that we are at the "two thumbs up" editing stage and that they should read their sentences for sense and ending punc just as they read mine.

Build Your Editor's Checklist Gradually

The items on the editor's checklist are not just there so that children will find them as they edit. The goal is that by focusing on the checklist items as children check the teacher's writing at the end of mini-lessons and by asking children to do a quick self-edit of their own writing each day, children will begin to incorporate these conventions as they write their first drafts. The question of when to add another item to the checklist can be answered by observing the first-draft writing of the children. If most of the children, most of the time, apply the current checklist items as they write their first drafts, it is time to add another item to the checklist.

Developing your editor's checklist is easy if you let your observations of children's first-draft writing determine what is added, the order in which it is added, and the speed with which it is added. Here are two examples of editors' checklists—one for primary and one for intermediate grades:

Common Core Connections: Editing

Writing Standard 5 requires students to edit and peer edit. It specifies that they should learn to edit for the mechanics and conventions included in Language Standards 1 and 2. Language Standard 1 specifies the grammar and usage expectations for writing at each grade level. Language Standard 2 specifies the capitalization, punctuation, and spelling expectations. You can use these expectations to help you determine what you need to include on your editor's checklist.

Our Editor's Checklist

1. Do all my sentences make sense?
2. Do all my sentences have ending punc?
3. Do all my sentences start with caps?
4. Are the words I need to check for spelling circled?
5. Do names and places start with caps?
6. Do all my sentences stay on topic?

Editor's Checklist

1. Do all the sentences make sense and stay on topic?
2. Do all the sentences start with caps and end with correct punc?
3. Are the words I need to check for spelling circled?
4. Do names, places, holidays, months, and days of the week start with caps?
5. Do words in a series have commas?
6. Do quotes have correct punc?

Teach Children to Peer Edit

Once children have had lots of experience editing the teacher's piece each day, they can learn how to edit with partners. You can introduce this by choosing a child to be your partner and role-playing how he or she will help with the editing. Here is how one teacher taught students to peer edit.

A Peer-Editing Mini-Lesson

I began by telling the class that we would soon start choosing some of their best pieces to publish and that once they had each chosen a piece, the first step in the publishing process would be to choose a friend to help with the editing:

> "Boys and girls, we are going to pretend today that I am one of the children in the class. I am getting ready to publish a piece, and I will choose one of you to be my editor."

I then wrote a short piece on the overhead as the children watched. Instead of letting the whole class read the sentences aloud and do "thumbs up or down," as we had been doing,

I chose one child to be my editor. As the children watched, my editor and I read my sentences one at a time and edited for the four things on the checklist. As we read each sentence, we decided if it made sense and had ending punc and a beginning cap. Next, we looked at the words and decided if any of them needed to be circled because we thought they were not spelled correctly. Here is what the edited piece looked like:

Polar Bears

Polar bears live in the arctic which is one of the coldest places on earth. Polar bears are the largest bears. Male polar bears are about 10 feet tall and weigh 1,100 pounds. Polar bears are fast movers, they can run 30 miles an hour. They are good swimmers too. Polar bears have a lot of fur and blubber to keep them warm. Polar bears eat fish, seals, careboo, berries and seaweed. People used to hunt polar bears, they were almost extink. only about 5,000 were left. Now, there are laws against hunting polar bears and there are about 40,000. Polar bears are amazeing animals.

For the next several days, I followed the procedure of choosing a child to be my editor and doing the partner-editing in front of the children. When I thought most of the children understood how to help each other edit for the items on the checklist, I partnered them up, assigning partners of similar writing ability to work together, and had each pair choose a piece and edit it together. I had several more peer-editing practice sessions before turning the children loose to peer edit without my supervision.

English Language Learners

Take special care in thinking about who to partner with your English language learners. Choose your most nurturing students and help them understand the supportive and encouraging role you want them to take when helping their English language learning peers to edit their writing.

Editing Tips: Editing = Fixing Up Your Writing

- Don't begin editing instruction until children are writing willingly and fluently—if not well!
- Observe children's writing to decide what mechanics and conventions they can do automatically and what things you need to focus on.
- Begin your checklist with one item. Let children edit your piece for this one item every day for several days.
- When the writing time is up, ask students to be their own editors. Praise their efforts at self-editing, but don't expect them to find everything.
- Add a second item when most of your students do the first item correctly most of the time. In your mini-lesson, sometimes make a #1 error and sometimes a #2 error—but do not make more than two errors in total.
- Continue to add items gradually, using the same procedure to teach each.
- Teach children to peer edit by role-playing, and then provide supervised practice as children peer edit with writers of similar ability.

Adding Conferencing, Publishing, and Author's Chair to Writer's Workshop

After your students understand how to edit and partner-edit with an editing checklist and are writing for about 15 minutes each day, you may want to add conferencing, publishing, and Author's Chair to your Writer's Workshop. (You should not wait until the editor's checklist is complete before beginning this, and, in fact, you will continue to add items to the checklist and do mini-lessons on editing conventions all year long.) Once publishing begins, you will spend the writing time holding conferences with your students to help them get their pieces ready to publish. (Since you cannot be in two places at one time, this means you will no longer be circulating and encouraging children as they write. Do not begin publishing until almost all your children are coming up with topics, spelling words for themselves, and writing willingly.)

Author's Chair

When children begin publishing, most teachers also shift from the informal circle sharing that has been happening each day at the end of Writer's Workshop to an Author's Chair format. One-fifth of the children share each day. They can share anything they have written since their last day in the Author's Chair. Of course, when they have published a piece, they share that. But they can also share a first draft or work in progress. After each child has read, he or she calls on class members to tell things they liked about the piece. The author can also ask if anyone has any questions and elicit suggestions to make the piece better. During Author's Chair, the focus is exclusively on the message that the author is trying to convey.

Here again, the role of the teacher model is extremely important. Useful comments include:

"I love the way you described …"

"I wondered why the character …"

"Your ending really surprised me."

"I learned a lot of new information about …"

"I loved the part about …"

"I can tell you know a lot about …"

When assigning children to days to share in the Author's Chair, you may want to assign one of your best and one of your most struggling writers for each day. The best writer might get an extra minute to share because these children often write longer, more complex pieces. Take a minute before Author's Chair each day to check in with your struggling writer and make sure he or she has selected something to share and is prepared to read or tell about it.

Publishing

Most elementary teachers tell children that they can choose a piece to publish when they have written three or four good pieces. They then teach mini-lessons in which they role-play and model, choosing a piece to publish and taking it through the process. Once the publishing part of the Writer's Workshop has been established, students will be at all different stages of the writing process each day. Those children who have just finished publishing a piece will be working to produce new first drafts, from which they will pick another one to publish. Other children will have picked a piece to publish and will be editing it with a friend. Some children will be having a writing conference with the teacher. Other children will have had their piece "fixed" during the writing conference and will be busy copying, typing, and illustrating the final product.

Since you can't help everyone publish at the same time, you may want to begin the publishing cycle by choosing five or six children to publish. This will allow you to conference with these children while the others continue to produce first drafts. Once these children are at the copying/typing/illustrating stage, you can continue to choose more children to begin the publishing process, until all the children have published something. From then on, the children will know that they can choose a piece to publish when they have three or four good first drafts. Many teachers post a chart like this to remind children of the publishing steps:

Common Core Connections: Publishing

Writing Standard 6 requires students to use technology to publish and share their writing. Third-graders are expected to use keyboarding skills and fifth-graders are expected to demonstrate their keyboarding skills by producing a minimum of two pages in a single sitting!

English Language Learners

If your children who are just learning English are hesitant to share in the Author's Chair, offer to be their voice. Let them tell you what they were writing and then use your voice to share this with the whole class.

Steps for Publishing

1. Pick one piece that you want to publish.
2. Choose a friend and partner-edit your piece for the items on the checklist.
3. Sign up for a writing conference.
4. Work with your teacher in a conference to edit your piece and fix spelling.
5. Copy or type your piece, making all the corrections.
6. Illustrate your piece.

The Writing Conference

Be sure that each child edits his or her piece with a friend before signing up for a writing conference with you. Children, of course, are at all different stages of understanding about writing and how to edit, and some children are much better editors than others. Peer editing for the checklist items is not perfect, and teachers often find things that should have been changed that weren't (and things that were changed that shouldn't have been!). But all the children become much better at being editors of their friends' and their own pieces as the year goes on, and they get in the habit of trying to edit before they publish and not leaving all the work for the teacher.

After the piece has been edited with a friend using the checklist, you should hold an individual conference with the writer and "fix everything!" Your goal in publishing is to have children experience the pride of being authors and having others read and enjoy their writing. This cannot happen if the final piece is not very readable. So, before the child goes to the publishing phase, sit down with that child and do a final edit. Fix the spellings of words, add punctuation and capitalization, clarify sentences that do not make sense, delete sentences that are totally off the topic, and do whatever else is necessary to help the child produce a "masterpiece" of writing!

You can generally do the "fixing" right on the first draft with a different-colored pen. To make this easier, have children write all their first drafts using every other line on the paper, leaving blank lines so that editing can occur. (Of course, some children can't write on every other line but most can, and they all get better at it as the year goes on.) If something must be inserted and cannot be clearly written between the lines, write it on a separate piece of paper and mark the insertion point. You should read each edited piece with each child, making sure he or she can read anything inserted and stopping to notice where to add punctuation, change spelling, and make other needed changes.

Give Additional Support to Your Most Struggling Writers

In almost every class, once you begin publishing, you will have a few children whose writing is really not "editable." (Like love, this is hard to describe, but you will recognize it when you see it!) You generally should not begin publishing until almost all the children are writing something "readable"—but *almost all* leaves a few children whose pieces are collections of letters with a few recognizable words and very few spaces to help you decipher the letters from the words! You might say these children simply aren't ready to publish and that they should just continue producing first drafts. But the message that these children will get from being left out of the publishing process is that, just as they thought, they "can't write!" Once you begin publishing, you need to include everyone in the process. Some children will publish more pieces than others. Some authors are more prolific than others! The goal is not for everyone to have the same number—and in fact, you should not count or let the children count. The goal is, however, for everyone to feel like a real writer because he or she has some published pieces.

Once you begin publishing, you should work with the most avid writers first, but when most of them have pieces published and are on their second rounds of first drafts, you should gather together the children who have not yet published anything. Help them choose pieces they want to publish and then give them the option of reading or telling what they want to say. Then, sit down individually with these children and help them construct their pieces. Get them to tell you again what they want to say. As they tell, write down their sentences by hand and later type them on the computer. After these children's sentences have been written, read the sentences with them several times to make sure they know what they have said. Then cut the sentences apart and have the children illustrate each one and put them all together into a book! They—like everyone else—are now real published authors, and they will approach their second round of first-draft writing with renewed vigor—confident that they, too, can write!

It is important to note here that you would not give this kind of support to the majority of your children. If more than a few children need this support, you are not ready to pull away during their writing time to hold individual and group conferences. But when most are ready and only a few lag behind, the solution just suggested works quite well in most classrooms and provides a big boost for your most struggling writers.

Keep the Publishing Process Simple

There are numerous ways to publish, but you don't want to spend too much of your or your children's time in publishing. In many schools, groups of volunteers create "skeleton books" for children to publish in. They cut sheets of paper in half and staple or bind them with bright-colored covers into books of varying numbers of pages. Children write (or type on the computer and cut and tape) their sentences on the pages and add illustrations. In other classrooms, the pieces are typed on the computer (by the child or an assistant/ volunteer) and then illustrated (with drawings, photos, or clip art) and displayed on the writing bulletin board. A variety of computer programs are available that make the publishing process a much less onerous one and help children produce professional-looking products. In many classrooms, children publish their pieces on the Web to share with the larger world.

English Language Learners

The procedure just described is exactly what you should use to help your children learning English publish their writing and feel proud of their products.

Tips for Publishing, Conferencing, and Author's Chair

- Don't begin publishing until most children are writing "editable" pieces and can edit for the items on the checklist.
- Don't let students publish every piece. Most of the learning in Writer's Workshop takes place as children participate in the mini-lesson and write their first drafts. Publishing is the "icing on the cake."
- Be sure that each student edits with a partner for the items on the checklist before conferencing with you.
- During the conference, fix whatever needs fixing—including things not yet on the checklist. Every child should produce a readable published piece to be proud of.
- Everyone does not need to publish the same number of pieces, but everyone does need to publish some pieces. Provide extra support so that your struggling writers can be proud of their writing and their status as authors.
- Let one-fifth of your children share each day in the Author's Chair. Model positive comments and good questions, and allow each author to choose one classmate to ask a question and one classmate to tell something he or she liked. When they have a new published piece, they will share that piece. Other days, they will share first drafts and even pieces they have not finished.

Adding Revising to Writer's Workshop

Editing is "fixing" your writing. *Revising* is making good writing *even better!* Because learning to do some basic editing is easier than learning to revise, teachers usually teach some editing rules first and then teach some revising strategies. After teachers have taught some revising strategies, students should revise their pieces before editing.

When you begin to teach revising, make sure your students understand that revising is not editing. *Editing* is fixing mistakes and making the writing easy for the reader to read. *Revising* is making the writing better—clearer—more interesting—more dramatic—more informative—more persuasive—more *something!* When a writer revises, he or she looks again at the writing, asking the essential question:

"How can I make this piece of writing *even better?*"

The word *even* in this question is important because it implies that the writing is good but can be even better! Using the phrase *"even better"* is part of the attitude adjustment your students may need to make about revising, since many children think that having to revise means you did not do a good job to begin with. All successful writers revise, and all published writing has been revised. Writers always begin revising by rereading their writing and thinking about how to make it *even better.*

Once they decide what is needed to make the meaning or clarity of their drafts even better, writers make revisions by adding, replacing, removing, or reordering. Sometimes they add, replace, or remove one or more words or phrases, or they reorder some words or phrases. Sometimes they add, replace, or remove one or more sentences or paragraphs, or they reorder some sentences or paragraphs. Occasionally, a writer will add, replace, or remove an entire section or reorder the sections that are already there.

To teach children how to revise, use the general revising strategies of adding, replacing, removing, and reordering. This will help them understand what revision is, how it is different from editing, and where to begin when trying to make the meaning of a selected piece of writing even better. As with editing, begin your revising instruction by teaching mini-lessons in which you select one of your writing pieces and revise it in front of the children. Of course, you want students to learn how to help each other revise, so you should teach some mini-lessons in which you pick a student to be your revising helper and role-play this peer revising as the other students watch. Next, partner up children with writers of similar ability and give them practice peer revising.

As with editing, revising strategies should be taught gradually, and when students have been taught only one strategy, they should be expected to use only that one strategy. As you conference with children getting ready to publish, remind them of the revising strategies you have taught so far and give them help implementing some of these with their pieces.

Steps for Publishing (Including Revising)

1. Pick one piece that you want to publish.
2. Choose a friend to help you revise.
3. Check your revisions with your teacher.
4. Partner-edit your piece for the items on the checklist.
5. Have a conference with your teacher to do a final edit.
6. Copy or type your piece, making all the corrections.
7. Illustrate your piece.

Teaching the Adding Revising Strategy

Adding is the easiest revising strategy, and thus you should teach it first. Children are often impressed with themselves when they write a long piece—and adding makes it even longer and more impressive! By starting with the adding revising strategy, you can capitalize on your students' affinity for length and start them off with a positive attitude toward revising.

If you have been writing on every other line during your mini-lessons and having your children write on every other line on their first drafts, adding just a word, phrase, or sentence will be easy to do and be seen right on the original piece. Adding longer sections will require cutting and taping—something children love to do and that also helps improve their attitude toward revising.

For your first adding mini-lesson, you may want to show students how adding words or phrases can make the meanings of their pieces clearer and more vivid. To do this mini-lesson, choose a piece you wrote recently. Tell the children that you want to revise this piece before you publish it and that one way to revise is to add a few words or phrases that will make the meaning clearer. Use a bright-colored marker and show children how you put a carat (^) and then insert a word or phrase in the empty line above at two or three different places to make what you have written better. Over the next several days, demonstrate adding words or phrases to revise with a few more of your pieces.

When you have done enough mini-lessons to be sure that most of your students understand how to revise by adding words or phrases, partner them so that children of

Walking My Puppy

Today, I went ^straight^ home from school to see my new

puppy. He came up to me and licked my ^whole^ face.

I ^quickly^ put his leash on and we went outside. We

saw a ^big, black^ dog. My puppy ran after the dog. The

dog ran away. Next he ran after a ^tiny^ squirrel.

The squirrel ran up a ^tall^ tree. Finally, he saw a

^gray^ cat. He ran after the cat. My dog ^just^ wanted to

play with the other animals but they all ^just^ ran

away.

relatively equal ability are working together. Ask each pair to choose pieces of their own writing and suggest words or phrases to each other that will make their writing clearer and more vivid. Give them brightly colored pens and christen them "revising pens." Collect the pens when children have finished revising their two papers and reserve them only for revising. The children will enjoy using these special pens, and this, too, will have a positive effect on their attitude toward revising.

As the children revise, go around and help the partners who seem to be having trouble adding words and phrases, as you have taught them in your mini-lessons. As you move around the room, monitoring and helping the partners, be on the lookout for particularly good additions. At the beginning of Author's Chair, take a few minutes and share some of the best revisions you have noticed.

Another way of making writing clearer and more vivid is to add dialogue. Again, take one of your pieces and use it as the first example. (You might want to plan ahead and write a piece with no dialogue but that would be improved by a few exact words so that you have a good example to use.) Tell the children that you want to revise this piece because after you wrote it, you realized that adding some dialogue—the words people or characters actually said—will make it "come alive." Use the same procedure that you used with adding words and phrases, and include a brief explanation of how quotations are punctuated.

Depending on the age and writing levels of your children, you may want to teach them how to revise by adding a missing part. To do this, write a first draft in which you purposely leave out some important information. Bring that piece out on the following day, and explain to the students that you realized you failed to include some very important information. As the students watch, cut your piece, write the new part on another piece of paper, and then tape it between the two parts of the original. Students of all ages will be intrigued by this idea that you can cut your writing piece and tape in a missing part. Encourage them to look at their own first drafts and find one that would be "even better" if it had more information. Then turn them loose with scissors and tape!

Teaching the Replacing Revising Strategy

Replacing is another revising strategy all writers use. While the adding strategy makes writing better by making it more elaborate and complete, the replacing strategy makes writing better by improving the quality of what is already there. As with adding, you can replace words, phrases, sentences, or a whole chunk of text. When replacing a small amount of text, use the special revising pens to cross out the text you want to improve and then write the new text clearly above it. When replacing large chunks of text in order to improve them, use the cut-and-tape procedure.

To prepare for your first replacing mini-lesson, write a first draft in which you purposely use as many "boring, tired, and common" words as you can. Don't tell the children your intent ahead of time. Just write it as you normally write during a mini-lesson. When you finish, have the class read it with you, and ask if they can think of any ways you can make your writing even better. Since you have already taught several lessons on revising by adding, children may suggest some words or phrases for you to add. It is all right to quickly add a few of the words suggested, but if no one suggests replacing some of your "overused" words, you will need to suggest it yourself in order to move your mini-lesson from the adding to the replacing strategy:

> "I notice that I have some common words here that don't create very vivid pictures. *Good,* for example, doesn't even begin to describe how wonderful the cookies were. I think I will cross out *good* and replace it with *scrumptious.*"

Continue replacing some of your boring, overused, or inexact words, eliciting suggestions from your students about which words need replacing and what you can use to replace them.

Just as with revising by adding, you probably will need to do several mini-lessons on replacing words or phrases before asking your students to use this strategy in their own papers. Again, when students try to apply this strategy to their own writing, have them work with partners as you move around helping individuals who are having trouble. Look for good examples of revision to share with everyone afterward.

"Show, don't tell" is a basic guideline for good writing. Unfortunately, many children (and adults!) are not sure what this guideline means. To teach your students what it means, you have to practice what you preach and *show* them how to "Show, don't tell," instead of taking the far easier road of *telling* them to "Show, don't tell!"

> ## My Birthday Party
>
> I had a ~~good~~ _wonderful_ time at my birthday party. It
>
> was a surprise party and I was surprised. My
>
> son, David, ~~came~~ _flew in_ from California. We went to
>
> a ~~good~~ _fancy_ restaurant and had a ~~good meal~~ _delicious dinner_. When
>
> we got home, I was ~~surprised~~ _amazed_ to see a new
>
> computer in the den. It was my birthday
>
> present and I ~~love~~ _adore_ it!

To teach children to replace *telling* words with words and sentences that *show,* you can use many of the procedures already described in this chapter. Write pieces in which you purposely tell rather than show, and then revise these pieces in mini-lessons with the children's help. You can also use paragraphs from the children's favorite authors as examples and rewrite them in mini-lessons by replacing the showing words with telling words and sentences. After identifying the places where the children wish the writer had shown them rather than told them, read the original and compare the telling version with the showing version. After several mini-lessons, partner the children and ask them to help each other find examples in their writing where they could make the writing come alive by replacing some of their telling words with showing words and sentences.

When the children understand how to replace boring and telling words with more interesting and showing words, you may want to teach them how to replace whole parts of their pieces. For most children, the first revision they do that replaces a chunk of text is when they make the beginning of that piece noticeably better. Your students need to understand that many authors routinely revise the beginning of a piece because once they have finished the piece, they realize what the beginning lacks.

Any writer can tell you that a good ending is hard to write! Children often solve the problem by stopping when they can't think of anything else to say and writing "The End."

Teaching students to revise by replacing the ending will help almost all of them to write better and more interesting endings.

> When my Grandpa died, I ~~was sad~~ ^moped around for a week,. One day,
>
> my mom asked me to take my Grandpa's dog
>
> for a walk. He ~~was happy to see me~~ ^jumped up and wagged his tail. We went ^when he saw me,
>
> for a long walk and ended up at the river. I
>
> threw sticks into the river and he swam in
>
> after them. When I took him back home,
>
> Grandma ~~was happy~~ ^smiled and thanked me,. I took Champ for a walk
>
> every day *and I felt better*. Walking Champ
>
> ^made me feel better and was ~~was fun and~~ something I could do for Grandpa!

To teach students to revise by changing the ending or beginning, you should once again contrive to write a piece in your mini-lesson that has a boring or not very informative beginning or ending. For the next day's mini-lesson, pull out your piece again,

Tips for Revising Beginnings and Endings

How to Make Your Beginning *Even Better*

- Include the background knowledge needed to understand the middle and end.
- If your piece is a story, be sure to describe the setting—time and place.
- Grab your reader's attention with an interesting question.
- Start with a real-life example.

How to Make Your Ending *Even Better*

- Answer any questions you posed in the beginning.
- Tie up all the "loose ends."
- Pose a question for your reader to think about.
- End with a surprise—but one that fits the rest of your piece.

and tell your students that after writing the piece, you realized how you needed to begin it—or you thought of a much better ending. Let them watch as you reread your ending or beginning, write a replacement, and then cut and tape the new part to the original piece. If you teach in a classroom in which you can write on the computer and have it projected on the screen, use the "Cut" and "Paste" functions on your computer to show your students how easy it is to replace text with the help of a word- processing program!

Teaching the Reordering and Removing Revising Strategies

Revising by *reordering* should not be taught until students can revise by adding and revise by replacing. Moreover, children cannot learn to revise by reordering until they have a firm sense of sequence and logical order, which many children do not develop until third grade.

Just as children like to add to their writing because it makes their pieces longer, they don't like to remove anything because they worked hard to write it and doing so shortens their pieces. Students are usually more willing to replace something than remove it. This is the reason that *removing* is the last of the four general revising strategies you should teach.

Often, however, when we finish writing something, we realize that something we included does not really add anything to our writing or distracts the reader from the point we are trying to make. None of us likes to delete the wonderful words we have written, but deleting or removing off-topic and distracting sentences or paragraphs is an essential revising strategy.

When your students are comfortable with revising by adding and replacing, you can teach reordering and removing just as you taught adding and replacing. Write some first drafts in which you purposely arrange things not in their logical sequence or include some extraneous information. Let students watch as you cut and reorder or remove sentences or paragraphs. Send them on a hunt for places in their writing they could make even better by reordering and removing, and provide guided practice with partners in using these strategies.

Revising Tips: Making Your Writing *Even Better*

- Look again at your writing. Pick a friend to look with you.
- Use special revising pens or cut and tape.
- Add:　　Words that make the writing more vivid or clearer
　　　　　Dialogue that makes the writing come alive
　　　　　Missing information

- Replace:　Boring words
　　　　　Telling with showing
　　　　　Beginnings that don't set up your piece or don't grab the reader's attention
　　　　　Endings that don't provide closure or are not very engaging

- Remove:　Sentences or paragraphs that don't stay on topic or distract the reader
- Reorder:　Sentences or paragraphs that are not in the right sequence

Revision is not an easy skill to learn, and although you want to teach children to revise and make sure they know how, you shouldn't expect a great deal of revision—particularly from first- and second-graders. The goal of revising should be to have children understand that meaning comes first—that authors often add, delete, or change things to make their writing more interesting, clear, or dramatic and that they should make whatever meaning changes they are going to make before they edit.

Focused Writing

Writer's Workshop is the appropriate venue for teaching students the writing strategies that apply to all writing. Simultaneously, students need to learn to produce specific types of writing. Common Core Writing Standards 1, 2, and 3 specify that elementary students learn to write opinion pieces, informative/explanatory pieces, and narratives. To learn how to write these specific genres, students need to be engaged in two types of lessons. First, the teacher teaches several prompt-based writing lessons that elicit the type of writing that the teacher is focusing on. Next, revision lessons are taught so that students learn how to revise their writing to meet the criteria for the type of writing they are doing. This cycle of lessons is demonstrated in the following sample lessons, which teach students how to write opinion pieces.

Prompt-Based Lessons for Opinion Pieces

This is the first opinion piece writing lesson this class has done. The teacher begins by asking his class:

> "Do any of you have a pet?"

He allows a few students to briefly tell about their pets. Then he says:

> "Let's think of what would be some unusual pets."

Students suggest animals that would make unusual pets. He records their suggestions and makes sure that everyone understands the difference between common and rare pets. Next, he displays the prompt the students will write to in this lesson:

> Pretend you would like to have a certain unusual pet. Write a note asking whoever takes care of you if you can have that pet.

Next, he reads a picture book to the class. It is *I Wanna Iguana* by Karen Kaufman Orloff and David Catrow. The story is told almost exclusively through a series of notes written back and forth between a boy named Alex and his mother. Alex explains why he wants to take a friend's baby iguana for a pet when his friend moves away. His mom expresses her doubts and concerns about him having an iguana for a pet.

When he finishes reading the book, he takes a few minutes to let his students talk about the story and what they liked about it. Then he points to the prompt and reminds them that in a few minutes he is going to want each of them to write a note asking for an unusual pet. He shows them a couple of the notes in the book again so they can see that a note is quite informal though it usually starts with "Dear …" and ends with the name of the person who wrote it.

This brings a flurry of questions about their writing from the students.

> "Do we write just one note or lots of notes like Alex did?"
> "Do I need to try to convince my mom like Alex did?"
> "Can the pet I ask for be an iguana?"

The teacher answers that they need only write one note and they do need to be convincing and that they cannot ask for an iguana. He then asks them to take one minute and think about what they will write.

> "Before you start writing, I want you to decide which unusual pet you are going to choose. You can't choose an iguana. The one you choose doesn't have to be one we've talked about, but it can be. Don't tell anyone, but decide in your own mind what unusual pet you are going to ask for. I'll give you one minute to decide and then we'll start writing."

The teacher uses the stopwatch on his smartphone as a timer. When the minute of "think time" is up, he points to the prompt and tells them he will leave it there while they write so they can refer to it at any time. He reminds them to skip every other line as they write. (From the first day of school, he has been having students skip every other line as they write first drafts because they don't know which ones they will choose to revise and edit. If they always skip lines when writing first drafts, they will have room to make their small revisions later by adding to or replacing what they have by writing in the empty lines above.) The students all write for about 10 minutes and then the volunteers tell which animals they have chosen and how they tried to convince the grown-up that this would be a good pet.

Over the next several days, the students write to several other prompts that will result in opinion pieces.

> Name the best book you have read so far this year and explain why you chose this book.
>
> We have been studying nutrition in science. Choose a healthy snack that you like and explain why you think this is a good and healthy snack.
>
> Write a letter to the school board and let them know why you think that Saturday make-up days is a good or a bad plan.

When all the students have several first draft opinion pieces, he teaches them a lesson in which they revise one of these first drafts.

Revising Opinion Pieces

The teacher begins the revising lesson by explaining to his students the purpose of the lesson.

> "Today you are going to revise one of the opinion pieces you have written. We have been revising during writer's workshop so you know that when we revise, we work to make what we have written even better. We don't edit while we are revising. Once we have made our revisions, we do our editing."

He then displays the *Opinion Piece Guidelines*, which has the first two of four items students will learn to revise opinion pieces for.

⦿ Our Opinion Piece Guidelines ⦿

1. Introduce the topic clearly and state your opinion about it.

2. Give good reasons supported by facts and details.

He asks the class to take out their writing notebooks and look at the four opinion first drafts they have written. He then leads them to determine the topic of each piece. The first opinion piece they wrote was about what unusual pet they might like to have, their second opinion piece was about the most interesting book they have read so far this year, their third was about the nutritious snack they like the best, and the last one gave their opinions about Saturday make-up days. Next, he displays a first draft opinion piece he has written on a different topic than any of them have written about. He tells the students that this opinion piece is one he might have written when he was their age.

> Roller coasters make me want to throw up! Pendulum rides get me so dizzy I can't walk straight when I get off. Drop towers scare me so badly I think I'm going to die. Swing rides also upset my stomach. They ought to pay me instead of me having to pay them to ride those things!

The students read his piece chorally and then he turns their attention to guideline #1.

1. Introduce the topic clearly and state your opinion about it.

After briefly looking over his opinion piece, he says:

> "Oh, dear, I didn't introduce my topic at all! I need to do that."

He writes a new first sentence in the space above the first line of his draft.

> I don't like most amusement park rides.
> Roller coasters make me want to throw up! Pendulum rides get me so dizzy I can't walk straight when I get off. Drop towers scare me so badly I think I'm going to die. Swing rides also upset my stomach. They ought to pay me instead of me having to pay them to ride those things!

He then asks students what the topic is and what his opinion on that topic is. They clearly understand that amusement park rides is the topic and that when he was a kid, he didn't like them. Students want to know if this is really the way he felt about amusement park rides when he was their age and if he still feels that way, and he assures them that these were his true feelings then and they haven't changed!

Now that the topic and his opinion about it are clearly stated, he asks them to help him think about the second guideline.

2. Give good reasons supported by facts and details.

The students decide that the fact the rides make him want to throw up and that he feels dizzy and scared he is going to die are indeed very specific details and good reasons for not liking them!

> "Now it's your turn to revise one of your opinion pieces. Pick any of the four and get with your partner. Read each piece together and decide if your piece introduces the topic clearly and gives your opinion about it. Change or add to your beginning if you need to. Next, look at your reasons. Do you have specific facts and details to support them? Write anything you want to add or change on the skipped lines and cross out anything you are replacing."

The students have been doing some revising during Writer's Workshop and they all have revising/editing partners. They get with their partners and begin looking at their pieces to choose the piece they want to revise. Two students' partners are absent and the teacher doesn't think they are close enough in writing ability to help each other much so he asks them to join him and the three of them work together to revise their pieces.

As students finish revising their pieces, they join the teacher and the two he has helped to revise and share some of the ways they made their opinion pieces even better by clearly introducing the topic and their opinion and providing specific facts and details to support their opinions.

Focused Writing Lessons for Informative/Explanatory Texts

Writing Standard 2 specifies that elementary students in grades one through five learn to write informative/explanatory texts. Fifth-graders are expected to introduce the topic clearly; develop the topic with facts, details, and examples; use linking words (also, another, in contrast, especially); use precise and domain-specific vocabulary; and provide a concluding statement or section. This is a very high expectation but an important one because the ability to write informative texts is critical to success in high school, college, and life! To teach students to do this, you can follow the same sequence of steps the teacher did in the sample lessons for opinion pieces. Begin by teaching several prompt-based writing lessons in which students write informational pieces.

● Our Opinion Piece Guidelines ●

1. Introduce the topic clearly and state your opinion about it.

2. Give good reasons supported by facts and details.

3. Use words like *because*, *for example*, *specifically*, *therefore*, and *consequently* to connect your opinion with your reasons.

4. Provide a concluding sentence or paragraph.

- Teach or review background knowledge needed to understand the prompt.
- Present the prompt and answer students' questions about it.
- For the first few lessons, provide students with a good example of an informational piece (an article for a magazine for children like *Time for Kids*, *Sports Illustrated for Kids*, or *National Geographic Kids*, an informational picture book or a short, well-written section from a science or social studies textbook).
- Have students individually plan their writing by having them talk to a partner about what they plan to include, or write down the three things they think are the most important.
- Have students independently write to the prompt, skipping every other line.

When students have written at least three informational pieces, teach revision lessons based on guidelines that gradually increase in length and sophistication.

- Show students one or two informational piece guidelines.
- Show students a piece of your writing that needs revision on the informational piece guideline that is the teaching point of your lesson.
- Tell students the purpose of the lesson. They are going to use the guidelines to revise one of their informational pieces so it will be "even better."
- For the first several revision lessons, and whenever you add a new guideline to the list, include the "I Do and You Watch" and "I Do and You Help" procedures to model for students what you want them to do.
- Have students work in partners ("You Do It Together and I Help") to revise their informational drafts for the guidelines that are currently on the list.

● Our Informational Piece Guidelines ●

1. Introduce the topic.

2. Give facts and details about the topic.

3. Have an ending statement or section. (After you have taught students to revise so they have an ending statement or section, keep moving this guideline down every time you add another one. So, this guideline will originally be #3, but then will become #4, then #5, and finally #6.)

4. Define a few important words if your readers might not know them.

5. Group related information together.

6. Use words like *also, another, and, more, but, in contrast,* and *especially* to connect related ideas together.

Focused Writing Lessons for Narratives

Writing Standard 3 requires that students learn to write narratives—stories that relate real or imagined events or experiences. As students go through the grades, they are expected to write increasingly sophisticated narratives with characters, settings, and plots. For many children (and adults) this is the most challenging type of writing because creating a story is not nearly as concrete as writing an opinion and informational piece that is supported with facts, details, and examples.

To teach your students to write narratives, follow the same sequence of lessons and steps described for writing opinion and informational pieces. Teach prompt-based writing lessons and then revising lessons. Add guidelines gradually and give students lots of practice with each guideline before adding another one. Here is a list of guidelines fifth-graders are expected to achieve in narrative writing. Students will need many prompt-based and revision lessons across several years to produce the level of narrative writing described in the Standards.

• Our Narrative Writing Guidelines •

1. Introduce the narrator, one or more characters, or both.

2. Describe the setting and situation your narrator or main character is in.

3. Have a sequence of events that feels natural to your readers.

4. Have an ending that follows from what happened and what the characters experienced. (After you have taught students to revise so they have an ending that meets this guideline, keep moving this guideline down every time you add another one. So, this guideline will originally be #4, but then will become #5, then #6, and so forth.)

5. Use dialogue and description to tell what happened.

6. Use dialogue or description to show how characters feel about what happened.

7. Use concrete words and phrases and sensory details to convey what happens.

8. Use some transitional words and phrases to convey the sequence of events.

Summary

Writer's Workshop is a powerful and versatile structure for teaching children to write. Beginning each day with a mini-lesson in which children watch you write allows you to model, demonstrate, and think aloud about all the "big" and "little" components that constitute good writing. In your mini-lesson, focus on just one aspect—choosing a topic, what to do about spelling, how to edit your writing, how to revise by replacing, or any of the other things writers must learn to do. As children write, encourage them in their writing or conference with them about how to make their writing better and more readable. Beginning your Writer's Workshop with only the mini-lesson, children writing, and sharing steps allows all children to get off to a successful start in writing. When the children are writing willingly (if not well), you can add editing to your workshop and then conferencing, publishing, and Author's Chair. Because learning to edit is easier than learning to revise, you should teach some editing rules before teaching revising strategies. When the children know some revising strategies, make sure they revise their pieces before doing any editing.

In Writer's Workshop, children are usually writing on topics of their own choosing in whatever form or genre they choose. After the children have achieved some comfort level with Writer's Workshop, begin to include some focused writing lessons. Building on the basics required by all good writing taught in Writer's Workshop, focus your students' attention on particular topics, forms, or genres. Teach mini-lessons in which you model the particular kind of writing you are focusing on, and then guide children through the steps of the writing process to produce published pieces. Children who engage in both Writer's Workshop and focused writing lessons throughout their elementary years will become ready, willing, and able writers.

In reviewing the research on writing, Hillocks (1986) found that natural process writing instruction is effective and that what has been called *environmental writing instruction,* in which students engage in various writing activities designed to teach them to learn and apply specific writing strategies and skills, is more effective still. The key to teaching writing, including the conventions of writing, appears to include being consistent with a developmental sequence that recognizes the commonalties of children as they move from early emergence to sophisticated ability (Dyson & Freedman, 2003; Farnan & Dahl, 2003; Hodges, 2003). Effective writing programs will look very different grade by grade and will have expectations for children at each grade that are appropriate to their development as writers. The best writing instruction teaches students how to plan, compose, revise, and edit their own pieces of writing, all within the context of inquiry, self-assessment, and self-regulation fostered by interaction with teachers and peers.

How Well Does Your Instruction Help All Children Learn to Write as Well as They Can?

1. Do I begin the year with Writer's Workshop in which I demonstrate that writing is telling and that the most important thing in my class is what they tell?

2. Do I help them stretch out words they need to spell and direct them to print in the room but refrain from spelling words for them when they are writing first drafts?

3. When students are used to deciding on their own topics and know what to do about spelling, do I teach them to edit by beginning an editor's checklist with just one item and adding to it gradually?

4. Do I teach some revising strategies they can use to make their writing "even better"?

5. Do I provide opportunities for children to share their writing in the Author's Chair and through publishing?

6. When my students have some basic editing and revising strategies, do I teach some focused writing lessons on how to write opinion, informational, and narrative pieces?

10

Reading and Writing Across the Curriculum

WE MADE THE ARGUMENT IN CHAPTER 8 that including reading instruction to help students learn to read informational text would result in better comprehension, increased subject-matter learning, and more total reading by all the students in your classroom. We would now like you to think about the benefits of including writing as part of your math, science, and social studies instruction. Writing requires thinking; that is the reason some people call writing "thinking made public." When you engage your students in writing tasks as part of your math, science, and social studies instruction, your students will think more about what they are learning. More and higher-level thinking will result in more learning. Just as with reading, when you include writing across your day, your students will write more. The more they write, the more fluent they will become in writing. This chapter will describe how you can incorporate writing into all the subjects you teach by using *Reading-Writing Connections* and *Think-Writes*.

Reading-Writing Connections

Chapter 9 began with the notion that writing is complex and that writers have to juggle a lot of different balls—ideas, vocabulary, spelling—when they are writing. Having students write about something they have read makes the writing task less complex. Students have the ideas and the vocabulary because they are writing in response to what they have just read. Spelling is less of an issue because they can refer to the text for the spelling of key vocabulary. In this section, we will describe some ways you can connect writing to some of the informational text lesson frameworks described in Chapter 8.

Main Idea Trees

Look at the completed main idea tree about snakes. Now imagine that you wanted students to write about snakes. Here is a sample lesson in which the teacher extends the main idea lesson to help students learn to write summaries. He begins the lesson by reminding

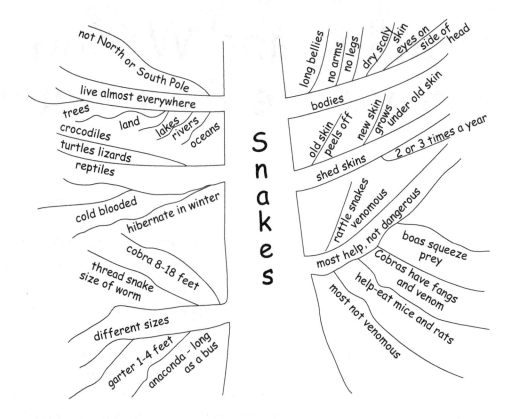

students that they created trees to organize the information they were learning about snakes. The topic, snakes, was written on the trunk of the tree and the main ideas they learned about snakes were written on the big branches with the supporting details on branches coming off the main branches. Then the teacher sets the purpose for the lesson.

"Now, we are going to write summaries telling everything we learned about snakes. Our snake tree has six big branches and we are going to write a paragraph for each branch. I am going to write the first one and you are going to help me write the second one. Then you are going to get in your trios and write one together. That will leave three main ideas that need to be summarized. Each of you will write a paragraph summarizing one of the remaining three branches."

The teacher looks at all six branches and then writes:

> Snakes are reptiles.

"Which main idea branch have I chosen to write about? That's right. The main idea is reptiles so I just turned that into a sentence to start my paragraph. Now I will add the details about reptiles. The details I want to include are that reptiles are cold blooded and hibernate in winter, and that crocodiles, turtles, and lizards are other reptiles. I am going to add these details to my paragraph but I need to turn them into sentences and explain a little more about each. I am going to tell that reptiles are cold blooded and explain what that means."

The teacher adds two sentences to the paragraph.

> Snakes are reptiles. Reptiles are cold-blooded animals. The body temperature of cold-blooded animals stays the same as the air temperature.

He then completes the paragraph with sentences explaining the other two details.

> Snakes are reptiles. Reptiles are cold-blooded animals. The body temperature of cold-blooded animals stays the same as the air temperature. If they live in cold places, they hibernate in the winter to stay warm. Other common reptiles include crocodiles, lizards, and turtles.

"Now, we are going to construct the next paragraph together. I want to write the next paragraph with the main idea about the sizes of snakes. Who can help me put this idea into a sentence?" The class decides that the first sentence should be:

> Snakes are many different sizes.

They then help him put the details into sentences and, jointly, the class constructs this paragraph.

> Snakes are many different sizes. A thread snake's size is only as big as a worm. Garter snakes are usually 1–4 feet long but cobras can be 8–18 feet long. The anaconda can be as long as a bus!

Having watched and then helped the teacher construct two paragraphs, the students are eager to construct their own paragraphs. They quickly assemble into their trios and choose one of the main ideas to work on together. The teacher circulates and assists but most trios have no difficulty constructing the paragraphs. Finally they divide the remaining three paragraphs among themselves and each student writes a paragraph. One trio has trouble deciding who will write which one. The teacher says, "If you can't decide, I will decide for you." As he suspected they would, they quickly make the decision themselves. The teacher knows who is apt to have trouble getting started on the individual paragraphs and moves around helping them formulate a first sentence if they need this help.

If it looks fairly easy to you for students to construct summary paragraphs based on the branches of the tree, you see how scaffolding the writing in this way makes the writing task less complex and allows all students to be successful. As a bonus, they will probably retain more of the facts you wanted them to learn about snakes because they have revisited that information and actively constructed their own internal summaries.

Time Lines

You can help students organize information in which the sequence of events matters by following-up your time line reading lesson with a writing lesson.

Time Line Space Exploration

1947	1949	1957	1961	1962						
^	^	^	^	^	^	^	^	^	^	^
fruit flies launched into space	Albert, a monkey, launched into space	Russia launched Sputnik 1 and Sputnik 2	Russian astronaut first human orbits Earth	JFK says America will get to the moon first and space race begins						

Use the same steps described for the snakes writing lesson to have students learn to summarize text with a sequential structure. Let the students watch as you construct a paragraph based on the first few events:

> In 1947, the first animals were launched into space. These animals were fruit flies. When they returned from their quick trip, scientists studied the effects of the flight on their bodies. The next animal to make the trip was a Rhesus monkey named Albert. Russia launched him into space in 1949. He flew 83 miles from the earth.

Let them help you construct a paragraph based on the next several events:

> In 1957, Russia launched two satellites into space. Sputnik 1 was followed by Sputnik 2. Along for the ride on Sputnik 2 was a dog named Laika, the first animal ever to orbit Earth. In 1961, the Russian astronaut Yurk Gararin became the first human to orbit Earth. President Kennedy was worried that the Russians were making all the breakthroughs in space exploration. In 1962, he promised that America would be first to get to the moon. The space race was on!

When students have watched you construct one paragraph and then helped you construct a second paragraph, divide up the remaining events and let students work together or individually to construct another paragraph.

Compare/Contrast Bubbles

You can help students learn to compare and contrast information by following up your *Compare/Contrast Bubbles* reading lesson with a writing lesson.

The teacher in this lesson reviewed the information on the double bubble, making sure that students understood that the similarities were in the intersection of the two bubbles and the differences were on the sides. She then wrote an introductory sentence:

> There are many similarities between China and Japan.

She invited students to suggest a second sentence based on the information in the intersection of the circles. After getting several suggestions, she added a second sentence to her paragraph and asked students to add at least two sentences to copy her first two sentences and add at least two more sentences describing similarities.

> There are many similarities between China and Japan. They are both on the continent of Asia and they both have forests and mountains.

As most children are finishing their paragraphs, she goes to the board and writes a starter sentence for the second paragraph.

> There are also many differences between China and Japan.
>
> "Now we are going to write a paragraph that compares China and Japan. Start your second paragraph like this. It's a new paragraph so don't forget to indent. Who can give me some ideas for my second sentence?"

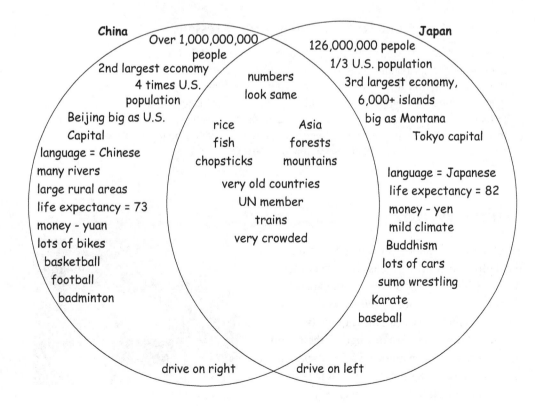

She listens to their suggestions and adds a second sentence. The students copy the first two sentences and add two or three sentences of their own.

> There are also many differences between China and Japan. China is much bigger than Japan and has almost ten times as many people.

As the children write, the teacher circulates helping them choose the differences that seem most important to them. Then she models how to conclude their summary with an opinion paragraph.

> "Now we need a short paragraph to complete our summary. So far we have included facts but I am going to end my summary with my opinion. I am going to tell you which country I would most like to visit and give you my reasons for this choice. Remember that we have learned to do persuasive writing in which we give reasons for our opinion to try to convince people we are right. As you watch me write my opinion and reasons, think about your own opinion and reasons."

> I would like to visit both China and Japan but if I could only visit one I would go to Japan. I like baseball and would love to go to a baseball game in Japan. I also like water and would love to visit a country made up of over 6,000 islands. Japan is much smaller than China and I think I could travel through lots of Japan in a week but I could only see a small part of China.

Before the children begin to write their opinion paragraphs, she removes hers so that they can't copy it. Her students always want to make their opinions known and so they eagerly write this final paragraph.

Common Core Connections: Reading-Writing Lessons

The focused writing lessons described in Chapter 9 teach students how to write the narrative, informational, and opinion pieces required in Writing Standards 1, 2, and 3. You can also teach students how to write informational and opinion pieces by connecting the writing to main idea trees, time lines, and compare/contrast bubbles they have constructed to help them organize informational text. The writing your students do based on their main idea trees will also help them meet Reading Information Standard 2, which specifies that students should be able to determine main ideas and supporting details and summarize the text.

Think-Writes

Think-writes are short, quick bits of writing that help your students focus and clarify their thinking. These quick bits of writing are often completed in two minutes and never take more than five minutes. We call these quick bits of writing "think-writes" to distinguish them from other more formal, extended writing experiences. Because think-writes are written not for others to read but for the writer to help clarify thinking,

Source: Patricia Cunningham

think-writes are not published and thus they do not require revising and editing. To make it very clear to your students that think-writes are writing they are doing just for themselves, have your students do their think-writes on scrap paper that we call "scraps."

Connection Think-Writes

Before your students begin to learn about a new topic in math, science, or social studies, do you ask them to share what they already know about that topic? When you pose the "What do you know about . . ." question, do the same hands always go up—and the same hands never go up? Do you wonder why some students' hands almost never fly into the air? Equally problematic (and more annoying!) are the students whose hands always fly up and then when they are the first person you call on, they ask, "What was the question?"

Connection think-writes can make your efforts at prior knowledge activation more productive for all your students. Imagine that your learning focus for today's lesson is on presidents. You begin your lesson by saying,

> "Today we are going to start learning about some of our nation's presidents. Take a scrap and write down everything you know about presidents. If you think you know something but you aren't sure, write it down anyway and we will try to find out. You have two minutes. Go!"

Your students grab scrap paper you have recycled from the copying room, torn into quarters and placed in small baskets at each table, and begin writing. You stand in front of the class and watch the clock, timing the students for exactly two minutes. Many of your students write as fast as they can, trying to "beat the clock" and write down many things. The children no longer ask you to spell things—as they did the first few times you did these think-writes—because they know what the answer will be:

> "Spell it as best you can. This writing is just for you to get your thoughts down. No one else needs to read it, so as long as you know what you wrote, we're good."

When exactly two minutes have passed, you say,

"Stop! Pens down! Who has something they want to share?"

Every hand is raised. You call first on a student who may not have much prior knowledge and that student proudly responds, "George Washington."

"Good thinking! George Washington was our first president."

You continue to call on students and affirm their responses.

"Yes, the president is the head of our nation."
"Yes, presidents get elected every four years."

Sometimes, you ask a follow-up question.

"Yes, Abraham Lincoln was a president. Does anyone know how Abraham Lincoln died?"

"The president does live in the White House. Who knows where the White House is? Have any of you ever been to the White House?"

"Good thinking. We did have two presidents named George Bush. We also had two other presidents with the same name. Does anyone have an idea who they might be?"

"Yes, Barack Obama is our first African-American president. Does anyone know where his father was born?"

Another student volunteers "George Washington" and you remind everyone that we need to listen and not repeat ideas, and then ask that student if he has anything on his list that hasn't been said. When students volunteer information that is clearly incorrect, you correct that information but affirm the response of the student.

"Benjamin Franklin was never president but he played a very important role in our government. Can anyone tell us what Benjamin Franklin did?"

When no more hands are raised, you congratulate your students on how much they already know about presidents and tell them that they will be learning many more interesting presidential facts and trivia in the coming days.

Think-writes to activate prior knowledge increase student engagement and motivation. Your most able students see it as a kind of race and they want to write as many ideas as they can in the two minutes. Your struggling students who may be reluctant to raise their hands are much more confident when they have had two minutes to think and when you are affirming of even a wrong answer or a misconception. Using think-writes forces you to do something we all know we need to do—but often find ourselves not doing. When we give students two minutes to write down ideas, we are forced to "wait" while they write. Both the quantity and quality of the responses you get will increase when you give your students wait-time. Two-minute think-writes make students think and teachers wait!

Once you start using think-writes, you will wonder how you taught without them. You can use think-writes to activate prior knowledge during math.

> "We are going to be learning more about measurement this week. You
> have two minutes to write everything you think you already know about
> measurement. Go!"

> "Our new math topic is fractions. I know you already know a lot about fractions.
> Take a scrap and write down what you know. You have two minutes. Go!"

Science topics also can be introduced with two-minute think-writes.

> "Our new science topic is on natural resources. Do you know any? What do
> you think you know about natural resources? You have two minutes. Go!"

> "Rocks is our science topic for the week. I know you know things about
> rocks. Let's see how much rock knowledge you can write down in two
> minutes. Go!"

You may even uncover some science misconceptions that are part of your students' prior knowledge. If someone tells you something you are sure is incorrect, make a mental note of that and respond by saying something like,

> "A lot of people think that—but we are going to find out that it actually
> works quite differently."

Here are some two-minute think-writes used to access prior knowledge in social studies.

> "What holiday do we celebrate in November? Right! Thanksgiving will soon
> be here. I know you know a lot about Thanksgiving. Grab a scrap and get
> those brains thinking. You have two minutes. Go!"

> "Immigration is our social studies topic. I am not sure how much you know
> about immigration but we will soon find out. You have two minutes. Go!"

For all these connection think-writes, the students are recording their ideas on scrap paper. This scrap paper is essential to successful two-minute think-writes for several reasons. First, it often takes a whole class of students more than two minutes to "get out a piece of paper." In two minutes, the think-write is done. Second, scrap paper is unintimidating. No one asks if they need to "head their paper" or if "this counts for the grade" when jotting down thoughts on a small scrap of paper. Finally, we are recycling paper that would have been thrown away and not wasting a perfectly good whole piece of notebook paper!

It is also important to specify and stick to the time limit. Two minutes is plenty of time for students to recall and jot down most of what they know. Students who don't know much don't get too squirmy in two minutes and students who know a lot enjoy racing to write down an impressive array of facts before the time is up.

Prediction Think-Writes

Prediction is another thinking process you can engage all your students in using think-writes. You will find numerous opportunities across your school day to use prediction think-writes. Science is a fertile area for prediction. In fact, prediction is one of the science processes we want all students to do regularly. Imagine that you are teaching a science unit on magnets and electricity and want your students to make some predictions and then test those predictions.

Talking Partners

On some days, instead of having your students write down their thoughts, seat them with their talking partners and give them a brief time to share ideas.

> "We are going to be learning about many of our nation's presidents this week. Turn and tell your partner everything you think you know about presidents. You have one minute."

> "Today we are starting a math unit on measurement. Have you ever measured anything? What can you use to measure things? Turn and share what you know about measurement."

> "In science today, we are going to experiment with these objects and see if they sink or float. I am going to hold up the objects one at a time and give you and your partner 30 seconds to decide if you think they will sink or float. At the end of 30 seconds, I will ask you to give me a 'thumbs up' or 'thumbs down' to show me your predictions."

> "Today we are going to learn more about Antarctica. Turn to page 67 in your social studies text. You have three minutes to mine the graphics with your partner. Talk about all the visuals on pages 67 to 70 and see what we can add to what we know about Antarctica."

Just as with think-writes, posing questions for talking partners to discuss gives your students the time and opportunity to gather and then share their connections and predictions. It forces you to do something most of us find very hard to do—wait! Wait-time has been shown to increase both the quantity and quality of student response. Incorporating think-writes and this talking partner routine, often called "Think-Pair-Share," into your lesson routines across the curriculum will result in much higher levels of talk, engagement, and thinking

> "Boys and girls, we are going to continue our unit on magnets and electricity today. In just a few minutes, you are going to get into your teams and test some materials and see if they will attract or repel the magnets. Before we test them, let's make some predictions. Grab a scrap and number it from 1 to 6. Next to number 1, write *ruler*. Then write either *attract* or *not attract* to show your prediction. Will the ruler be attracted to the magnet?"

The prediction think-write continues as you hold up each object your students are going to test. Students write the name of the object and their guess of "attract" or "not attract" next to each. Some students are hesitant to guess and claim they don't know. You push them, however, by saying something like the following:

> "You're not supposed to know. That's what a guess is. When you test them, you will change any guesses to the correct answers. Make your best guess. I'm not going to let you join your team to test the objects until you have made a prediction for each."

Prediction is a powerful motivator but students are often afraid of being wrong. When they learn that you don't care if they are wrong or right and that they are expected to change incorrect guesses to correct answers, and if you make it clear they will not move forward in the activity until they have some guesses, they will put something down. Once they have a prediction, human nature kicks in and they are eager to "see how they did." Think about the science units you teach and the science activities your students engage in and you will quickly envision many prediction think-write possibilities.

> "Which objects will sink and which will float?"
> "Will more water in the glass make the pitch higher or lower?"

> "When we roll all these round objects down the ramp, which one will hit the ground first?"
>
> "Today, we are going to test clay soil, loamy soil, sand, and pebbles to see how quickly water flows through them and how much water is absorbed. Take a scrap and order these four from slowest movement to quickest movement. Then order them from absorbs most water to absorbs least water."

In math, we also want students to learn to predict and we refer to these predictions as *estimates*. Teachers often ask their students to give oral estimates before doing math activities. Having the students write their predictions on scrap paper increases the participation and engagement for all students.

> "We are continuing to work with measurement today and we are going to measure and compute some areas and perimeters. We will use our metric rulers, so our answers will be in centimeters. As I show you each object you are going to measure, write down the name of the object and your guess of the perimeter and area of that object, making sure your guess is in centimeters."

Prediction think-writes also work well in social studies, although they take a very different form from those done in science classrooms. You learned in Chapter 8 that informational text has a lot of special features including photographs, maps, charts, graphs, and other visuals. The *Text Feature Scavenger Hunt* lesson framework teaches students how to interpret and learn from all these visuals. You can help students establish the habit of studying the visual in a text first by doing a prediction think-write before they read. Imagine that you are about to read a piece on Ecuador in your *Time for Kids*, *Scholastic,* or *Weekly Reader*.

> "We are going to read a short piece about Ecuador today. Before we read, I am going to give you exactly three minutes to mine the graphics. Look at all the graphics—photos, illustrations, maps, charts, graphs, anything visual— and write down as many things as you can that you think we are going to learn about Ecuador. You can use the labels, captions, and other quicktext that go with the graphics but don't waste your three minutes reading the longer pieces of text. Take a scrap and get started. You have three minutes to write down as many things as you can about Ecuador. You may start now!"

When the three minutes are up, have your students put the text out of sight and ask them to volunteer what they learned about Ecuador from the graphics. Just as in the connection think-write, you accept their answers and ask expanding or clarifying questions as appropriate.

> "Yes, Ecuador is on the equator. Does anyone remember what the equator is?"
>
> "Yes, bananas are a major crop. Do you think they keep all the bananas they grow there or export them?"
>
> "Right, Ecuador is about the size of Nebraska. Do you think that makes it larger or smaller than our state?"

As your students share information and think about your expansions on their ideas, they are going to want to return to the piece again and point out more information from the graphics. You explain that they will be reading the whole piece soon but until then you want them to focus on how much they were able to glean from the graphics in just three minutes. If you catch someone sneaking a peek, you remove the text from that student and return it when it is time to read. You adhere firmly to your "no sneak peeks" rule during the first several

three-minute prediction think-writes, knowing that your students will learn to make maximum use of their three minutes in future lessons.

Think-Writes for Summarizing

Connection and prediction think-writes are usually done before students read. You can also use think-writes to help your students do the thinking processes they use while they are reading. Imagine that you give your students three minutes to mine the graphics and write down what they think they are going to learn about Ecuador, as described in the previous section. Next, your students will read the text. Before letting them reopen the text, give each student three sticky notes for marking the three most important facts they learn about Ecuador. Show them how to write a brief sentence or phrase telling what they think is important and place the sticky note right on the place where they found that information.

The first time you do this with your students, they will probably use their sticky notes quickly and ask for more. Make it clear that there is a lot of information about Ecuador in this short piece and that they can't sticky-note everything. Their job is to pick three important facts they think everyone should know about Ecuador. Don't give them any additional sticky notes. Letting them cover the piece with sticky notes would defeat your purpose of helping them learn to think about what information is most interesting and important. You may want to have your students work in partners to read and sticky-note the text, partnering struggling readers with stronger readers who will help them with difficult words.

When students complete the reading, gather them together and go through each part of the text, asking who has a sticky note on this page. Have them read what they wrote on the sticky note and explain why they think this is an important fact. You can use three sticky note think-writes in any subject area when students are reading informational text and you want them to think about what information is most important or interesting to them.

You can also use a paragraph frame such as this one to help your students summarize what they have learned after reading informational text. Here is the frame one teacher uses followed by one student's completed paragraph after reading about Ecuador.

I have learned many interesting facts about _____. I learned that _____. I also learned that _____ and _____. But the most interesting fact I learned about _____ is that _____.

I have learned many interesting facts about Ecuador. I learned that Ecuador is a medium-sized country in South America that borders Peru and Columbia. I also learned that Ecuador exports oil and bananas. But the most interesting fact I learned about Ecuador is that the Galapagos Islands are in Ecuador and the Galapagos giant turtle can weigh 500 pounds!

Think-Writes for Concluding, Evaluating, and Imagining

The thinking process of concluding or inferring requires the reader to take information in the text and "figure out" an idea that the text does not directly state. Our brains draw many different conclusions as we read, but often these conclusions are drawn by comparing our world and experiences to the new world or experiences we are learning about. To use think-writes to help your students draw conclusions, pose a question that requires that kind of thinking. For Ecuador, you might have students write the words *climate, size,* and *geography* on a piece of scrap paper. Tell them that as they read, you want them to try to figure out how similar the climate of Ecuador is to the climate of the state in which they live. For size, they should try to figure out if Ecuador is larger or smaller than the state in which they live. And for geography, they should think about the different regions of Ecuador and how these are similar to or different from the regions of their state. Tell the students to jot down notes on these three topics as they read. After they read, have students share their comparisons and support their ideas with information from the Ecuador article and information they have previously learned about their state.

Everyone loves to give their opinions! Kids are no exception to this rule. If the kind of thinking you want your students to do falls into the evaluate/opinion category, ask them to decide something and justify that decision with facts from what they read. Here are some examples of opinion think-writes.

"Your mom or dad has the chance to take a job in Ecuador. Your whole family would move to Quito and live there for two years. You would go to school there and learn to speak Spanish. Your family has decided that everyone gets a vote in this important decision. How will you vote and what reasons will you give to support your opinions?"

"Imagine that you are grown up and have just been elected to the United States Senate. The deficit is large and the president has proposed eliminating the space program. How will you vote? Support your vote with facts you learn about what we have learned from space exploration."

"As you are reading about sea turtles, you will discover that they are endangered in many parts of the world. Different people have ideas about how to save sea turtles from extinction. Which ideas do you think would work best and why do you think so?"

Common Core Connections: Think-Writes

Writing Standard 10 requires that students write routinely over extended and shorter time frames for a range of tasks, purposes, and audiences. Incorporating think-writes into your instructional routines across the school day can greatly increase the amount of writing (and thinking) your students do.

Even the thinking process of imagining can be prompted with a think-write. Give your students a large index card and ask them to "sketch" what they are reading about. Tell them to use pencils—not crayons—because you want them to focus on what they see in their "mind's eye," not on an artistic creation. Some of your more verbal students will experience some frustration with this task because they are used to processing information with words only. But your spatial and artistic students will enjoy this novel way to think about what they are reading. Maybe instead of a think-write, this activity should be called a *think-draw!*

Concluding is figuring it out. *Evaluating* is deciding "what *you* think." *Imagining* is putting yourself into the text and "being there." Your students will approach informational text with much higher levels of engagement if you include some higher-level think-writes—and think-draws—to your comprehension tool kit!

Summary

Just as the more you read, the better and more fluently you will read, the more you write, the better and more fluently you will write. Chapter 9 described how to use Writer's Workshop and focused writing lessons to teach students how to write. This chapter suggests ways you can "piggyback" writing lessons to your informational text comprehension lessons. Writing paragraph summaries after construction of main idea trees, time lines, or compare/contrast bubbles is actually easier for students than other writing because the information they need is available to them in an organized form. The graphic organizer they refer to while writing also helps ease the spelling burden and allows them to write more fluently.

Think-writes are another way of connecting reading, writing, and subject learning. Think-writes can be constructed to prompt students to make connections and predictions before they read and to prod them to use the thinking strategies of summarizing, concluding, evaluating, and imagining as they read.

Research confirms that having students write during science, social studies, and other subjects increases their learning in all these subjects, and having students write regularly produces the greatest gains (Bangert-Drown, Hurley, & Wilkinson, 2004; Graham & Perin, 2007).

How Well Does Your Instruction Integrate Writing with Reading and Other Subjects?

1. Do I provide opportunities to connect reading and writing by having students write based on something they have read?
2. Do I incorporate writing into my teaching of math, science, and social studies by teaching focused writing lessons connected to these subjects and by including quick think-writes across the school day?

11

Assessment

ASSESSMENT IS PART OF EVERYTHING we do in life. Most of us make an assessment of the weather each morning to decide what to wear. We assess the food, service, and atmosphere as we dine at a new restaurant. We assess our new neighbors as we watch them interact with each other and move their furniture in. This chapter provides some examples of how you can make assessment an extension of your teaching, rather than just one more chore that has to be done.

What Is Assessment?

Sometimes, it is easier to define something by beginning with what it is not. Assessment is *not* grading—although assessment can help you determine and support the grades you give. Assessment is *not* standardized test scores—although these scores can give you some general idea of what children have achieved so far. Assessment *is* collecting and analyzing data to make decisions about how children are performing and growing.

Caldwell (2015) describes four steps for assessment. First, identify what you want to assess. Second, collect evidence. Third, analyze that evidence. And fourth, make a decision and act on that decision. Caldwell suggests three main purposes for reading assessment: to determine student reading level, to identify good reading behaviors, and to document student progress.

Determining Student Reading Level

Reading level is affected by individual factors within each child, such as prior knowledge and interest, as well as by instructional factors, such as type of prereading instruction, amount of support provided by the reading format, and whether a first reading or a rereading of a selection is being considered.

Despite the fact that reading level is not static, you still need to determine an approximate reading level for each of your students. Knowing the levels at which students are reading early in the school year serves as a benchmark against which to judge how well your instruction is helping your students raise their reading levels. Knowing their reading levels also helps you determine whether the books your students are choosing for independent reading are too hard or too easy, so you can guide them toward more appropriate choices. Having a general idea of each child's reading level can help you decide how much support each child needs to experience success during comprehension lessons. Finally, you need to determine reading levels because many schools and parents expect you to know the reading level of and document progress for each student.

To determine reading levels, have individual students read passages at different reading levels. Many reading series include graded passages with their reading textbooks. Some school districts and states have created graded passages or selected benchmark books that you can use to assess reading levels. The Developmental Reading Assessment (DRA) (Beaver, 2012) and a number of published Informal Reading Inventories (IRIs), such as the Basic Reading Inventory (Johns, 2012) and the Qualitative Reading Inventory (Leslie & Caldwell, 2010), also include graded passages. These reading passages are graded in various ways. Traditionally, passages were specified as preprimer (early first grade), primer (middle first grade), first grade, early second grade, late second grade, third grade, fourth grade, and so on. Recently, books and passages have been divided into more levels. In the Reading Recovery system, for example, books are divided into many levels; levels 16 through 18 are considered end of first grade.

Regardless of the source or leveling system of your graded passages, you can use these passages to determine the approximate reading level of each student. Generally, you have the child read a passage aloud, beginning with one you think he or she can handle. As the child reads, you mark the reading in some way that errors can be counted and analyzed. After the child reads the passage, you ask the student to retell the passage or you ask questions to determine how much was comprehended.

> Once there was a farmer who lived with his wife and their
> ten children in a very small farmhouse. The farmer and his
> family were miserable. They were always bumping into
> each other and getting in each other's way. When the
> children stayed inside on rainy days, they fought all the
> time. The farmer's wife was always ~~shooing~~ *shooting* children out of
> the kitchen so she could cook. The farmer had no place to
> sit ~~quietly~~ *SC quickly* when he came in from *his* work. The farmer (finally)
> could stand it no longer. He said to his wife, "Today I am
> going ~~into~~ *to* the village to talk with a wise man about our
> crowded house. He will know what to do."

Once you have made a record of the child's oral reading and a determination about comprehension from the retelling or the answers to questions, you decide what level of oral reading accuracy and comprehension is adequate. Most experts recommend that a child have an oral reading accuracy level of about 95 percent and demonstrate comprehension of 75 percent of the important ideas in the passage. The passage about the farmer and his wife has approximately 100 words. If you do not count the self-correction (which we would not because self-correcting is a good reading behavior that indicates the child is self-monitoring), the reader made four errors, giving him an accuracy rate of 96 percent. If the child's retelling indicates comprehension of most of the important ideas in this short passage, we will know that this reader can read text at this level quite adequately. We will not, however, know that this is the just right, or instructional, level for the child.

Instructional level is generally considered to be the highest level of text that a reader can read with at least 95 percent word accuracy and 75 percent comprehension. To determine instructional level, you must continue to have the child read harder and harder passages until word identification falls below 95 percent or comprehension falls below 75 percent. Instructional level is generally considered to be the *highest* level of text for which the child can pass both the word and comprehension criteria.

When you know the approximate reading levels of all your students, you can use this information to choose materials for comprehension lessons and decide how much support your different readers will need with the various materials. Remember that prior knowledge and interest have a large influence on reading level. Remember that during comprehension lessons, you build both interest and prior knowledge (including meaning vocabulary) before children read. You then choose your lesson framework to provide enough support so that they can be successful at meeting the purpose for the lesson. Children can read text that is a little beyond their level if they are given the appropriate support before, during, and after reading. Remember also that the size of the "leaps"

Determining Reading Levels

1. Use passages or books that have been determined to get increasingly more difficult.

2. Have the child begin reading at the level where you think that child might be.

3. To get a measure of word reading accuracy, record oral reading errors as the child reads.

4. After the child reads, remove the text and ask the student to retell what was read or answer some comprehension questions.

5. If the child's word reading accuracy is at least 95 percent and comprehension is approximately 75 percent, have that child read the next harder passage. If the child's word reading accuracy is below 95 percent or comprehension is below 75 percent, have that child read the next easier passage.

6. Continue to have the child read until you determine the highest level at which the child can read and still meet the 95 percent word accuracy and 75 percent comprehension criteria. This is the best general indicator of that child's just right, or instructional, reading level.

children make has limits. If you determine that a child's reading level is late first grade, that child can usually be given enough support to feel successful with some second-grade-level material. However, material written at the third-grade level is probably not going to be accessible for that child.

Why Not Use Standardized Tests to Determine Reading Levels?

In many schools, children take a variety of tests that yield a grade equivalent. Teachers get a printout that tells them that Billy reads at 2.5 and Carla reads at 5.5. Being trusting, logical people, they assume that this means Billy's instructional reading level is middle second grade and Carla's instructional reading level is middle fifth grade. Unfortunately, life is not that simple. If Billy and Carla are both in the second grade, most of the passages they read on the test are second-grade passages. Billy's score of 2.5 means that he did as well on the test as average second-graders reading second-grade text. Carla read the same passages and she did as well as the average fifth-grader reading second-grade passages would have done. We can certainly say that Carla is a good reader—certainly a better reader than Billy. But we cannot say that her instructional reading level is fifth grade because she did not read any fifth-grade passages!

Another reason that we cannot use standardized tests to determine individual reading level is that all tests have something called a *standard error of measurement (SEM)*. Look in the manual of any test and it will tell you what the SEM is. If the SEM is five months, then the score a child achieves is probably within five months of the true score. Billy's score of 2.5 has a 68 percent chance (one standard deviation) of actually being somewhere between 2.0 and 3.0. If we want to be 95 percent sure, we have to go out two standard deviations. Then we will know that Billy's score is almost surely somewhere between 1.5 and 3.5.

Across groups of children, these SEMs balance out. One child's score is higher than his actual ability, but another child's score is lower. If your class average score is 2.5, you can be pretty sure that your class reads about as well as the average class of second-graders on which the test was normed. Standardized scores provide information about groups of children but give only limited information about the reading levels of individual children. To determine the reading level of a child, we must listen to that child read and retell and find the highest levels at which he or she can do both with approximately 95 percent word accuracy and 75 percent comprehension. Unfortunately, no shortcut will get us where we need to go.

Once you understand how to listen to a child read and retell to determine instructional level, you can use this knowledge during your weekly independent reading conferences. You won't want to do formal oral reading records during these conferences. Rather, listen as the child reads a part he or she has selected, and then ask that child to tell about the most interesting part of the book or what has been learned so far. As the child reads and tells you about his or her reading, your informal 95 percent/75 percent meter is running, and if you realize that a child is choosing books that are way too easy or way too hard, you can steer that child toward some "just right" text.

Identifying Good Literacy Behaviors and Documenting Student Progress

There are three types of assessment commonly used in classrooms. Determining reading levels is an example of diagnostic assessment. It is done at a certain point in the school year—usually early in the year and its purpose is to "diagnose" student reading levels. The second type of assessment you will see in most classrooms is summative assessment. Summative assessment is usually the end of something and little if any instruction takes place as result of summative instruction. The Friday spelling test, the end of unit science test, and the end-of-grade tests are all examples of summative assessment. The third—and most important for learning—type of assessment is formative assessment. Formative assessment can take many forms—a "ticket out the door" response completed by all students; a writing sample; a student–teacher conference; a teacher eavesdropping on student discussion as they work with partners or in trios to complete a task; a checklist to guide observation of good behaviors. What makes all these assessments formative is not what they are but rather what the teacher does with the results. Formative assessments can take many forms but they are all intended to inform instruction. Formative assessment can tell you which strategies students lack or misconceptions they hold, alert you to the need for reteaching parts of a lesson, help you document progress students are making toward meeting certain goals and show you who may need some small group or one-to-one interventions.

Day in and day out, you need to be assessing and monitoring how well your students are reading and writing. To do this, you have to know what you are looking for. What are the good reading and writing behaviors? Throughout this book, we describe instruction that develops good literacy behaviors. In this section, we suggest ways to use formative assessment to monitor how well your students are developing these behaviors as they engage in literacy activities.

Assessing Emergent Literacy

Chapter 3 describes many activities for building the foundation for literacy and concludes that there are seven signs of emergent literacy. Emergent readers can "pretend read" favorite books, poems, songs, and chants. They can "write" and read what they have written—even if no one else can read it. They can track print and know print jargon. They can read and write some concrete words. They can name most common letters and know the common sounds for these letters. They are developing phonemic awareness and can blend and segment short words and tell you which words rhyme. The seven signs are the reading behaviors we look for as indicators that each child is moving successfully into reading and writing. These behaviors form the basis for our assessment of beginning readers. You can assess these behaviors as your students engage in their daily literacy activities.

If you teach young children, you may want to keep a checklist of emergent literacy behaviors. Each day, put the checklists of two or three children on your clipboard and observe and talk with these children as they engage in independent reading and writing to determine how well they are developing critical behaviors. Use a simple system, a minus (−) to indicate the child does not have that behavior, a question mark (?) when the behavior is erratic or it is unclear that the child has the behavior, and a plus (+) to indicate the

• Emergent Literacy Behaviors •

Name _____   **Dates Checked (− ? +)**

"Pretend reads" favorite books, poems, songs, and chants   __ __ __ __ __ __

"Writes" and can "read back" what was written   __ __ __ __ __ __

Tracks print   __ __ __ __ __ __

      Left page first

      Top to bottom

      Left to right

      Return sweep

      Points to each word

Knows reading jargon   __ __ __ __ __ __

      Identifies one letter, one word, and one sentence

      Identifies first word, first and last letter in a word

Reads and writes some concrete words   __ __ __ __ __ __

      Own name and names of friends, pets, family

      Favorite words from books, poems, and chants

Demonstrates phonemic awareness   __ __ __ __ __ __

      Counts words in oral sentence

      Claps syllables in words

      Stretches out words in attempt to spell

      Blends and segments words

      Identifies rhymes

Demonstrates alphabet awareness   __ __ __ __ __ __

      Names many letters

      Knows some words that begin with certain letters

      Knows many common letter sounds

child does seem to have developed that behavior. Three pluses on three different dates is a reliable indicator that the child has indeed developed that behavior.

Assessing Word Identification Strategies

As children move from the emergent literacy stage into the beginning reading and writing stages, you need to monitor and assess their development of fluency, sight words, decoding, and spelling strategies. Chapters 4 and 5 contain many activities for developing these strategies. Your assessment, however, must take place while the children are actually reading and writing. The goal of word instruction is to teach children words and strategies they can actually use when they are reading and writing. What you want to know is *not* how your students spell words during the daily word wall activity, but how quickly they recognize these words when reading and how correctly they spell these words when they are writing.

There are many opportunities throughout the day to make these observations. During your weekly independent reading conferences with children, ask them to read aloud a short part of what they have chosen to share with you. Listen for how fluently they read; how automatically they identify the word wall words; and how they use patterns, context, and other cues to figure out unknown words. When your students are reading in partners or trios, circulate to the different groups and ask them to read a page to you. Notice how they are using what you are teaching them about words as they actually read text.

Whenever you have the opportunity to observe the oral reading of a student, make a record of their word-identification accuracy so that you can then analyze errors, hesitations, and self-corrections to determine what word strategies the student is actually using while reading. After listening to Erin read on 10/17, her teacher concluded that Erin was monitoring her reading well and probably using context to self-correct. Because hesitating or mispronouncing common words can really interfere with fluency, the teacher created a personal word wall for Erin and provided practice with the high-frequency words she was mispronouncing or hesitating on. She decided that Erin and the rest of her third-graders could profit from some instruction on big words and provided that instruction to everyone. The teacher plans to analyze Erin's oral reading again in about a month and puts the 11/7 date on her record sheet as a reminder.

Word-Identification Analysis for Oral Reading				
Name: Erin				
Date	High-Frequency Words	Analysis	Low-Frequency Words	Analysis
10/17	them (pronounced they, self-corrected)	Self-correcting based on context	performing (hesitated, decoded correctly)	Needs more work with big word parts
	could (pronounced cold, self-corrected)		numerous "numer"	
	although (hesitated, pronounced correctly)		popular (hesitated, decoded correctly)	
			traditional "tradi"	
11/7				

Looking in the writing notebooks of your students and analyzing their spelling errors will give you a wealth of information about the word strategies they are actually using. Because writing results in a visible, external product, it is easier to determine what skills your students are actually using. By looking at two or three writing samples done a month or more apart, progress in word development is easy to determine.

To examine a writing sample to gain information about phonics knowledge, record all words misspelled and how the word was spelled. Analyze the errors and see if there is a pattern to the types of errors made. Look at your students' spelling of high-frequency words. Remember that many common words do not follow spelling patterns and students just have to learn how to spell them. Look at their attempts at spelling less frequent words. Do their invented spellings indicate that they can hear sounds in words and know what letters usually represent those sounds? Are the letters in the correct order? Are they spelling by pattern rather than just putting down one letter for each sound? Are they adding endings correctly and applying spelling changes when needed?

Looking at Toby's errors in his 9/7 writing, we can conclude that he misspells many common words, including confusing common homophones. If other students have similar misspellings of high-frequency words, these words could be gradually added to the class word wall. If Toby's errors are unique, you might want to create a personal word wall for him. His misspellings of less frequent words indicate that he is primarily spelling words by putting down a letter for each sound he hears. That spelling strategy works in Spanish where letters almost always represent the same sound, but in English words are spelled by pattern. Toby also needs work with prefixes and suffixes, and spelling changes required when endings and suffixes are added to words.

Spelling Errors in Writing Sample

Name:_Toby_____

Date	High-Frequency Words	Analysis	Low-Frequency Words	Analysis
9/7	thay (they)	Misspells many common words, including common homophones	sumer (summer)	Spells one letter = one sound. Needs work with prefixes, suffixes, spelling changes.
	to (too)		vacashun (vacation)	
	frend (friend)		speshul (special)	
	there (their)		complan (complain)	
	were (where)		hotest (hottest)	
	accept (except)		swiming (swimming)	
			flots (floats)	
			eckspensive (expensive)	
			crouded (crowded)	
10/12				

• Comprehension/Thinking Strategies •

Name: _____   **Dates Checked (– ? +)**

Makes text/prior knowledge connections   — — — — — — —

Predicts and asks questions while reading   — — — — — — —

Makes inferences and draws conclusions   — — — — — — —

Imagines and visualizes information   — — — — — — —

Summarizes most important ideas and events   — — — — — — —

Expresses a personal reaction/opinion   — — — — — — —

Monitors comprehension and uses fix-up strategies   — — — — — — —

Assessing Comprehension Strategies

As with emergent literacy behaviors and word strategies, you can monitor and assess your students' development of these behaviors as you interact with them during comprehension lessons and in your independent reading conferences. Because comprehension is so dependent on prior knowledge and interest, it is not possible to feel secure in our judgments that a child can—or cannot—use a particular comprehension strategy. Often, children recall much information and respond to that information in a high-level way when the topic is familiar and of great interest, but demonstrate little comprehension of less-familiar, uninteresting topics. Chapter 7, "Comprehension," describes seven thinking strategies readers use to comprehend. You can use a checklist of general comprehension strategies to periodically check on your students' use of these comprehension/thinking strategies. Many teachers analyze the anecdotal records for one or two children each day. Alternatively, you can keep anecdotal records only for those students who appear to have difficulty comprehending and observe these students more frequently.

• Comprehension Strategies—Story •

Name: _____   **Dates Checked (– ? +)**

Names and describes main characters   — — — — — — —

Names and describes settings   — — — — — — —

Describes the goal or problem in the story   — — — — — — —

Describes major events that lead to resolution   — — — — — — —

Describes the resolution to the story   — — — — — — —

Determines the point of view of characters   — — — — — — —

Determines the moral, theme, or lesson learned when appropriate   — — — — — — —

Compares and contrasts characters, settings, or themes   — — — — — — —

• Comprehension Strategies—Information •

Name: _____   **Dates Checked (– ? +)**

Reads closely to determine facts and details   — — — — — — —

Makes logical inferences   — — — — — — —

Determines main ideas   — — — — — — —

Describes sequential and causal relationships   — — — — — — —

Compares and contrasts information   — — — — — — —

Determines author's point of view and evaluates reasons   — — — — — — —

Uses visuals and other special features of informational text   — — — — — — —

As described in Chapters 7 and 8 and recognized in the Common Core Standards, comprehending narrative text and informational text requires some different strategies. In addition to analyzing your students' ability to use the seven general comprehension strategies, you will want to observe how well they comprehend as they read stories and informational text.

Assessing Writing

As described in Chapter 9, writing is perhaps the most complex act people engage in. The best way to determine how well students write is to observe them each day as they are writing, to look at first-draft writing samples, and to interact with them during writing conferences.

You can observe many aspects of writing as you move around the classroom. Do students struggle to identify topics for writing? Do students do some planning first when asked to write? Is handwriting easy for them? Are they using resources in the room and spelling patterns they know to spell words? Are they automatically using some of the mechanical and grammatical conventions they have been learning? Do students move confidently through a first draft? Do students revise and edit some as they write, or do they wait until they are publishing a piece? To record these observations, you may want to make a checklist similar to the previous examples but specific to the age and starting point of your students.

In addition to the observations you record, you may want to take a focused writing sample during the first week of school. Give your students a prompt to which they all can relate, such as "What Third Grade Is Like" or "My Three Most Favorite and Least Favorite Things." Analyze these samples to determine where individual children are in their writing development and what the class as a whole needs to work on. Put this sample somewhere where you can find it in January. After the winter holidays, have your students write on the same prompt again. When your students have written the second time, return the first samples to them and let each child analyze the writing growth made. You can also analyze the second samples, comparing them to the first for each child and looking for indicators of things the class needs to work on. Repeat the same procedure once more at the end of the year and you and your students will be able to document the growth they have made.

Writing is a very complex process. No matter how good we get, there is always room for growth. Because writing is complex, it is easy to see only the problems children still exhibit in their writing and not the growth they are making. Having three writing samples on the same topic across the school year provides tangible evidence of growth to both teacher and student.

In addition to observing their general writing behaviors, you will want to observe their progress toward learning to do the three types of writing described in the Common Core Standards. You can use the guidelines described in Chapter 9 to develop checklists appropriate for your grade level to evaluate how well your students are writing opinion, informational, and narrative pieces.

Assessing Attitudes and Interests

It is hard to overemphasize the importance of children's attitudes toward and interests in reading and writing. If developing avid readers and writers is one of your major goals, you need to collect and analyze some data so that you can identify needs and document progress.

Early in the year, it is important to determine what your students like to read and how they feel about reading. Many teachers start the school year with the following homework assignment: "Next Monday, bring to school the three best books you read all summer." They encourage students to go back to the library to check out a book previously read. If children can no longer find the book, the teachers ask them to tell why they thought it was such a good book. Young children are encouraged to bring favorite books they like to have read to them.

When the children bring their books, encourage them to tell what they like about the books. As they share, note the titles of the books they bring and their reasons for liking them. This tells you a lot about their current reading interests and also suggests selections for read-aloud books to try to broaden interests.

Some children do not bring three books, or they bring books but have nothing to say about them and may not have liked or even read the books. This tells you a lot about the current interests, attitudes, and home environment of these children. It also lets you know that all the efforts you plan to make to encourage and support reading are truly important and needed. You might want to follow up this "best books" assignment with another homework assignment to bring in magazines and parts of the newspaper the children have read. Again, follow up this assignment with group sharing and make notes about what each child brings (or does not bring).

To document your students' progress in becoming "readers," you may want to have your students complete a reading attitude assessment such as the "Reading and Me" assessment on pages 14 and 15. If you do this during the first week of school, in January after the holiday recess, and at the end of the year, you will have evidence of the growth your students have made in becoming readers—not just people who can read but people who do read!

Just as with any kind of assessment, your assessment of reading interests and attitudes should be ongoing. By linking your assessment directly to your instruction, you ensure that your assessment is valid. By assessing interests and attitudes on a regular schedule, you get a more reliable indicator than if you assess only once or twice a year. Also, as in any assessment, you can use a variety of methods to assess interests and attitudes. One of the best methods of assessing is to observe what your students actually do. Many teachers fill out checklists for everyone early in the year and then fill them out again for one-sixth

Reading Interests and Attitude Summary

Name: _____   **Dates Checked (– ? +)**

Seemed happy when engaged in reading   — — — — — — —

Seemed happy when engaged in writing   — — — — — — —

Talked about reading at home   — — — — — — —

Talked about writing at home   — — — — — — —

Showed enthusiasm when sharing a book with peers   — — — — — — —

Showed enthusiasm when sharing a piece of writing   — — — — — — —

Showed enthusiasm during independent reading conference   — — — — — — —

Showed enthusiasm during writing conference   — — — — — — —

Chose to read rather than engage in another activity   — — — — — — —

Chose to write rather than engage in another activity   — — — — — — —

of their class each week. If you do this all year, you should have six or seven indicators of reading attitude throughout the year and should be able to document which students have better attitudes at the end of the year than they did at the beginning.

Summary

Three types of assessment are commonly used in classrooms. Diagnostic assessment is used with individual students to determine their instructional reading levels. For children who struggle with reading, diagnostic assessments can determine which part of the complex process of reading is keeping them from making progress. You will learn much more about diagnostic assessment in Chapter 12, which describes how to diagnose your struggling readers' strengths and weaknesses and target your instruction to their specific needs.

The second type of assessment you will see in most classrooms is summative assessment. Summative assessments are used to provide evidence of student achievement in order to make judgments about student competence or program effectiveness. Summative assessments rarely lead to changes in instruction and the results of some of these assessments, such as end-of-grade tests, are not usually available until students have moved on to other grades or classrooms.

Formative assessment is assessment that informs our instruction. While the term *formative assessment* has only recently entered the educational jargon, good teachers have been doing formative assessment for years. You are doing formative assessments when you ask students to write down the most important thing they learned in a lesson today or something they are confused about or how they can apply what they learned to their own lives as a "ticket out the door." By looking at these brief responses, you can figure out how well your students are learning whatever you are focusing on and adjust your instruction for tomorrow. You can decide to make these adjustments for the whole class, a small group, or an individual. Technology can help us get "real-time" information as students use "clickers" to respond to questions. The responses that appear on the screen for everyone to see are anonymous so no one is embarrassed by a wrong answer, but the teacher's responses show which students gave correct and incorrect responses. When you look at writing samples and decide which parts of the writing process to focus your mini-lessons on, you are doing formative assessment. During individual conferences with students, you gain information that affects what you do next for that student and sometimes for your whole class of students. You are doing formative assessment when you stop and listen in on the discussion your students have as they work with others to complete a task. Using a checklist to guide your observation of good reading behaviors as described in this chapter is formative instruction. A test can be formative assessment if, in addition to grading it, you analyze the results and decide what you need to reteach and for whom. What makes all these assessments formative is not what they are but rather what you do with the results.

Dylan Williams (2011) has written a wonderfully "informative" book called *Embedded Formative Assessment* in which he gives many practical examples of formative assessment in all subjects and at all grade levels. He also summarizes research done throughout the world that shows that the students of teachers who regularly use formative assessments to inform their instruction achieve standardized test scores 15 to 25 percent higher than students in other classrooms (Black and William, 1998).

12

Differentiation and Interventions for **Struggling Readers**

"The more different ways I teach, the more children I reach."

WE DON'T KNOW who the author of this quote is but we all recognize (and research supports) the common sense truth it communicates. The children you teach are all individuals and they differ on any dimension you can name. We know from the research on multiple intelligences that children differ in the ways they learn. To meet the needs of your kinesthetic learners, you need to provide hands-on, concrete learning experiences. Your interpersonal learners thrive when you include small-group and partner activities as a regular feature of your literacy instruction. In today's multicultural classrooms, there are many cultural differences among our students. They have different cultural heritages and racial backgrounds, and they come to school speaking a variety of languages. In addition to cultural differences and differences in how your students learn, they also differ in how much they like to read and write and thus approach literacy activities with very different levels of engagement. The most obvious difference you probably notice among your students is their reading levels. Regardless of what grade you teach, your most achieving students probably read and write at levels several years beyond the levels of your struggling students. Although we have not used the word *differentiation*, the concept of teaching in a variety of ways to meet the needs of all your students has been an important agenda in all the preceding chapters of this book. Before we suggest some additional ways you can differentiate your instruction for your struggling readers, think back to the possibilities already described.

This book began by inviting you into the classrooms of unusually effective teachers—teachers who year in and year out got better-than-expected results from their students. Common across all these classrooms was the variety factor. Teachers used a wide variety of materials, a wide variety of lesson formats, and a variety of student groupings. Another common factor was student engagement. Discipline problems were few and far between because the teacher viewed the classroom as a community and taught students to work together and to help and respect one another. Quantity of reading and writing was another common factor in successful classrooms. Students spent a lot of time reading and writing— not only when the schedule said "reading" and "writing" but also during math, science, and social studies time. The research reviewed in Chapter 1, "Creating Classrooms That Work," suggests that the most effective teachers know that "one size does not fit all" and that their instruction across the day incorporates the basic principles of differentiation.

The chapters that have followed Chapter 1 also incorporate the basic principles of differentiation. The essential question of Chapter 2, "Creating Independent Readers," focuses on how you can increase the quantity of reading done by *all* your students. Including some informational books and magazine articles in your teacher read-aloud and adding more informational pieces to your classroom library is a differentiation strategy, because males often prefer nonfiction. Including multicultural books provides additional differentiation for your students of varying cultural and racial heritages. During your weekly independent reading conferences, you differentiate your instruction for both struggling and avid readers by spreading struggling readers out across the days and spending an extra minute or two with them, steering them toward materials at their optimal reading level. The most obvious way you differentiate your instruction during independent reading time, however, is by letting your students choose what they want to read. When they can choose, they will differentiate for themselves.

Glance through the activities for building the literacy foundation suggested in Chapter 3 and think about how they are differentiated. It is not by accident that many of the activities center on the names of your children. When you use your children and their names to build beginning literacy concepts, your children can view each lesson as "all about them!" When your fledgling readers choose what they want to read during independent reading time and write in the Writing Center, they are differentiating their own instruction by their choices.

The focus of Chapters 4 and 5 is on helping all children become fluent readers and writers who can automatically and quickly read and spell common words, and who have strategies for quickly identifying and spelling unfamiliar words. In these chapters, differentiation is accomplished through quantity, variety, and choice. Everyone can find things that are easy for them to read because you have accumulated and created a wide variety of "everyone" books. Across the week, you engage your children in rereading through choral reading, echo reading, and reading along with recorded books they have selected. By having your word wall words always visible, you are supporting your visual learners. Auditory learners learn these important words as they chant them. The learning style of your kinesthetic learners is supported as they write the words.

The decoding and spelling activities in Chapter 5, "Teaching Phonics and Spelling Patterns," are carefully designed to move all your students forward in their understanding of spelling patterns. During Guess the Covered Word activities, the words are always read in the context of a sentence or paragraph. Children learn how to use word length, all the beginning letters, and known words to figure out unknown words. In every Guess the Covered Word lesson, beginning sounds are reviewed for children who need more practice with beginning sounds. Advanced readers often learn to read all the words in the sentences used in Guess the Covered Word activities—greatly increasing the number of words they can read. Each Making Words lesson begins with short, easy words and progresses to longer, more complex words. Children who still need to develop phonemic awareness can do this as they "stretch out" words while making them and as they decide which words rhyme while sorting them. Using Words You Know, lessons begin with short, familiar words and proceed to longer, more complex words.

Differentiation in the vocabulary and comprehension activities described in Chapters 6, 7, and 8 is supported by the great variety of activities and lesson formats you can use to help your students build their vocabularies and hone their thinking strategies. Beginning the year with Writer's Workshop, as described in Chapter 9, "Writing," and letting your students choose their topics allows all your students to write about what they know about and care about. When you form revising and editing partnerships by pairing writers with similar abilities, you are using these partner groupings to differentiate your writing instruction. As you meet with individual students in writing conferences, you can tailor your conference to the individual needs of each writer. This writing conference provides the "teachable moment" in which both advanced and struggling writers can be nudged forward in their literacy development. During Writer's Workshop, children choose their topics and write about what matters to them. Many children thrive during Writer's Workshop but other children struggle to come up with their own topics. These children are more likely to enjoy and progress in writing during your focused writing lessons in which topics are assigned and they learn to write opinion, information, and narrative pieces. Including think-writes and reading-writing connections, as described in Chapter 10, gives all your students more and varied opportunities to learn to read and write as you incorporate comprehension and vocabulary instruction into your math, science, and social studies instruction.

Assessment is essential to differentiation. Only when you know what your individual students can do and cannot yet do, can you make good decisions about how to spend your instructional time and what kind of lessons and groupings will move all your students forward.

If you are incorporating many of the ideas from the previous chapters into your daily instruction, you already have a lot of differentiation going on in your classroom. This differentiated and varied instruction represents ideally what all children would experience in their classrooms. In 2004, as part of the reauthorization of the Individuals with Disabilities Education Improvement Act, response to intervention (RTI) was born (U.S. Department of Education, 2004). RTI mandates that before considering that a child has a learning disability, the school must demonstrate that the child has had appropriate classroom instruction and instruction specifically targeted to his or her needs (Johnston, 2010). RTI is generally implemented as three tiers of instruction. Tier 1 instruction occurs in the regular classroom. If assessments demonstrate that children are not making adequate progress in spite of focused and differentiated classroom instruction, these students are to be given Tier 2 instruction. Tier 2 instruction is in addition to the Tier 1 classroom instruction. Tier 2 instruction is often delivered in small groups or tutoring formats and is targeted to specific instructional needs. Children who do not show adequate progress in Tier 2 instruction can be evaluated for a learning disability and move into Tier 3 instruction, often delivered by a teacher specifically trained to teach children with learning disabilities.

Partner Older, Struggling Readers to Tutor Younger, Struggling Readers

All struggling readers, regardless of why they struggle, need to do some easy reading. Getting them to do this easy reading, when they often claim to "hate reading," is not easy. Webster Magnet School in Minnesota (Taylor, Hansen, Swanson, & Watts, 1998) solved this problem by setting up a tutoring program in which fourth-graders who were reading at beginning third-grade level tutored second-graders, most of whom were reading at primer level. The second-graders were all participating in an early-intervention program in their classroom in which they read books on their level. The fourth-graders spent 45 minutes on Monday and Tuesday with the reading coordinator or with their classroom teacher preparing for their 25-minute tutoring sessions on Wednesday and Thursday. On Monday, the fourth-graders selected a picture book to read to their second-grader and practiced reading the book. They also practiced word-recognition prompts that they would use when their second-grader read to them. On Tuesday, they practiced again and developed extension activities to develop comprehension strategies, including story maps and character sketches. They came up with several good discussion questions based on the book they were planning to read.

On Wednesday and Thursday, the fourth-graders met with their tutees. During this session, they listened to their second-grader read the book currently being read in their classroom's early-intervention program. While listening, they helped their second-graders identify words by giving them hints: "Look at the picture," "It starts with *pr*," "Sound it out in chunks—what would this part be (covering all but the first syllable)?" Next, they read from the picture book they had chosen, built meaning vocabulary from the book, led a discussion based on their discussion questions, and did the comprehension extension activity.

On Friday, the fourth-graders had debriefing sessions with their teacher in which they discussed how their tutees reacted to the book, how well their word-recognition prompts were working, the success of their discussion and comprehension activities, as well as problems encountered and progress noticed. They also wrote a letter to project coordinators detailing the successes and problems of that week. They received a response to their letter on Monday.

Data reported on this project show that both the second- and fourth-grade struggling readers made measurable progress. This is not surprising because this program combines all the elements essential for reading growth. Second-graders were getting daily guided reading instruction in materials at their level in their classrooms. In addition, during the tutoring session, they were reading material at their level to someone who knew how to help them with word recognition. They were also increasing their knowledge stores and comprehension strategies as they listened to their fourth-grade tutor read the picture book to them and as they engaged in the discussion and comprehension activities. Fourth-graders got a lot of practice using the material at their instructional level, reading the picture book, and learning word-recognition and comprehension strategies, as they prepared and carried out the tutoring with their second-graders.

Targeted Tier 2 Interventions for Struggling Readers

Michael is a fifth-grader who has struggled with reading since first grade. Achievement test scores and assessments done by his teachers indicate that Michael reads approximately two years below grade level. At the beginning of fifth grade, he can read most materials at second-grade level and some third-grade materials. What kind of instruction does Michael need so that he can read materials closer to his grade level? Because reading is a complex process, there is no simple answer to this question.

As adults, we have been reading for so long we are unaware of all the different actions our brains are orchestrating as we read. At the most basic level, our eyes have to focus on the print and use the spaces to separate the words. We have to begin on the left and move across the line to the right and at the end of the line, our eyes have to jump back to the left side and start again. As we read, we quickly recognize almost every word, pronouncing it aloud or in our minds if we are reading silently. Occasionally, we encounter an unfamiliar word such as *pluvial* and use our phonics knowledge to decode it. Often the unfamiliar word is one we haven't heard before. If *pluvial* is not a word you have a meaning for, you won't know the difference between a pluvial lake and other kinds of lakes unless the text goes on to clarify the meaning of *pluvial*. If you cannot associate meaning for several of the key vocabulary words in a passage, your comprehension will be impaired because associating meanings with words is critical for comprehension. As you are reading, you must also read fairly quickly and give the words the kind of phrasing and expression you would give them if you were speaking the words. This fluent reading allows you to get meaning from phrases of words and promotes comprehension.

Reading is multidimensional and requires your brain to perform many functions simultaneously. As you have been reading these first paragraphs, you have been using your print tracking skills to move your eyes smoothly across the page, your immediate word identification skills to instantly recognize most of the words, your phonics skills to decode an unfamiliar word such as *pluvial*, your fluency skills to read phrases with appropriate expression, your meaning vocabulary skills to quickly access the meaning of words, and your comprehension skills to piece together the meaning of what you have been reading.

No matter what kind of text you are reading, print processing, automatic word identification, decoding, fluency, and meaning vocabulary are essential to comprehension. In addition, different kinds of text require different strategies. Most children read stories better than they read informational texts. Because so much of their reading has been stories, they have learned what it is important to pay attention to. Stories have characters and settings and problems to be solved or goals to be reached. Texts that compare and contrast the kind of animal and plant life found in deserts and in rain forests have none of these story features. Nor do texts that explain how the water cycle works or why climate change is an issue we should all be concerned about. Reading is the most complex subject we teach because comprehension is what matters and comprehension depends on all these parts working smoothly together.

You may be wondering what this explanation of the complexity of the reading process has to do with Michael. Actually, it has everything to do with Michael because until we know which parts of the reading orchestration he does well and which parts don't work for him, we won't know how to target our instruction to the part holding him back!

Michael has a younger sister, Erin, who is five years old and just starting kindergarten. Erin loves to be read to but she can't read these books yet. Why not?

Because Erin does not know how to read most of the words in these books. For most young children, the reason they can't read is simple: they don't know the words! Because word identification is the major reason young children can't read, we often assume word identification is the problem for all children who struggle with reading. Research does not support this commonly held idea.

In 1998, test results in Washington State indicated that 43 percent of fourth-grade students had not met proficiency on the state reading assessment. The Washington State Legislature allocated $9,000,000 to K–2 classrooms to be used for instructional materials and professional development, and districts were encouraged to adopt instructional materials and approaches that emphasized phonics.

Buly and Valencia (2002) did reading profiles on a sample of 108 of the fourth-graders who had scored below proficiency on the Washington assessment. They found that less than half of these struggling readers had a weakness in word identification relative to the rest of their scores. The researchers concluded that:

> "Mandating phonics instruction . . . for all students who fall below proficiency would miss large numbers of students (more than 50% in our sample) whose word identification skills are fairly strong yet who struggle with comprehension, fluency or language." (p. 233)

A more recent study by Lesaux and Kieffer (2010) confirms these results. These researchers gave a standardized reading comprehension test to 581 urban sixth-graders and found that 45 percent of them scored at or below the 35th percentile. These 262 struggling readers were then given a battery of tests to determine their relative strengths and weaknesses on the major components of reading. Decoding as measured was above average for 79 percent of the struggling readers and a relative strength for the majority of the rest. Fluency was at least average or a relative strength for the majority of them. What the struggling readers had most in common was low meaning vocabulary knowledge.

So, why does Michael read two years below grade level? It is possible that he is not able to identify words accurately and quickly, but research with older struggling readers suggests that it is more likely that Michael has a limited meaning vocabulary and can identify words at a higher level than he can comprehend. This makes sense, actually, when you recall that vocabulary research summarized in Chapter 6 indicates that most new word meanings are learned through reading and that children who read more have larger meaning vocabulary stores. Michael struggles with reading and probably only reads when he is forced to, and thus has fewer opportunities to learn new word meanings.

Determining Areas of Greatest Need for Struggling Readers

Because Michael is not making adequate progress in his reading with the good Tier 1 instruction he is receiving in his classroom, Michael needs to be given some additional Tier 2 instruction. This instruction can include individual tutoring as well as small group instruction, but it must be targeted to Michael's needs. How can a teacher determine which part of the reading orchestration Michael is most in need of? Just because most older struggling readers have relative strengths in word identification and fluency and relative weaknesses in meaning vocabulary and comprehension does not mean that this is Michael's profile.

Chapter 11 describes how to use graded passages to determine instructional reading levels. Instructional level is defined as the highest level at which a student can accurately read at least 95 percent of the words and can comprehend at least 75 percent of the meaning of the passage read. To determine the area of greatest need for struggling readers, we can modify the procedures described in the previous chapter. Here is how we will determine the area of greatest need for Michael—and others who read at least a year below grade level.

Using some set of graded materials, have the student read silently and retell or answer questions without looking back at the passage. Begin with a passage that is one level below the level you think the student can succeed with. If the student demonstrates adequate comprehension on the first passage, have the student read a passage at the next higher level. If comprehension is inadequate, have the student silently read and retell or answer questions on a passage that is a level lower. Continue to have the student read and retell or answer questions until you find that student's comprehension level.

Before students read, be sure to tell them that they should think about what they read because you will ask them to "retell" the major facts or events of what they read. When students finish reading, take the passage away and say:

"Now tell me everything you remember from your reading."

Listen while they tell you and ask questions if you are unsure of how much they comprehended. You may want to record what they tell you or make notes of their recall. Rate their comprehension on a four-point scale. Their comprehension level is the highest level for which they score a Level 3 or 4 on the Comprehension Scale.

Comprehension Scale	
Level 4	Recalls most of the important events or facts and no misinformation
Level 3	Recalls a lot of events or facts and little misinformation
Level 2	Recalls some events or facts and may include some misinformation
Level 1	Recalls little except the topic

Michael's teacher had him start with the second-grade level passage. He read it silently and then told what he remembered and responded successfully to questions the teacher asked about information he had not included in his retelling. He included no misinformation. Having achieved a comprehension level of 4 on the second-grade passage, the teacher then had him read the third-grade passage.

Michael read the third-grade passage silently. Based on his retelling and responses to follow-up questions, the teacher rated his comprehension as a 3 and now has him read the fourth-grade passage. After reading the fourth-grade passage, his recall is minimal and the teacher rates it at a 2 on the comprehension scale. Since comprehension level is the highest level at which a student achieves a rating of 3 or 4, the teacher determines that Michael's comprehension level is third grade.

Why is Michael unable to comprehend the passage at the fourth-grade level? To determine this, the teacher has Michael read the fourth-grade passage aloud and marks his reading as he reads. She uses this simple marking system shown on page 194. She writes any word Michael substitutes for another word, circles words he omitted, carets in words he added, and writes an SC for self-corrects above any errors he made and then self-corrected. When Michael finishes reading, she counts the errors made in the first 100 words. Michael made only one error in the first 100 words giving him a word identification score of 99 percent. Clearly, Michael's inability to comprehend this fourth-grade passage is not because he could not decode the words!

As he reads, she also listens to how fluently and expressively he reads. Some students read as if they are reading words in a list—one word at a time—ignoring punctuation and lacking the expression readers normally read with. She uses an oral reading fluency scale to determine his level of fluency. Michael's reading sounds like speech and she gives his oral reading fluency a rating of 4.

Oral Reading Fluency Scale	
Level 4	Reads in phrases with expression that sounds like speech
Level 3	Reads mostly in phrases and with some expression
Level 2	Reads mostly word by word with some phrases but little expression
Level 1	Reads like reading words in a list, word by word with little or no expression

Targeted Tier 2 Instruction for Michael

Now that Michael's teacher knows that comprehension—not word identification or fluency—is what keeps Michael from reading better, she can target Michael's instruction to that area. She or someone else can tutor Michael individually or she can form a group with Michael and two or three other students who struggle with reading and have comprehension as their greatest need and focus this tutoring or small-group instruction on comprehension. (For this example, we will assume that she is tutoring Michael but she could also use the same procedures with a small group of struggling readers who have comprehension as their area of greatest need.)

To ensure Michael knows the different thinking strategies readers use to comprehend, she does some think-alouds (page 104) to demonstrate for Michael

Seven Thinking Strategies
● **Call up** and **connect** to what you know.
● **Predict** and ask yourself **questions** about what you will learn or what will happen.
● **Visualize** or **imagine** what things look, feel, sound, taste, and smell like.
● Decide on the **most important** ideas and events and **summarize** or **recap** as you read.
● Make **inferences** based on what you read and what you know.
● **Monitor** your comprehension and use **fix-up** strategies when you are confused.
● **Evaluate**, make **judgments**, and form **opinions**.

how to use thinking strategies while reading. She makes a list of these strategies and gives it to Michael.

She then reads aloud and stops periodically to tell Michael what her brain is thinking. Then she asks Michael to tell her what thinking strategy he thinks she is using.

Next it is Michael's turn to read and think aloud. He quickly gets the idea and enjoys sharing his thinking and having his teacher guess what thinking strategies he is using. Across the next two weeks, they do these shared think-alouds with both story and informational text. During each session, the teacher reads and thinks aloud about the first half of the text and Michael guesses which thinking strategy her brain is using. Then they reverse roles, with Michael reading and thinking and the teacher guessing. For the first few think-alouds, Michael's think-alouds are almost always connections and predictions. His teacher includes a few connections and predictions in her think-alouds but tries to include more of the higher-level thinking skills of inferring, visualizing, summarizing, and evaluating. Soon, Michael begins to include some of these higher-level thinking skills in his think-alouds. Monitoring is the hardest strategy to get Michael to use. The teacher is not surprised at this. Michael has always struggled with reading and, like most struggling readers, does not like to admit he is having any problems. To get Michael to monitor, the teacher chooses some harder text with some vocabulary terms she in not familiar with. When she is reading, she models this monitoring by saying things such as:

> "I don't know what an aerie is. I will reread and see if I can figure it out. Maybe the picture will help."

She then proceeds to use fix-up strategies to figure out the meaning of *aerie*. By choosing some text in which she can frankly admit to not understanding the meanings of some words and needing to stop and use fix-up strategies, she makes it "okay" for Michael to monitor and use fix-up strategies in his reading.

As the tutoring sessions continue, the teacher uses the think-aloud lesson framework on some days but adds in other types of lessons when she notices specific comprehension issues Michael demonstrates. In spite of her modeling, Michael does not like to admit to not understanding the meanings of some words and often reads right past these words without stopping. His teacher plans some lessons using the Word Detectives framework (page 93) to help him learn to use context, pictures, and morphemic clues to figure out the meanings of unfamiliar words and to learn a new meaning for a multimeaning word. Michael is also not good at making inferences and so she does some Find It or Figure It Out lessons (page 126) to focus explicitly on making inferences. She uses a variety of short text to teach these lessons and makes sure to include both story and informational text.

As she and Michael work together, she realizes that he is better at comprehending story text than he is at comprehending informational text. To focus his attention on the special features of informational text, she creates some scavenger hunts (page 142) in which Michael has a limited amount of time to find as many answers as he can, using only the visuals, headings, and other special features of informational text. Michael loves the "beat the clock" nature of these hunts and soon learns that you can get a lot of information if you focus on these visuals and other special features. One day, he remarks that he never knew how to read those charts and other things and that big words are easier to pronounce if you read the translation in the parentheses after the word. "I used to just skip all those graphs and big words and now I can figure them out!"

Michael also enjoys working with his teacher to construct main idea trees, time lines, and compare/contrast bubbles (pages 131–136) to organize information in informational text. At first, the teacher told him what kind of graphic organizer they would make. After he became good at creating these, he and the teacher would preview the text together and decide which of these organizers to use.

Knowing that in addition to targeted instruction, struggling readers need lots of practice to become good readers, Michael's teacher searches for some reading material Michael would read on his own. They go to the library at the end of one of the tutoring sessions and the teacher suggests some books on his reading level that she thinks he might like. Michael is less than enthusiastic but finally checks out a book, probably more to please the teacher than because he will read it! As they are leaving the library, Michael spots the new issue of *Sports Illustrated for Kids*, which has just arrived. He picks it up and turns to an article about basketball—his favorite sport. Unfortunately, magazines cannot be checked out so he doesn't get to read the article. The teacher, however, acts on this information and orders her own subscription to the magazine. A few weeks later, she pulls out the magazine at the end of a tutoring session and she and Michael spend a few minutes "grazing" in it. For the next several tutoring sessions, she ends each session by letting Michael choose an article from the magazine which they read together. When the next issue arrives, they use this new one for their end-of-tutoring reading and she gives Michael the old issue to keep. As the tutoring continues, Michael realizes that if he picks up the pace (and doesn't procrastinate!), there is more time at the end of a tutoring session for reading in his magazine! He is especially eager to get to the reading when a new issue sits there tantalizing him! Just before the end of the school year, Michael arrives at the tutoring session waving a *Sports Illustrated for Kids* in his hand—his "graduation" from elementary school present from his mom, who never thought she would see Michael reading voluntarily!

Targeted Tier 2 Instruction for Jenny

Like Michael, Jenny is a fifth-grader whose test scores and teachers' observations indicate that she is reading at least two years below grade level. Unlike Michael, Jenny's records and her mom indicate that she was a good reader in first and second grade and began to struggle with—and avoid—reading about halfway through third grade. To determine what is keeping Jenny from progressing in reading, Jenny's teacher uses the same diagnostic procedures she used with Michael but with very different results.

The teacher began by having Jenny read a second-grade passage silently and then having Jenny retell what she read and answer questions about information she left out of her retelling. Jenny read the passage quite quickly and recalled most of the important information so the teacher rated her comprehension at level 4 and moved on to the third-grade passage.

Comprehension Scale	
Level 4	Recalls most of the important events or facts and no misinformation
Level 3	Recalls a lot of events or facts and little misinformation
Level 2	Recalls some events or facts and may include some misinformation
Level 1	Recalls little except the topic

Jenny read the third-grade passage more slowly and asked the teacher to pronounce several words for her. The teacher explained that she couldn't help her with the words and that Jenny should just try to figure them out or continue with the reading. Jenny's retelling included some facts but she was unable to answer any of the questions the teacher used to probe for information she had not included in her retelling. The teacher rated Jenny's comprehension on the third-grade passage at level 2 and thus decided that Jenny's comprehension level was second grade. She then asked Jenny to read the third-grade passage aloud. Jenny had eight errors in the first 100 words—almost all of them longer words that she hesitated on and then skipped over. The eight words she could not pronounce were **celebrate, eagerly, promotion, wouldn't, unwrapped, explained, listening,** and **joyfully.**

Because Jenny could not correctly identify at least 95 percent of the words on the third-grade passage, the teacher had Jenny read the second-grade passage aloud, Jenny made three errors in the first 100 words, once again longer words—**yourselves, basement,** and **cricket**—that she hesitated on and then skipped. The teacher decided that Jenny's word identification level, like her comprehension level, was second grade and that her inability to decode longer words was the reason she was not progressing in reading.

Except for hesitating on longer words, Jenny's reading was fluent and expressive and the teacher rated her oral reading fluency at level 4.

Oral Reading Fluency Scale	
Level 4	Reads in phrases with expression that sounds like speech
Level 3	Reads mostly in phrases and with some expression
Level 2	Reads mostly word by word with some phrases but little expression
Level 1	Reads like reading words in a list, word by word with little or no expression

As the teacher finished the diagnostic tests with Jenny, she marveled at the fact that two fifth-graders could struggle with reading but for such different reasons. Michael's word identification was excellent but he struggled with comprehension and had a limited meaning vocabulary. Jenny, on the other hand, struggled with word identification and not being able to identify longer words impeded her comprehension. Jenny's teacher recalled Jenny's mom's observation that Jenny was a good reader until third grade, and this made sense because third grade is the level at which multisyllabic words become more common.

The Tier 2 instruction Jenny's teacher began with focused on teaching her how to chunk larger words into syllables and use patterns she knew from one-syllable words to decode these longer words, building Jenny's bank of sight words that contained the prefixes, suffixes, and spelling changes common to big words and teaching her to use context and pictures, along with the morphemes she was learning, to decode big words.

Jenny's teacher had observed in listening to Jenny read aloud that she had no difficulty identifying short one-syllable words, including uncommon words such as **blew, whale,** and **hatch.** But she could not pronounce words such as **basement** and **cricket,** the syllables of which are common syllables from one-syllable words. To get Jenny off to a quick, successful start with decoding longer words, Jenny's teacher decided to use the Using Words You Know lesson framework (page 64) and to focus the instruction on two-syllable words.

For the first lesson, Jenny' teacher gave Jenny four sticky notes on which she had written four words she knew Jenny could easily read—**cat**, **ape**, **snake**, and **ant**. She then explained to Jenny the decoding strategy she could use to figure out big words by thinking of words she knew that ended like the big word. Jenny looked skeptical but she agreed to try. The teacher wrote the word **pancake** on a sheet of paper and asked Jenny to put the sticky note with the word that she thought rhymed with the end of the word she had written. Jenny quickly placed **snake** next to **pancake** and used **snake** to pronounce **cake** and then looked at the rest of the word, and in a surprised tone of voice pronounced "pancake?" "Exactly," said the teacher. "Now let's try another one." The teacher wrote (but did not pronounce!) the word **eggplant**. Jenny placed the sticky note with the word **ant** next to **eggplant**, pronounced **plant**, looked at the remaining part of the word, and said, "**eggplant**?" Jenny's confidence and excitement mounted as she quickly matched the last syllable and then correctly pronounced **enchant**, **earthquake**, **escape**, **transplant**, and **acrobat**!

In this first lesson, Jenny caught on quickly to using known rhyming words to figure out the last syllable of a longer word, and then looking at the chunk that was left and decoding the word by putting the chunks together. The teacher did two more lessons with the sticky notes to build Jenny's confidence. In the second lesson, Jenny wrote the words **black**, **neck**, **sick**, **rock**, and **truck** on sticky notes and then used these words to decode the words the teacher wrote: **toothpick**, **woodchuck**, **padlock**, **roadblock**, **racetrack**, **ship-wreck**, and **homesick**. In the third lesson, Jenny used **late**, **Pete**, **kite**, **vote**, and **cute** to decode **donate**, **translate**, **athlete**, **parachute**, **promote**, **dynamite**, and **invite**.

By the end of this third lesson, Jenny's teacher knew that Jenny understood how she could use the words she knew to decode the last syllable of a word and, with that chunk decoded, she could look at the rest of the word and use her phonics knowledge to figure out the first part and then put the chunks together. The teacher also knew that Jenny would not automatically use that strategy when she was reading and came to a word she did not immediately recognize—especially if, as the teacher suspected, Jenny had developed the habit of just skipping over longer words when she was reading on her own. Jenny liked the *Magic Tree House* books and she was reading a chapter at home each night and telling the teacher about what she had read at the beginning of each tutoring session. The teacher got a new *Magic Tree House* book—one Jennie had not read before and which she intended to let Jenny keep. She went through the first chapter and highlighted longer words she thought Jenny could decode based on words she knew. The words she highlighted in the first chapter were **flashlight**, **downstairs**, **enchantress**, **adventure**, **backpack**, **whisper**, and **silent**. Jenny was quite excited to see the new *Magic Tree House* book and surprised the teacher had highlighted words right in the book—which she assumed was a school book. The teacher assured Jenny that the highlighting was okay because this was a book she meant to let Jenny keep when they were finished using it to practice decoding big words. Jenny looked at each highlighted word and then explained how she could decode it.

"This one is easy because I know light and a-s-h is ash—flashlight"

"This one is easy, too, it's just stairs and down!"

"This is harder but t-r-e-s-s is like dress and c-h-a-n rhymes with an, e-n is like ten—enchantress?"

"T-u-re is like sure and then v-e-n is like ten and it starts with ad—adventure?"

"Backpack, really easy"

"P-e-r is per and w-h-i-s is like is and his—whisper"

"L-e-n-t is lent—silent!"

For the next four tutoring sessions, Jenny decoded words the teacher had highlighted in the next four chapters of the book. Jenny whizzed through the highlighted words in Chapter 5, declaring that they were all easy! At the end of this tutoring session, the teacher gave Jenny the book. Jenny read all of the five first chapters overnight and proudly showed the teacher the word in Chapter 6 that she had highlighted and explained how she had figured them out on her own!

In addition to the Using Words You Know lessons each day, Jenny's teacher was helping her build a bank of known words she could use to decode longer words that have special parts not found in one-syllable words. She decided to gradually teach Jenny to spell the words on the Nifty-Thrifty-Fifty List (pages 79–80), which contained an example for all the common prefixes and suffixes and endings with spelling changes. She began her teaching of these words with the words **richest**, **prettier**, and **happiness**. She divided a page in a notebook into three columns and headed the three columns with these words. She explained to Jenny that many big words are just smaller words with endings, suffixes, or prefixes and that today, they would work on learning to spell these three words and other words that have the same parts. Three words would be added each tutoring session until Jenny had 50 big words that would help her read and spell hundreds of other words.

The teacher then worked with Jenny to learn to spell the three words. She led Jenny to say the word and chant its spelling three times as she pointed to the letters.

"richest r-i-c-h-e-s-t; r-i-c-h-e-s-t; r-i-c-h-e-s-t richest"

Then Jenny closed her eyes and spelled the word. When she could successfully spell each word with her eyes closed, they went on to the next word.

"prettier p-r-e-t-t-i-e-r; p-r-e-t-t-i-e-r; p-r-e-t-t-i-e-r prettier"
"happiness h-a-p-p-i-n-e-s-s; h-a-p-p-i-n-e-s-s; h-a-p-p-i-n-e-s-s happiness"

When Jenny could spell all three words with her eyes closed, the teacher wrote the words **rich**, **pretty**, and **happy** above each related word and they talked about how when a word ended in *y*, you changed the *y* to *i* before adding an ending. Jenny and the teacher then made up a sentence that used both words and showed the meaning of the words with the endings added.

"Now it is time to start seeing how spelling these three words can help you read and spell lots of other words. I will tell you a word that has one of these endings. You will decide which ending it has and how to spell it and then write it in the column with the word that ends the same." The first several words the teacher said—richer, faster, fastest, slower, slowest, shortest, shorter, taller, tallest, goodness, kindness—needed no spelling changes and Jenny quickly wrote them in the correct column.

"Now, I am going to say some words that need the spelling change we talked about." The teacher said the words *prettier, happier, happiest, lazier, laziest, laziness, uglier, ugliest,* and *ugliness* and Jenny wrote them in the appropriate columns.

For the next tutoring session, the teacher reviewed the three words from the first lesson and Jenny added *funnier, funniest, sadness,* and *fitness* to the first day's list. Then the teacher headed three columns on a new notebook page with the words **beautiful**, **hopeless**, and **patiently**. Jenny pointed to the letters of each word and chanted the spelling of the words three times. Then she spelled each word with her eyes closed. She had trouble with the word *patiently* but after several practices was able to spell it. The teacher wrote the words **beauty**, **hope**, and **patient** above their related words. To focus Jenny's attention

rich	pretty	happy
richest	prettier	happiness
fastest	richer	goodness
slowest	faster	kindness
shortest	slower	laziness
tallest	shorter	ugliness
happiest	taller	sadness
laziest	prettier	fitness
ugliest	happier	
funniest	lazier	
	uglier	
	funnier	

beauty	hope	patient
beautiful	hopeless	patiently
hopeful	painless	richly
painful	restless	happily
restful	useless	sadly
useful		angrily
		lazily

on meanings, they made sentences with the words and then the teacher reminded Jenny of the "y to i" spelling change, which she needed to change **beauty** to **beautiful**. Then, the teacher said some words that ended with these suffixes—*richly, happily, hopeful, painful, painless, sadly, restful, restless, angrily, useful, useless, lazily*—and Jenny wrote them in the appropriate columns.

During each tutoring session, the teacher added three new words that Jenny learned to spell and then used these words to spell other words dictated by the teacher. They also went back to a few of the previous lists of words and added a few more words Jenny could spell. When Jenny had learned to spell the 50 words on the Nifty-Thrifty-Fifty list, they counted all the words she had spelled and Jenny was proud to realize she had over 700 words!

During the Using Words You Know and Nifty-Thrifty-Fifty activities, Jenny was learning to decode words based on patterns from other words. The teacher also wanted Jenny to learn that you could decode words if you used a combination of letter-sound patterns, pictures, and context. To teach Jenny this, the teacher used the Guess the Covered Word lesson format (page 63). Jenny liked to learn about things and she was particularly interested in animals and other countries. The teacher used some of the Gail Gibbons animal books and some articles from their student magazines about other countries as the source for these lessons. She chose some of the big words from the book or magazine and covered all but the first chunk of the word with teeny sticky notes. Jenny read the sentence in which the word occurred and used the first chunk, context, and sometimes picture to guess the word. Then she removed the sticky note to discover that most of the time she had guessed correctly. Here are the sentences the teacher used from an article about Ecuador.

> The giant tor▮▮ can weigh more than 500 pounds.
> Many animals live in Ecuador's moun▮▮▮ and rain for▮▮.
> These animals include par▮▮, arm▮▮▮ and mon▮▮.
> Bananas are one of Ecuador's top ex▮▮.
> Ecuador won its free▮▮ from Spain in 1822.

Now you didn't have the pictures to help you as Jenny did, but could you use the context and the first chunk to figure out the words *tortoise, mountains, forests, parrots, armadillos, monkeys, exports,* and *freedom?*

While working with the student magazine article and Gail Gibbons books with Jenny, the teacher noticed that they both contained pronunciation guides for unfamiliar words in parentheses after the words.

The capital of Ecuador is Quito (**kee**-toh)

Cotopaxi (ko-toe-**pahk**-see) is the tallest active volcano in the world.

Jenny delighted in using these guides to pronounce words that even the teacher had no idea how to pronounce!

Jenny's big word decoding roadblock was much more specific than Michael's comprehension/meaning vocabulary roadblock. She learned to use the word identification strategies her teacher taught her and enjoyed reading the *Magic Tree House* and Gail Gibbons books and the student magazine articles about countries. Jenny went on to middle school equipped to tackle the big words she would find there and much more confident in her ability to read.

Targeted Tier 2 Instruction for Noah

Noah is a fourth-grader who readily tells you that he hates reading and writing but that he loves math! He is new to the school and his records don't give any indication of his reading level. Noah's teacher begins her testing of him by asking him to read the first-grade passage to himself and think about what he is reading. Noah points to each word and mouths it as he reads. When he finishes reading, he is not able to tell much about what he read or correctly respond to the questions. The teacher gives him a comprehension level of 1 and then asks him to read the passage aloud. Noah reads the words aloud with little expression and ignoring punctuation. In fact, if you heard him read, you

might

assume

he

was

reading

words

in

a

list

not

sentences

Noah's fluency level is clearly a 1. He identifies all but two of the words correctly but he reads the words as you would read a shopping list.

Oral Reading Fluency Scale	
Level 4	Reads in phrases with expression that sounds like speech
Level 3	Reads mostly in phrases and with some expression
Level 2	Reads mostly word by word with some phrases but little expression
Level 1	Reads like reading words in a list, word by word with little or no expression

To see how good his word identification is, Noah's teacher has him read a second- and a third-grade passage aloud. He reads these in the same expressionless way but meets the 95 percent word identification accuracy criterion. Noah is a bright and verbal child and a whiz at math, and the teacher suspects that his comprehension of the passages would be quite good if he were reading in phrases with the expression that gives meaning to individual words. To check this out, she reads the second- and third-grade passages to him after explaining to him that she wants him to listen carefully so that he can retell and answer questions about what she read. His comprehension when listening was excellent and she rated it a 4 for both the second- and third-grade passages.

Noah's teacher has never seen a child with such an extreme fluency problem before but she knows that if she can teach Noah to read with expression, he can make rapid progress in reading because of his strong word identification and language comprehension. Noah is quite a "ham," so his teacher decides to use plays and do some echo reading (page 49) with Noah. She searches the Internet for plays for children and is delighted to find several sites with free plays. When Noah comes for his first tutoring session, she and he go to one of these sites and look at the possible plays. He chooses *Jack and the Beanstalk* and she prints out a copy for them to share. In addition to a narrator, *Jack and the Beanstalk* has four characters: Jack, Jack's mom, the giant, and the giant's wife. The teacher tells Jack that they will read the play together a few times, and then they will read the play with Jack being any two characters he chooses and the teacher being the narrator and the other two characters.

As they echo read the play, the teacher assumes a "television announcer" voice as the narrator and then different voices for Jack's mom, Jack, the giant's wife, and the giant. The narrator's sentences are quite long and the teacher does not expect Noah to echo her voice for these sentences. The characters all have short sentences and Noah can easily echo her voice for these. After they have read the play together twice, she lets Noah choose the two characters he wants to be. It is no surprise that Noah chooses Jack and the giant. They read the play through twice more and Noah is quite expressive as he plays Jack, "Mother, get an ax!" and the giant, "Fe, Fi, Fo, Fum. I smell the blood of an Englishman!" At the end of the session, the teacher gives Noah the play script and a homework assignment he will actually enjoy. Noah and his family will read the play, with Noah reading the parts of the giant and Jack and assigning the other parts to his mom and sister.

The next four tutoring sessions follow the same format. Noah and his teacher read *The Grasshopper and the Frog*, *The Gingerbread Boy*, *Rumplestilskin*, and *The Little Red Hen* together twice. Then Noah chooses two characters for himself and they read the play twice more. Noah then takes the play scripts home and the family reads the plays together.

Once Noah has the idea of what it means to read with expression, the teacher decides to help Noah transfer this ability to other text. She knows that this transfer will not be automatic because Noah has established the habit of reading text one word at a time as if it were a list. She decides to help him make the transition by choosing stories that have a lot of dialogue. She also wants to choose a series of books, hoping that after they read a few together, Noah will want to read the others on his own. She looks through her books that are series books and notices that the *Magic Tree House* books have a lot of dialogue. When Noah arrives for his tutoring session, he finds four *Magic Tree House* books sitting on the table. The teacher asks him if he has read any of these books and he says he knows about them but he hasn't read them. He then reminds the teacher that he hates to read! Undeterred, the teacher tells him that he might like these books because they are like plays because the characters do a lot of talking. She then tells Noah that she is going to read to him the first chapter of each of the four books and that he can choose which one they will read together. Noah listens attentively as she reads the first chapter of each book and when she has finished, he chooses *Polar Bears Past Bedtime*. The teacher tells him that they will start reading it during the next session.

Before starting to read *Polar Bears Past Bedtime*, the teacher and Noah look at all the pages in the first chapter and find all the words that are in quotation marks. The teacher explains that the quotation marks show what the characters say and that because Jack is so good at sounding like different characters, the parts in quotation marks will be what he reads and she will read all the rest.

On the first page, the teacher reads everything until they get to the sentence in which the owl says, "whoo." She pauses at this word and waits for Jack to read that one word. On the following pages, the teacher pauses each time there are quotation marks and waits for Noah, who quickly assumes an owl voice and different voices for Jack and Annie. Sometimes he reads the things Jack and Annie say in a flat word-by-word voice the first time but he quickly reads them again, this time with quite dramatic expression. When he gets to the sentence in which Annie whispers something, he reads it in his normal Annie voice but when the teacher finishes the sentence by reading, *Annie whispered*, Noah re-reads Annie's words in a whispering voice.

It takes three tutoring sessions for the teacher and Noah to finish reading *Polar Bears Past Bedtime*. When they finish, Noah asks if they can do another one and chooses *Buffalo Before Breakfast*, which they finish in two tutoring sessions. When he asks the teacher if they can read a third one, she tells him that they have other things they need to do during the tutoring time, but he is welcome to choose one to read at home. Over the next several weeks, Noah—who still declares he hates to read except for *Magic Tree House* books—reads all these books he can find and then goes back to reread the two they read together! Reading the *Magic Tree House* books provides Noah with the easy reading that along with repeated readings are essential for readers to develop fluency.

Once Noah is developing some fluency in reading and doing some easy reading, his teacher decides it is time to help Noah read some grade-appropriate text that does not have a lot of dialogue. She decides to begin this by offering Noah the chance to read some of the nonfiction companion texts that provide information related to the *Magic Tree House* books. Noah chooses *Polar Bears and the Arctic*, which is the companion text to the first *Magic Tree House* book he read, *Polar Bears Past Bedtime*. The teacher reads the first chapter to Noah and they notice that there are no characters or dialogue but that there are a lot of interesting facts about polar bears and the Arctic. The teacher reminds Noah that Jack kept a notebook in which he made lists of facts and they look back at a few of these books and the facts he wrote in his notebooks. The teacher then gives Noah a new note-book and tells him that they will learn lots of facts from these books and that they, like Jack, will write these facts in a notebook. She labels the first page *Facts about Polar Bears and the Arctic*. She and Noah look back at the first chapter and start their list of facts. The teacher and Jack then read the second chapter silently, a paragraph at a time. When they finish each paragraph, they decide if they learned a new fact and, if so, they add it to the *Facts about Polar Bears and the Arctic* page. As Noah is reading the first several para-graphs silently, he "mouths" the words and the teacher notices him occasionally slipping back into his word-list reading habit but then he rereads. Clearly, he is trying to focus on meaning so he can have a fact to add to the list.

It takes four tutoring sessions to finish reading *Polar Bears and the Arctic* but they have quite an impressive four-page list of facts. When they finish, Noah wants to do another one and chooses *Space*, the nonfiction companion to *Midnight on the Moon*. Before they finish reading and recording facts about *Space*, he asks to take the notebook and *Rain Forests* home so that he can work on two books at the same time! When he makes this choice, the teacher knows that she was right about assuming Noah could make rapid progress in reading once he learned to read in phrases with expression, since he had good word identification and language comprehension. When they finish *Space*, the teacher assesses Noah's reading comprehension by having Noah read a fourth-grade passage silently and retell and answer questions. He recalls most of what he read and achieves a score of 3 on the comprehension scale. She then asks him to read it aloud. He reads it mostly in phrases and with some expression, and the teacher decides he is almost a 3 on the oral reading expression scale. Halfway through fourth grade, Noah is reading on grade level and no longer declares he hates to read!

Targeted Tier 2 Instruction for Tyrone

Tyrone is a second-grader who was retained in first grade. His second-grade teacher is not surprised to find that Tyrone reads at a beginning first-grade level, since she has taught many children who had repeated first grade and not done much better the second year than they did the first year. She uses the diagnostic procedures to confirm that Tyrone has a comprehension, fluency, and word identification level of early first grade. On the first-grade passage intended for the middle of first grade, Tyrone makes 10 errors in the first 100 words. She analyzes these errors and discovers that four errors were confusions for common sight words. He read "saw" for *was*; "want" for *went*; "them" for *then*, and "who" for *why*. In spite of the fact that the sentences made no sense with these substituted words, Tyrone did not self-correct any of these errors when he finished the sentences. His other six errors were omissions. He hesitated and then skipped the words *garden*, *ground*, *weeds*, *seeds*, *thought*, and *growing*.

The diagnosis for Tyrone is straightforward. He is not progressing in reading because he confuses common words and is unable to use his phonics skills and context to decode less common words. The teacher plans a program for Tyrone that includes having him read books at his instructional level of early first grade and coaching him to figure out words using letter-sound knowledge and context, having him write a sentence or two about the book he read each day, and developing a personal word wall for him of common words he misreads during reading or needs to spell during writing.

Tyrone is very interested in animals and often looks at a Gail Gibbons animal book or a *Zoo Book* magazine during independent reading time. These books and magazines are too hard for him to read but the teacher decides to capitalize on his interest in animals and downloads printable books about animals at early first-grade level from several websites. During the first tutoring session, she and Tyrone look at these books together and Tyrone chooses the first three he would like to read. The teacher then gives him a notebook and tells him that after they read a book, they will write a sentence or two telling something they learned from that book. She also shows him that she has divided the inside cover into sections for each letter and that with Tyrone's help with reading or spelling some words, she will write them under the letter they begin with.

For the first tutoring session, Tyrone has chosen a book about bears. The book has lots of pictures and before asking Tyrone to read the book, the teacher and Tyrone take a picture walk in which the teacher prompts Tyrone to expect certain words based on the pictures. This is what the vocabulary prompting during the picture walk sound like:

Teacher: "What do you see on this page?"

Tyrone: "Three big bears."

Teacher: "Do they all look like the same kind of bear?"

Tyrone: "No, they are different."

Teacher: "How are they different?"

Tyrone: (pointing to bears) "This one is brown and this one is black and this one is white."

Teacher: "Let's see if you can find the words that describe these bears. What letter does *brown* and *black* begin with?"

Tyrone: "B."

Teacher: "Look at the words and see if you can find the words *brown* and *black*."

Tyrone: (pointing to the two words) "Here they are."

Teacher: "Yes, those are the words, but which one do you think is *black* and which one is *brown?*"

Tyrone: "I don't know."

Teacher: "Say the words *brown* and *black* slowly and listen for the letter you hear after the *b*."

Tyrone stretches out these words with the teacher's help and figures out that there is an *r* in *brown* and an *l* in *black*. He then triumphantly decides which word is *brown* and which one is *black*. Spurred on by this success, he then decides to hunt for the word *white*, but doesn't find it. The teacher asks him if he knows what kind of bear the white bear is and he responds that he thinks it is a polar bear and quickly finds the word *polar*.

The teacher and Tyrone continue to look at the pictures and the teacher prompts him to find the words *fish, cubs, paws, claws, climb,* and *trees*.

Finished with the picture walk, the teacher and Tyrone take turns reading pages. When Tyrone reads, he miscalls a few words. The teacher waits until he finishes the sentence and then takes him back to the word he missed and helps him use the context that follows the word to self-correct. For example, Tyrone reads the sentence *Bears can climb trees* as "Bears came climb trees." The teacher stops him at the end of the sentence.

"Wait a minute. You read 'Bears came climb trees.' That doesn't sound right to me. Go back and look at this word again (pointing to *can*). It starts like *came* but *came* doesn't make sense with 'climb trees.'" After some thought, Tyrone reads, "Bears can climb trees?" "Right," the teacher says. "Lots of words look alike but when you finish the sentence and it doesn't sound right, you need to go back and try to figure out what word would sound right in the sentence." As Tyrone reads, his teacher takes him back to self-correct by pointing out that what he reads doesn't make sense.

In addition to confusing some similar words, Tyrone stopped at several words and looked to his teacher to pronounce them for him. The teacher remembered that when she was testing Tyrone, he regularly skipped words without trying to pronounce them. She wants him to get in the habit of looking at all the letters and trying to decode words so, instead of pronouncing words for him, she coaches him to figure them out. When he stops on the word *track*, the teacher asks him to say all the letters in the word. Tyrone points to and names the letters "t-r-a-c-k" but still can't figure out the word, so the teacher reminds him of a rhyming word he knows.

"Remember you read the word *black*. *Black* is spelled b-l-a-c-k. This word is t-r-a-c-k. Can you make this word start with the *tr* sound and rhyme the word with *black?*"

She cues him in the same way when he stops at *drop*. "You know that s-t-o-p spells *stop*. This word is spelled d-r-o-p. Can you make this word start with the *dr* sound and rhyme with *stop?*"

With the teacher's prompting, Tyrone can do this but he needs a lot of scaffolding. The teacher decides to do some Using Words You Know (page 64) with him to teach him how he can use words he knows with the same rhyming pattern.

When Tyrone stops at a word for which he probably doesn't have a rhyming counterpart, the teacher prompts him to finish the sentence or look at the picture and then go back and look at the word and see if he can figure it out.

For the word *winter*, she says, "Look at the picture. There is lots of snow on the ground and it looks cold. What season do you think it is?"

For the word *catch*, she prompts, "Finish the sentence and see if you can figure out what this word is." Tyrone finishes reading the sentence—*Bears can catch fish*—and figures out the word *catch*. His teacher decides to include some Guess the Covered Word lessons (pages 61–63) in future tutoring sessions to teach Tyrone to use beginning letters—which he knows quite well—and context to decode words.

When Tyrone finishes reading the book, she gives him his notebook and explains that each day, when they finish reading, they will each write a sentence or two about what they learned and that he can take the notebook home and read the sentences to his family and illustrate them if he likes. Tyrone does not look too excited about writing but he does like to draw!

The teacher opens the notebook and turns the page so that there are two facing pages. She then writes these two sentences on one of the pages.

> Some bears are black and some bears are brown. Polar bears are white.

Tyrone reads these sentences as she writes them and declares he will draw a brown bear, a black bear, and a polar bear on that page.

Next, Tyrone tells her what he wants to write on his page. He decides to write:

> Bears can climb trees and catch fish.

The teacher prompts him to spell words by starting them with the appropriate letters and then finding the rest of the spelling in the book.

At the end of the tutoring session, the teacher draws his attention to the inside covers of the notebook. As she writes the letters of the alphabet, she explains, "This is where we will make your spelling dictionary. We will add words you choose and words that are confusing and that you will need a lot in writing. Each time we meet, we will add four words to your dictionary, two you choose and two I choose. What words do you want in your dictionary?" There are a lot of words Tyrone would like to add but he settles on *bears* and *climb*. The teacher writes these words under the letters they begin with along with *they* and *them*, two words Tyrone had confused when he was writing.

At the beginning of the next tutoring session, Tyrone reads the bear book he read in the previous session. This time, he reads all the pages and pronounces most words accurately. When he does miscall or hesitate on a word, the teacher has him finish the sentence and then use the context to self-correct. Tyrone's teacher congratulates

Aa	Bb	Cc
	bears	climb
Dd	Ee	Ff
Gg	Hh	Ii
Jj	Kk	Ll	Mm
Nn	Oo	Pp	Qu
Rr		Ss
Tt			Uu
them
they
Vv	Ww	Xx	Yy	Zz

him on his good reading and asks him if he would like to take the book home to read to his family. Tyrone is pleased to do this and shows her the pictures he drew to go with the sentences they wrote in his notebook. "I can read the book to my little brother," he declares. "He likes bears, too, and he says I can draw really good bears!"

From here on, the tutoring sessions follow a predictable pattern. Tyrone rereads the book he read during the previous session and then takes it home to read to him little brother. Tyrone and the teacher then read a new book, alternating pages that they read. Before reading, they picture walk the book and the teacher uses the pictures to teach Tyrone that thinking about the pictures on a page can help him figure out words on that page. Tyrone identifies the great white and tiger sharks and the teacher has him find the words *tiger*, *great*, and *white*. He tells the teacher that there are clams and crabs in the water and then finds the words *clams* and *crabs* on that page. Other words that are cued by the pictures that Tyrone finds are *ocean*, *teeth*, *fins*, and *mouth*. Tyrone is clearly pleased (and amazed) that you can use the picture to help you figure out words and, by the fifth tutoring session, is taking the lead in identifying things in the picture and then hunting for those words in the text. Most of the time, he can quickly find the words and his reading confidence builds each time this happens.

For each new book, Tyrone and the teacher alternate reading the pages. The teacher wants to model good reading and she realizes that reading the whole book would be overwhelming for a child like Tyrone, who has experienced two years of reading failure. When Tyrone is rereading a book before taking it home, however, Tyrone reads the entire book.

Once they have read the book, Tyrone and the teacher each write a sentence or two in his notebook. After reading about sharks, they wrote these sentences.

Sharks live in oceans, rivers, and lakes. They eat fish, clams, and crabs.
There are many different kinds of sharks. great white sharks, tiger sharks, and bull sharks are the most dangerous.

After writing the sentences, they each chose two words to add to Tyrone's spelling dictionary. Tyrone chose words he liked and the teacher chose common words he confused in his reading or needed to learn to spell.

In addition to the book work, the teacher did a quick Guess the Covered Word or Using Words You Know lesson using words from the book read that day and in previous days. For the first lesson, the teacher wrote the words *black, shark,* and *tank* on three small index cards. She gave these to Tyrone who quickly read them. Then, she wrote nine words with the same rhyming patterns—*dark, Jack, crack, bark, bank, park, stack, crank, prank*—on nine index cards and Tyrone used the three words he knew to decode the nine rhyming words. They stored these 12 words in an envelope and used them—and other sets of rhyming words—to play a quick match game when they had a few minutes at the end of a tutoring session.

Tyrone made rapid progress in reading as a result of this targeted Tier 2 instruction and the good Tier 1 instruction he received in his classroom. By the end of second grade, he was reading at a mid-second-grade level and was finding books he could read during independent reading and at home. His writing also improved greatly and he used the spelling dictionary in his writing notebook to spell words during the classroom writing time. Tyrone's kindergarten brother was an appreciative audience for Tyrone's reading and was in awe of his big brother's drawing abilities. Hopefully, all the positive reading experiences he was having with his brother would result in his having more success in learning to read in first grade.

Summary

Differentiation is essential because children differ on so many dimensions. Faced with all the differences children in one classroom exhibit, teachers often feel overwhelmed and frustrated that they cannot give every child the amount of individual attention each child deserves. Differentiation cannot be achieved with any single strategy or program.

The most effective teachers use *variety* as one of their main tools for diversifying their instruction. They seek out and use a wide variety of materials. They use a variety of grouping structures, including whole-class teaching, various collaborative grouping arrangements, and individual instruction during conferences. Knowing that students have individual learning styles, effective teachers use a wide variety of lesson formats so that across the day and week, all students experience success and enjoyment as they participate in different activities.

Choice is another principle you can use to differentiate your instruction. When students can make choices about what to read during independent reading time and what to write during Writer's Workshop, they are differentiating that part of your instruction by their choices.

Increasing the *quantity* of reading and writing activities your students do by including literacy activities as you teach math, science, and social studies increases the amount of differentiation you provide. When you include reading, writing, and vocabulary activities in the different subject areas, you have additional opportunities to use a variety of lesson frameworks and collaborative groupings.

In spite of good, balanced Tier 1 instruction, some students will need additional instruction beyond what they are being provided in the classroom. Tier 2 instruction is usually delivered to individuals or in very small groups of students that have the same targeted needs. To determine which interventions are most appropriate for struggling readers, you need to do some individual diagnosis to determine their areas of greatest need. To do this, you need to use some graded passages and determine the struggling readers' comprehension, word identification, and fluency levels. Here is the most efficient way to use graded passages to determine reading levels and the area of greatest need.

- Have the student read a passage silently that you think is at that student's instructional reading level. Tell the student to try to think about what he (or she) is reading so that he can retell the major facts or events and answer some questions about it.

- When the student has finished reading, take the passage away and ask the student to tell everything he (or she) remembers. After the student's retelling, ask follow-up questions to probe for important ideas not included in the retelling. You may want to record or make notes about the student's retelling and answers to questions.

- Use a comprehension scale and rate the comprehension of this passage.

Comprehension Scale	
Level 4	Recalls most of the important events or facts and no misinformation
Level 3	Recalls a lot of events or facts and little misinformation
Level 2	Recalls some events or facts and may include some misinformation
Level 1	Recalls little except the topic

- If the child's comprehension score is a 3 or 4, have that child silently read a passage at the next-higher level. If the score is a 1 or a 2, have the child read a passage at the next lower level.

- Continue having the child read, retell, and answer questions until you find that child's comprehension level—the highest level at which he (or she) can achieve a score of 3 or 4 on the comprehension scale.

- To determine the child's word identification level, have the child read aloud a passage one level higher than that child's comprehension level. Record the reading errors made and calculate the child's word identification score, the highest level of text the child can read with 95 percent word accuracy. Do not count any self-corrections as errors.

- Rate the child's oral reading fluency on an oral reading scale.

Oral Reading Fluency Scale	
Level 4	Reads in phrases with expression that sounds like speech
Level 3	Reads mostly in phrases and with some expression
Level 2	Reads mostly word by word with some phrases but little expression
Level 1	Reads like reading words in a list, word by word with little or no expression

- Compare the child's comprehension, word identification, and fluency scores to determine which of these is the area of greatest need for this child.

- Provide tutoring or small group instruction targeted to the child's area of greatest need.

References

Allington, R. L. (2009). *What Really Matters in Fluency: Research-Based Practices Across the Curriculum.* Boston: Allyn & Bacon.

Allington, R. L. (2013). What really matters when working with struggling readers. *The Reading Teacher, 66,* 520–532.

Allington, R. L., & Johnston, P. H. (Eds.). (2002). *Reading to Learn: Lessons from Exemplary Fourth-Grade Classrooms.* New York: Guilford.

Artley, S. A. (1975). Good teachers of reading—Who are they? *The Reading Teacher, 29,* 26–31.

Bangert-Drown, R. L., Hurley, M. M., & Wilkinson, B. (2004). The effects of school-based writing to learn interventions on academic achievement. *Review of Educational Research, 74,* 29–58.

Baumann, J. F., Kame'enui, E. J., & Ash, G. E. (2003). Research on vocabulary instruction: Voltaire redux. In J. Flood, D. Lapp, J. R. Squire, & J. M. Jensen (Eds.), *Handbook of Research on Teaching the English Language Arts* (2nd ed., pp. 752–785). Mahwah, NJ: Erlbaum.

Beaver, J. (2012). *Developmental Reading Inventory* (2nd ed.). Boston: Pearson.

Beck, I. L., McKeown, M. G., & Gromoll, E. W. (1989). Learning from social studies texts. *Cognition and Instruction, 6,* 99–158.

Beck, I. L., McKeown, M. G., & Kucan, L. (2002). *Bringing Words to Life.* New York: Guilford.

Becker, W. C. (1977). Teaching reading and language to the disadvantaged—What we have learned from field research. *Harvard Educational Review, 47,* 518–543.

Biemiller, A. (2004). Teaching vocabulary in the primary grades. In J. F. Baumann & E. J. Kame'enui (Eds.), *Vocabulary Instruction* (pp. 28–40). New York: Guilford.

Biemiller, A., & Slonim, M. (2001). Estimating root word vocabulary growth in normative and advantaged populations: Evidence for a common sequence of vocabulary acquisition. *Journal of Educational Psychology, 93,* 498–520.

Blachowicz, C., & Fisher, P. (2015). *Teaching Vocabulary in all Classrooms* (5th ed.). Boston: Pearson.

Black, P., & D. William. (1998). Inside the black box: Raising standards through classroom assessment. *Phi Delta Kappan, 80*(2), 139–148.

Bond, G. L., & Dykstra, R.(1967). The cooperative research program on first-grade reading instruction. *Reading Research Quarterly, 2*(4), 4–152.

Buly, M., & Valencia, S. W. (2002). Below the bar: Profiles of students who fail state reading assessment. *Educational Evaluation and Policy Analysis, 24,* 219–239.

Caldwell, J. (2015). *Reading Assessment: A Primer for Teachers and Tutors* (3rd ed.). New York: Guilford.

Calkins, L. (1994). *The Art of Teaching Writing.* Portsmouth, NH: Heinemann.

Chomsky, C. (1971). Write first, read later. *Childhood Education, 46,* 296–299.

Cocca-Leffler, M. (1999). *Missing: One Stuffed Rabbit.* Morton Grove, IL: Whitman Publishing.

Cooper, H., Nye, B., Charlton, K., Lindsay, J., & Greathouse, S. (1996). The Effects of Summer Vacation on Achievement Test Scores: A Narrative and Meta-Analytic Review. *Review of Educational Research, Fall 1996, Vol. 66 no. 3* 227–268.

Cunningham, A. E., & Stanovich, K. E. (1998). What reading does for the mind. *American Educator, 22*(1&2), 8–27.

Cunningham, P. M. (2006). High-poverty schools that beat the odds. *The Reading Teacher, 60,* 382–385.

Cunningham, P. M. (2007). *Six Successful High-Poverty Schools: How they Beat the Odds. 56th Yearbook of the National Reading Conference,* 191–207.

Cunningham, P. M. (2013). *Phonics they use: Words for Reading and Writing* (6th ed.). Boston: Allyn & Bacon.

Cunningham, P. M., & Hall, D. P. (2001). *True Stories from Four Blocks Classrooms.* Greensboro, NC: Carson-Dellosa.

Cunningham, P. M., Hall, D. P., & Defee, M. (1991). Nonability grouped, multilevel instruction: A year in a first grade classroom. *The Reading Teacher, 44,* 566–571.

Duke, N. K., & Pearson, P. D. (2002). Effective practices for developing reading comprehension. In A. E. Farstrup & S. J. Samuels (Eds.), *What Research has to Say About Reading Instruction* (3rd ed., pp. 205–242). Newark, DE: International Reading Association.

Durkin, D. (1979). What classroom observations reveal about reading comprehension instruction. *Reading Research Quarterly, 14,* 481–533.

Dyson, A. H., & Freedman, S. W. (2003). Writing. In J. Flood, D. Lapp, J. R. Squire, & J. M. Jensen (Eds.), *Handbook of Research on Teaching the English Language Arts* (2nd ed., pp. 967–992). Mahwah, NJ: Erlbaum.

Ehri, L. C., & Wilce, L. (1987). Does learning to spell help beginners learn to read words? *Reading Research Quarterly, 22,* 47–65.

Ellis, N., & Cataldo, S. (1990). The role of spelling in learning to read. *Language and Education, 4,* 47–76.

Farnan, N., & Dahl, K. (2003). Children's writing: Research and practice. In J. Flood, D. Lapp, J. R. Squire, & J. M. Jensen (Eds.), *Handbook of Research on Teaching the English Language Arts* (2nd ed., pp. 993–1007). Mahwah, NJ: Erlbaum.

Fisher, D., Frey, N., & Nelson, J. (2012). Literacy achievement through sustained professional development. *The Reading Teacher, 65*(8), 551–563.

Gamse, B. C., Jacob, R. T., Horst, M., Boulay, B., & Unlu, F. (2008). *Reading First Impact Study: Final Report* (NCEE 2009–4038). Washington, DC: National Center for Education Evaluation and Regional Assistance, Institute of Education Sciences, U.S. Department of Education.

Graham, S., & Perin, D. (2007). A meta-analysis of writing instruction for adolescent students. *Journal of Educational Psychology, 99,* 445–476.

Graves, D. H. (1995). *A Fresh Look at Writing.* Portsmouth, NH: Heinemann.

Graves, M. F. (2004). Teaching prefixes: As good as it gets? In J. F. Baumann & E. J. Kame'enui (Eds.), *Vocabulary Instruction* (pp. 81–99). New York: Guilford.

Graves, M. F. (2006). *The Vocabulary Book.* Newark, DE: International Reading Association.

Graves, M. F., & Watts-Taffe, S. M. (2002). The place of word consciousness in a research-based vocabulary program. In A. E. Farstrup & S. J. Samuels (Eds.), *What Research has to Say About Reading Instruction* (3rd ed., pp. 140–165). Newark, DE: International Reading Association.

Guthrie, J. T., & Humenick, N. M. (2004). Motivating students to read: Evidence for classroom practices that increase motivation and achievement. In P. McCardle & V. Chhabra (Eds.), *The Voice of Evidence in Reading Research* (pp. 329–354). Baltimore: Paul Brookes Publishing.

Hart, B., & Risley, T. R. (1995). *Meaningful Differences in the Everyday Experiences of Young American children.* Baltimore: Paul H. Brookes.

Hattie, J. (2009). *Visible Learning: A Synthesis of Over 800 Meta-Analyses Relating to Achievement.* New York: Routledge.

Hemphill, F. C., and Vanneman, A. (2010). *Achievement Gaps: How Hispanic and White Students in Public Schools Perform in Mathematics and Reading on the National Assessment of Educational Progress* (NCES 2011-459). National Center for Education Statistics, Institute of Education Sciences, U.S. Department of Education. Washington, DC.

Hillocks, G., Jr. (1986). *Research on Written Composition: New Directions for Teaching*. Urbana, IL: National Conference on Research in English/ERIC Clearinghouse on Reading and Communication Skills.

Hodges, R. E. (2003). The conventions of writing. In J. Flood, D. Lapp, J. R. Squire, & J. M. Jensen (Eds.), *Handbook of Research on Teaching the English Language Arts* (2nd ed., pp. 1052–1063). Mahwah, NJ: Erlbaum.

Hutchins, P. (1971). *Rosie's Walk*. New York: Alladin

Ivey, G., & Broaddus, K. (2001). "Just plain reading": A survey of what makes students want to read in middle school classrooms. *Reading Research Quarterly, 36*, 350–377.

Johns, J. J. (2012). *Basic Reading Inventory* (11th ed.). Dubuque, IA: Kendall/Hunt.

Johnston, P. H. (2010). A framework for response to intervention in literacy. In P. H. Johnston (Ed.), *RTI in Literacy: Responsive and Comprehensive* (pp. 1–9). Newark, DE: International Reading Association.

Juel, C., Biancarosa, G., Coker, D., & Deffes, R. (2003). Walking with Rosie: A cautionary tale of early reading instruction. *Educational Leadership, 60*, 12–18.

Juel, C., & Minden-Cupp, C. (2000). Learning to read words: Linguistic units and instructional strategies. *Reading Research Quarterly, 35*, 458–492.

Keene, E. L., & Zimmerman, S. (1997). *Mosaic of thought: Teaching Comprehension in a Reader's Workshop*. Portsmouth, NH: Heinemann.

Knapp, M. S. (1995). *Teaching for Meaning in High-Poverty Classrooms*. New York: Teachers College Press.

Lesaux, N. K., & Kieffer, M. J. (2010). Exploring sources of reading comprehension difficulties among language minority learners and their classmates in early adolescence. *American Educational Research Journal, 47*, 596–632.

Leslie, L., & Caldwell, J. (2010). *Qualitative Reading Inventory* (5th ed.). New York: Longman.

Manning, G. L., & Manning, M. (1984). What models of recreational reading make a difference? *Reading World, 23*, 375–380.

Mason, J. M., Bewell, D., & Vogt, M. (1991). *Responses to Literature*. Newark, DE: International Reading Association.

Mason, J. M., Stahl, S. A., Au, K. H., & Herman, P. A. (2003). Reading: Children's developing knowledge of words. In J. Flood, D. Lapp, J. R. Squire, & J. M. Jensen (Eds.), *Handbook of Research on Teaching the English Language Arts* (2nd ed., pp. 914–930). Mahwah, NJ: Erlbaum.

Miller, D. (2009). *The Book Whisperer: Awakening the Inner Reader in Every Child*. San Francisco, CA: Wiley.

Nagy, W. E., & Anderson. R. C. (1984). How many words are there in printed school English? *Reading Research Quarterly, 19*, 304–330.

National Center for Educational Statistics. (2010). *NAEP 2009 Reading: A Report Card for the Nation and the States*. Washington, DC: U.S. Department of Education.

National Governors Association Center for Best Practices & Council of Chief State School Officers. (2010). *Common Core State Standards for English language Arts and Literacy in History/Social Studies, Science, and Technical Subjects*. Washington, DC: Authors. Accessed at www.corestandards.org/assets/CCSSI_ELA%20Standards.pdf on February 21, 2014.

National Reading Panel. (2000). *Teaching Children to Read: An Evidence-Based Assessment of the Scientific Research Literature on Reading and its Implications for Reading Instruction: Reports of the Subgroups* (National Institute of Health Pub. No. 00-4754). Washington, DC: National Institute of Child Health and Human Development.

Nye, B., Konstantopoulos, S., & Hedges, L. V. (2004). How large are teacher effects? *Educational Evaluation and Policy Analysis, 26*(3), 237–257.

Palmer, B. M., Codling, R. M., & Gambrell, L. B. (1994). In their own words: What elementary children have to say about motivation to read. *The Reading Teacher, 48*, 176–179.

Pearson, P. D., & Gallagher, M. (1983). The instruction of reading comprehension. *Contemporary Educational Psychology, 8*, 317–344.

Pressley, M., Allington, R. L., Wharton-McDonald, R., Block, C. C., & Morrow, L. (2001). *Learning to Read: Lessons from Exemplary First-Grade Classrooms*. New York: Guilford.

Pressley, M., & Wharton-McDonald, R. (1998). The development of literacy, Part 4: The need for increased comprehension in upper-elementary grades. In M. Pressley (Ed.), *Reading Instruction that works: The Case for Balanced Teaching* (pp. 192–227). New York: Guilford.

Rasinski, T. V. (2003). *The Fluent Reader*. New York: Scholastic.

Rasinski, T. V. & Padak, N. D. (2013). *From Phonics to Fluency* (3rd ed.). Boston: Allyn & Bacon.

Rasinski, T. V., Reutzel, D. R., Chard, D., & Linan-Thompson, S. (2011). Reading fluency. In M. L. Kamil, P. D Pearson, E. B Moje, & P. P. Afflerbach (Eds.), *Handbook of Reading Research* (Vol. 4, pp. 286–319). New York: Routledge.

Read, C. (1975). *Children's Categorization of Speech Sounds in English*. Urbana, IL: National Council of Teachers of English.

Share, D. L. (1999). Phonological recoding and orthographic learning: A direct test of the self-teaching hypothesis. *Journal of Experimental Child Psychology, 72*, 95–129.

Stahl, S. A., Duffy-Hester, A. M., & Stahl, K. A. D. (1998). Everything you wanted to know about phonics (but were afraid to ask). *Reading Research Quarterly, 33*, 338–355.

Stahl, S. A., & Nagy, W. (2006). *Toward Word Meanings*. Mahwah, NJ: Erlbaum.

Stanovich, K. E. (1986). Matthew effects in reading: Some consequences of individual differences in the acquisition of literacy. *Reading Research Quarterly, 21*, 360–401.

Stanovich, K. E. (1991). Word recognition: Changing perspectives. In R. Barr, M. Kamil, P. Mosenthal, & P. D. Pearson (Eds.), *Handbook of Reading Research* (Vol. 2, pp. 418–452). New York: Longman.

Stanovich, K. E., & West, R. F. (1989). Exposure to print and orthographic processing. *Reading Research Quarterly, 24*, 402–433.

Sulzby, E., & Teale, W. (1991). Emergent literacy. In R. Barr, M. Kamil, P. Mosenthal, & P. D. Pearson (Eds.), *Handbook of Reading Research* (Vol. 2, pp. 727–757). White Plains, NY: Longman.

Taylor, B. M., Hanson, B., Swanson, K., & Watts, S. (1998). Helping struggling readers in grades two and four: Linking small-group intervention with cross-age tutoring. *The Reading Teacher, 51*, 196–209.

Taylor, B. M., Pearson, P. D., Clark, K., & Walpole, S. (2000). Effective schools and accomplished teachers: Lessons about primary grade reading instruction in low-income schools. *Elementary School Journal, 101*(2), 121–166.

Topping, K., & Paul, T. (1999). Computer-assisted assessment of practice at reading: A large scale survey using Accelerated Reader data. *Reading and Writing Quarterly, 15*, 213–231.

U.S. Department of Education. (2004). Building the legacy: IDEA, Washington, DC: U.S. Government Printing Office.

Visser, C. (1991). Football and reading do mix. *The Reading Teacher, 44*, 710–711.

Wharton-McDonald, R., Pressley, M., & Hampston, J. M. (1998). Literacy instruction in nine first-grade classrooms: Teacher characteristics and student achievement. *The Elementary School Journal, 99*, 101–128.

Williams, D. (2011). *Embedded Formative Assessment*. Bloomington, IN: Solution Tree Press.

Wylie, R. E., & Durrell, D. D. (1970). Teaching vowels through phonograms. *Elementary English, 47*, 787–791.

Yopp, R. H. & Yopp, H. K. (2004). Preview-Predict-Confirm: Thinking about the language and content of informational text. *The Reading Teacher, 58*, 79–83.

Yopp, R. H. & Yopp, H. K. (2007). Ten important words plus: A strategy for building word knowledge. *The Reading Teacher, 61*, 157–160.

Index